MW00626645

John Stark of
Rogers' Rangers

John Stark of Rogers' Rangers

A Famous Ranger and His Associates During the French & Indian War

The Life of General John Stark
of New Hampshire

Howard Parker Moore

With Biographies from Memoir and Official
Correspondence of General John Stark

Caleb Stark

LEONAUR

John Stark of Rogers' Rangers
A Famous Ranger and His Associates During the French & Indian War
The Life of General John Stark of New Hampshire
by Howard Parker Moore
With Biographies from Memoir and Official Correspondence of General John Stark
by Caleb Stark

FIRST EDITION

Leonaur is an imprint of Oakpast Ltd

Copyright in this form © 2020 Oakpast Ltd

ISBN: 978-1-78282-974-4 (hardcover)
ISBN: 978-1-78282-975-1 (softcover)

http://www.leonaur.com

Publisher's Notes

Contents

The Life of General John Stark

In 1745 the fall of Louisburg served to bring to a temporary close the inciting of the Indians by the French to depredations in the Merrimack Valley, though in Suncook one McQuade was shot and killed, his companion, Burns, escaping to spread the terror. The Starks saw pass their hamlet a regiment of some 800 men that Col. Theodore Atkinson of Portsmouth headed, destined for Canada. The ill-conceived plan ended in the wintering of the large force on one of the bays or outlet lakes of Winnepesaukee. From December, 1745, till April, 1746, Capt. John Goffe (living a few miles South of the Starks) had his men out, most of the time on snow-shoes.

In May two men were killed and one was captured by the stealthy red men, biding their time until they could strike. Watchfulness and alarm prevailed in the Derryfield hamlet, in the direct path, successively, of the explorers, the scouting parties and venturesome settlers. Everything passed the doors of the Stark homestead. There the first news of every foray was received and relayed. The last act for the time (Potter said, the last in the Merrimack valley) was when the Indians attacked Epsom, 16 miles as the crow flies, from Derryfield, capturing Mrs. McCoy. By Oct. 1748, (Treaty of Aix-la-Chapelle) the incursions had practically ceased.

James Rogers (father of the famous Ranger, Robert Rogers) and Joseph Putney had built temporary log houses about 1746. When these were burned by the Indians they retired to Concord for a time. In 1749 Capt. Wm. Stinson (born, Ireland, 1725) built his permanent log cabin and by 1751 John Hogg and Thomas Mills had built in the western part of the forest wilderness. At the tavern of Samuel Rankin, Londonderry, in 1751 Archibald Stark, John Hogg and Hugh Ramsay were authorized to call the meeting and the names of the principal landholders were disclosed (1752). The Starks included Archibald, William, John and Archibald, Jr. "of a place called Amoskeag".

Caleb Page, Jr. and others were "of Hampstead". Title to lands about six miles square had been acquired in 1751 from "the assigns of John Tufton Mason" (*Hist. Dunbarton*) Archibald Stark being the first named, and from that fact, rather than from the size of the family's holdings, it was named and for the first 14 years carried the name, "Starks town". Captain Caleb Page (born 1705) of pure English descent, came at this time and at once assumed a prominent place, by 1753 being appointed with Col. Zacheus Lovewell and Major John Talford, by the New Hampshire authorities, "to survey and make a road to Coös". On the list of the men they engaged are found, as of March 1753, the famous names of John Stark, Pilot, (who collected the same pay as the three leaders, 35 shillings a day) and Robert Rogers.

Archibald Stark's financial troubles were slowly growing and eventually overwhelmed him but did not deter his taking an interest in Dunbarton. In 1748 he gave two notes to Samuel Rankin. One for £57 shows his signature as clear and distinct as when written just 200 years ago (No. 19834, N.H. Hist. Soc. archives) the other being for £37, and for both of which, being unpaid in 1750, Rankin sued. In 1750 Archibald gave a note to James Dwire (Dwyer), apparently a truckman or teamster and followed it with three others, all small amounts. Dwyer waited seven years, then got out a writ and Sheriff Thomas Packer attached a chair in Stark's house. Such legal proceedings were very common and it is seldom that the outcome, damages collected or what not, is now evident.

A serious affair in 1751, as the result of some argument or clash Archibald Stark and John McNeil, his neighbour, became involved in a case having far reaching consequences. Archibald swore that McNeil, assisted by Daniel McNeil, used "clubs and stones" in an assault and that he suffered "great pain, incurred charges for nursing and doctors and was hindered from any labour or business from 14th April till Aug. 3rd, 1751" claiming his "life was for a long time despaired of." Three Arbitrators awarded Stark "for trespass and all other controversies" the sum of £34 and Robert Boys, Justice of the Pease, fined John McNeil 20 shillings. Perhaps the physical disabilities may have been, as usual, exaggerated, but an actual assault on a 60 year old man by a huge bully is proven by the legal outcome. The Stark boys, aged 27, 25 and 23 could not have been around or they would have seen that their father was not knocked about.

There are three accounts of John Stark captured by the Indians 1752, the first being a brief one by Stickney, son-in-law of the general, printed in the *Patriot*, Concord, 1810, barely two score lines; the principal feature this:

I have had many hours of high enjoyment in hearing the old

gentleman relate anecdotes of his captivity. Stark remained with the Indians three or four months; and he says he received from them more kindness than he has ever seen prisoners of war receive from any civilized nation, and that they practice the moral virtues in general much more than the Europeans.

By 1831 when Caleb (1805-1864) son of Major Caleb (1759-1838) wrote his inadequate *Memoir* of his grandfather (the general), he, of course, enlarged on Stickney, but as he personally scarcely knew his grandfather, living in another town and being only 17 when the general died, his account, which it is better to give (as it is the earliest) must have been derived from father Caleb, who may not have checked it, containing, as it does a mis-statement, that John, was the second son of Archibald, when he was actually the third.

In 1736 Mr. Stark removed to Derryfield, now Manchester, upon Merrimack River and commenced a settlement near Amoskeag falls. John, his second son, the subject of this *Memoir*, resided with his father, at this place, till 1752. At that time (in company with his brother, William, Messrs. David Stinson and Amos Eastman) he went upon a hunting expedition to Baker's River, in Rumney, N.H. On the 28th of April they were surprised at this place by a scout of ten St. Francis Indians. Signs of them had been discovered two days before and the party were in consequence about leaving the hunting ground. John, separated from his companions to collect the traps and while thus engaged fell into the hands of the enemy. On being interrogated respecting his comrades he pointed a contrary direction and led them two miles out of the way. His friends, alarmed at his long absence fired several guns, which discovered them to the savages, who, proceeding some distance down the river, turned their encampment and formed an ambush to intercept their boat.

The hunters, suspecting what had taken place, were proceeding down the river William Stark and Stinson in the canoe, and Eastman on the bank; when, about sunrise the latter fell into the ambush, and was taken by the savages, who then directed John to hail the others He did so; informed his friends of his situation and advised an escape to the opposite shore upon which four of the Indians fired into the boat.

At this critical moment he had the temerity to strike up two of their muskets, and upon the others preparing to fire, did the same and told William to escape, as they had fired all their guns. He profited by the advice and made good his retreat Stinson, his companion, was killed. This conduct of their prisoner so exasperated the Indians, that they beat him severely, made prize of his furs and proceeded to Coös, near where Haverhill, N.H. is now situated, where they had left two of their party to collect provisions for their return. Here they tarried one night, and continued their route to upper Coös; whence they despatched three of their party with Eastman to St. Francis.

The remainder employed themselves sometime in hunting upon a small stream called John's River. The prisoner was liberated during the day, but confined at night. While he, Stark, was directed to try his fortune at hunting, he succeeded in trapping one beaver and shooting another, and received the skins as a reward for his skill.

On the 9th of June the Indians reached St. Francis where he remained six weeks was well treated and obtained a knowledge of their modes of attacking and annoying their enemies. Mr. Wheelwright of Boston and Capt. Stevens of Number Four, who were sent by Massachusetts to redeem prisoners, arrived about this time at the village, and not finding those they expected from Massachusetts, released both the captives, and returning by way of Albany, reached Derryfield in August following.

Mr. Stark paid for his freedom $103, and Eastman $60. These sums were never repaid by the state. Massachusetts, directed by a more just and liberal policy, redeemed all her captives. It may not be improper to remark that the scout which captured these prisoners came to Albany in company with this returning party, and sold the furs taken from them, without molestation.

During this captivity Stark acquired that thorough knowledge of the Indian character, and of their stratagems of war, which he turned to such good account against them, and their allies, the French, in the war that ensued. It is a custom with the Indians, to impose all their labour and drudgery upon their captives and squaws. They accordingly directed Stark to hoe corn. He first proceeded to cut down the corn, carefully sparing the weeds; but this, not answering his purpose of relieving himself of the labour, he threw their hoes into the river, telling them, "it was the business of squaws and not warriers to hoe corn".

Instead of being irritated at this, they were pleased at his boldness, called him "young chief and he was accordingly adopted as the son of their *sachem*. In the latter days of his life he used to relate with much humour, the incidents of his captivity; observing that he had experienced more genuine kindness from the savages of St. Francis, than he ever knew prisoners of war to receive from any civilized nation.

When Eastman and Stark arrived at St. Francis, they were compelled to undergo the ceremony of running the gauntlet. The young men of the village ranged themselves in two lines, each armed with a rod, to strike the captives as they passed along. Eastman was severely whipped; but Stark, thinking one good turn deserved another, snatched a club and made his way through the lines knocking the Indians down, right and left whenever they came within his reach; and escaped with scarcely a blow, to the great delight of the old men, who sat at a distance enjoying the sport at their young men's expense.

In 1834 Edward Everett followed, almost word for word the 1831 account, except that there was some improvement in the language, as would be expected. Everett commented severely:

The unhappy want of political concern between the Colonies at this period is curiously illustrated by the fact, that the party of Indians, who had plundered and captured Stark and his companions, travelled with them to Albany, and there, without molestation, made sale of the very furs, which had been taken from these citizens of a sister province in time of peace; for this adventure preceded by four years the breaking out of the war of 1756.

Though Everett was 28 years old at the time of Gen. Stark's death, he seems to have contributed little in his life in knowledge acquired otherwise than in print.

Observing the development of the spirited story of Stark's capture; Potter in his *Manchester* took occasion, with his great knowledge of the Indian life, to improve on Caleb Stark's story: Stark when first discovered by the Indians, had his attention arrested by a sharp hiss; "upon William's return to the settlement a party from Rumford, consisting of Nathaniel Eastman, Timothy Bradley and Phineas Virgin started for the scene of the disaster, found the body of Stinson, scalped, buried it in the woods nearby and returned in safety"; for the gauntlet the prisoners were instructed in their parts, being taught to repeat some

11

sentence as they passed through the lines and being "furnished with a pole six or eight feet in length, upon the top of which was placed the skin of some animal"; Stark's pole was furnished with a loon skin; "Stark started off at a deliberate trot singing out at the top of his voice "*Nutchipwuttoonapishwameugnonkkishguog*" which means "I will kiss all your young women", Eastman having repeated some gibberish, probably improvised by Potter, meaning "I will beat all your young men".

Having seen this in 1856, Caleb Stark for his 1860 volume of *Memoirs* and correspondence, added something himself, but more conservatively, the furs had a value of five hundred and sixty pounds sterling; the chief was Francis Titigaw; author did not repeat that 1831 foot-note, that the follow-up party, burying Stinson, "brought home one of the paddles of the canoe, which was pierced with several shot holes; it was preserved a long time by the Eastman family". But Caleb, influenced by the pole story, replaced his own, Stark "snatched a club", a more probable weapon than a long pole in close attack, in view of the effective use Stark made of it. Caleb was not impressed into repeating Potter's 38 letter equivalent of the kissing threat but did add "Stark stated that the first one that struck him was a youth, whom he knocked down; and that he did not see him again while he was at the village".

Stark's opinion of Albany morality had its origin when he first saw the place, a redeemed captive, in the summer of 1752. He never got over his resentment, as he needed the money to reimburse Massachusetts and had to find it the hard way later. Albany was not less curious to the eyes of Stark and Eastman than Montreal had been, each having characteristics greatly different from New England towns. They saw old Dutch buildings, all sorts, brick and wood mixed together, steep gables on the street sides, stockades still standing, a fort on the hill within them. One Kalm, a traveller from Sweden, had visited the place in 1749 and described the customs and costumes in detail (Foster's trans. 3 vol. 1771) but see Justin Smith "Our Struggle" for vivid, if "constructive" portrayal.

At 24 Stark was keen and observant but his mental vision could have hardly conjured up a picture of himself during a long war with Great Britain a quarter century later, as a general in command of the Northern Department, of an army of colonists throwing off a foreign yoke. The place had grown fast; the County in 1731 having had 8573 inhabitants, growing four years after Stark's first visit into 14,805. The number of slaves more than doubled; 1222 to 2619. But the two young men had neither the time nor the money to enable them to tarry on their homeward journey. The route and the events have never been found in print, but the men reached Derryfield and Dunbarton, respectively, in safety.

The real price of Stark's redemption came out in Butler's address to the Legislature of Vermont (1849):

> For it was not for $103 but for an Indian pony. I copy the following from the original journal of the officer who redeemed the captive. 'July 1, 1752, this day was John Stark brought to Montreal by his Indian master. He was taken a hunting this spring. He is given up for an Indian pony for which we paid 515 *livres'*.

In the 1810 story Stickney had something about Stark having been given a deceased chief's widow for a "mother" and a daughter for a "wife", doubtless quite symbolic acts. Bancroft had a comprehensive paragraph, all that a general history could give;

> Danger lowered on the whole American frontier. In the early Summer of 1752 John Stark of New Hampshire, as fearless a young forrester as ever bivouaced in the wilderness, of a rugged nature, but of the coolest judgment, was trapping beaver along the brooks of his native highlands, when a party of St. Francis Indians stole upon his steps and scalped one of his companions. By courage and good humour, he won the love of his captors, was saluted by their tribe as a young chief, and, for a ransom, was set free.

While Stark and his companions were on their Baker River Hunt in 1752 a party (called a Committee, but whose make-up has not survived) looked into the Coös (pronounced co-oss) country with a view to forestalling any French lodgements. But the real work was done in 1753 with Stark as "pilot" because he had been through with the Indian party of his captivity, and, no doubt, because of his recognised skill. The fifteen men would have been able, in the short time (19½ days) to have done little more than blaze a trail. The Indian word *"Co-has"* stood for a wide and level valley of the Connecticut where the river, flowing past the towns of Haverhill and Newbury forms the famous "ox-bow" of fertile farms and lovely villages today.

It was a winter job, necessarily on snow-shoes, the party reaching Concord on its return on March 31st, 1753. It was a small beginning for Stark. In what month Caleb Stark's 1831 book does not indicate, but it was probably later in the year, April, 1753, that an honourable obligation to repay a ransom was undertaken.

Our adventurer repaired the next season to the River Androscoggin to pursue his vocation and raise the means to discharge his redemption debt. Upon this occasion he was very successful and returned with a valuable load of fur.

It was a long and arduous journey beyond the White Mountains possibly, and was not one to be made alone, as danger from roaming Indians would be enhanced on such a long quest. Without knowing it John Stark was in training for valorous deeds.

There were border attacks in 1753 on the Merrimack River settlements. In Canterbury, inhabited but a few years, two familiar and hitherto friendly Indians, Sabbatis and Plausawa, acted in a threatening manner and were killed by two settlers, Morrill and Bowen, to prevent outrages. They were tried, being deemed by some little better than murderers, but were delivered from jail by friends, in disguise. The menace was not averted; it was accentuated.

There was (1753) another family item, a note given by Archibald to Richard Ayer of Haverhill, Mass. a tanner, a suit following it eventually, Hugh Stirling, Stark's future son-in-law being co-maker.

The year 1754 saw on Feb. 22nd the first marriage, William Stark to Mary, sister of the pioneer, Capt. William Stinson, at Dunbarton, his parents and John probably being present to celebrate the first alliance of the family, one that influenced the future life of William Stark in a dark and fatal way. There may have been there a brown eyed girl from the house of Capt. Page in whom a young scout from Derryfield was taking an interest.

In July, 1754, the colonies sent delegates to a conference or congress at Albany, the first great conclave, abortive of immediate and tangible results, but showing the feasibility of coming together on subjects of mutual interest. The men, some of whom met for the first time, would form almost a roster of the leaders of their respective colonies. One object, treaty making with the chiefs of the "Six Nations" was partly achieved. The Indians, lavishly entertained, with feasting and speechmaking, prevented the important York state tribes from affiliating with the French. In the course of the next six years this meant much to John Stark. New Hampshire's bill, (still extant) for cloth, vermillion, a cow, liquor and "printing Mr. Peters' sermon"; some £83, date; Dec. 26, 1754.

Capt. John Webster's list of 20 scouts sent to capture the Indians, who in May, 1754, took Nathaniel Meloon's family at Stevenstown, did not include the name of John Stark, but another scout under Capt. Peter Powers of Hollis, starting from Pennacook June 15th, probably had him, judging from the 1831 and 1860 paragraphs:

> In 1754 the report was current that the French were erecting a fort at the upper Coös and Capt. Powers was despatched by Gov. Wentworth with 30 men and a flag of truce to demand their authority for so doing. He applied to Mr. Stark to accompany him, who conducted the party to the Upper Coös by way of the little Ox-bow by the same route he had travelled two years before as a captive to the Indians.

At Canterbury on May 31st Col. Blanchard, as a Justice of the Peace, took a joint deposition by John Stark and Amos Eastman after having taken one by those two men with William Stark added, because of the expectation that a council would be held at Casco involving restitution, the three setting up claims for £560 "at least". John and Amos deposed:

> That the said Amos was sold to the French and for his redemption paid sixty dollars to his master besides all his expenses of getting home. That the said John purchased his redemption of the Indians for which he paid one hundred and three dollars besides all his expenses in getting home. That there was ten Indians in company who captivated the deponents and lived at St. Francis they often told the deponents it was not peace. One Francis Titigaw was the chief of the scout. There was in their scout one named Peer they called a young Sagamore that belong to St. Francis.
>
> And the deponents further say that in their return from Canada they were at Crown Point, a negro named Tom was there who told them he was captivated at Canterbury that year by Sabbatis and Christo and that they sold him to a Frenchman at that fort for four hundred *livres* which sum Capt. Phineas Stevens and Mr. Wheelwright then offered for his redemption in order to return him to his master James Lindsay but the Frenchman his master refused his Liberty unless they would pay him six hundred *livres* which they refused to do. (Provincial Papers VI)

Mrs. McCall was tomahawked on her doorstep at Stevenstown and a scout of 24 horsemen were sent there as a guard, the commander, Lt. John Goffe, taking young Caleb Page (26) and nine Derryfield men, including young Archibald Stark (24) but no Indians were seen. John Stark seems not to have been on this or a larger one (State Papers VI and Potter, 1866,11) though Robert Rogers was one of the scouts.

15

Potter concluded that:

> The promptness of Gov. Wentworth in this emergency and the effective force detailed preserved the inhabitants of the Merrimack valley from any further molestation.

There being no domestic items of the Stark family until the summer of 1757, William and John being in the Ranger service in the French and Indian War, the closing year in the life of Archibald Stark will be related, out of order.

On Aug. 9, 1757, a one year old black colt, with a white spot on its forehead, the property of James Wallace of Londonderry, and valued at 14 pounds, old tenor, while in the custody of Robert Anderson, in some manner got into the field of Archibald Stark. The court papers show 14 documents (N.H. His. Soc. archives). John McNeil heard Anderson tell Stark he would not pay the damages claimed at the moment he was leading the colt out of the field, namely 11 or 12 pounds, but would pay reasonable damages. Matthew Patten gave a "warrant of appraisement to Daniel McNeil and Wm. Eliot to apprise three colts said Stark had pounded for which he gave me £4, O.T.", as to "Rye, barley and grass", the appraisers considered £20 O.T. proper damages to Archibald Stark.

The colts were sold at auction at Stark's instance on August 20th. Two days later an action looking like reprisal was started by Wallace who had Stark arrested as he had "converted and disposed of to his own use knowing it to be the property of James Wallace" the colt in question. The trial at Portsmouth on Sept. 6th was attended by Matthew Patten who "sit in the sessions the afternoon" and the next day, gave his testimony. Put over till the next term (December) the jurors found for Wallace but only in the amount of seven ponds odd.

On appeal Stark lost the action in June 1758, in spite of the ability of hired legal talent in Squire A. Livermore, whose bill afterward, not showing up, might indicate that he got cash. Presented were numerous affidavits; Ann Stark, eldest daughter made her mark, Isabel Stirling signed "Isabell Starling" for all we know her sole surviving signature. The girls swore to seeing the colt taken out of their father's field by him and an apprentice boy, John Johnson. Patten earned good fees out of the unfortunate case.

The controversy had caused him much time, and also money he could ill afford to spare. The talk of the community had worried him, culminating in the gall and bitterness of a lost case. The whole took its inevitable toll of the ageing man's vital forces. Hot weather and fatigue may also have been factors. He had tried to get home from Portsmouth. A hurried horseback journey may have been the immediate cause of his death, as a similar one was destined to kill his grandson, Caleb, in Ohio.

But for one obscure item posterity would have been none the wiser as to his being taken deathly sick at Kingston, on the way home. On June 22nd he hurriedly made his will, describing himself as weak, witnesses, Caleb Towle, Caleb Towle, Jr., and Benjamin Sleeper. The signature of Archibald Stark, his last, was a feeble effort but is well preserved, brown ink practically unfaded, linen paper durable.

It was during the heat of midsummer that Archibald Stark's body was brought home. The duty fell to Samuel, recently married, living at home, for the 32 year old son had no help from William and John then at Lake George in the final stages of the Abercrombie campaign. When the rude cart bearing the body, pulling hard in deep sand, bumping over ledges and rocks, creaking through many a stretch of pine woods, finally reached the old home and the never ending roar of the falls, the remains were received amid subdued voices and placed by restrained and reverent hands in the front room of the house he had built twenty years before.

The last journey was over, forty miles. Eleanor, the bereaved wife, grieving over one who, however wrongheaded at times, had been

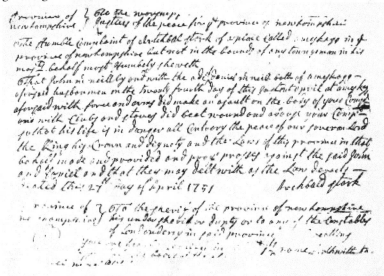

Archibald Stark's Charge of Assault, 1751

her loyal companion for more than two score years of poverty, joy, prosperity, affliction and now at last, disaster, had daughters and sons to help her bear her burden. The burial was in the little cemetery by Christian Brook, in sight of the home. A few of the early settlers had preceded him. When William and John came home they were shown the new made grave.

The envelope containing the Will and the estate papers (*N.H. Hist. Soc.*) is filed with hundreds of others of that early period. He left to wife, "Eliner" one third of the income, everything else to the children (without favouritism, so common at the time), William, Samuel, John, Archibald, Nancy, Isabel Stirling and Jean Stinson. After feebly making his signature he had only three days to live (grave stone inscription, June 25, 1758). When Executor John Stark (William, co-executor, seems not to have been active) filed his accounting Oct.21, 1765, more than seven years afterward, it included "$100 to convey the body of the Deceased from Kingstown (where he died) to Derryfield, and the funeral charges". By August 11th, 1758 John Stark had arrived home for Patten wrote in his book:

I with Thomas Hall apprised Archibald Stark's estate and got 19¾ pounds of beef at 4s from John Stark and pd him.

Patten and Hall eventually collected over £88 for their work. The lands were down at £8000, personal at £1618, but the estate was "insolvent" some 21 persons having claims among them Matthew Thornton (later a "Signer") and though a physician it was probably not for medical attendance. John Stark had the principal claim, "me, the subscriber, £441" and it implies he had been giving his father sums out of his pay as a ranger Captain. Patten had many more entries due to the estate settlements.

A stone was erected over the body of Archibald Stark, reading:

HERE LYES THE BODY OF MR. ARCHIBALD STARK
HE DEPARTED THIS LIFE JUNE 25TH, 1758, AGED 61 YEARS.

What remained of it was destroyed or covered up when the "Stark Park" idea was being carried out about 1900, by persons unknown. Potter's *Manchester* gave the date of Stark's birth as in 1693. But fortunately, the Bible in possession of a descendent of William Stark's line, Harold M. Stark of Detroit, gives the exact date as "July 8, 1687", the only record known and conforming to other evidence. A year before she died, Mrs. Jennie L. Osborn, born 1858, told the author that when she was a little girl she went with her mother, Mrs. Susan Abbott,

(1834-1910) to the Valley Cemetery, to which the few bodies iden-
tifiable by stones had been removed in 1854 (when the locomotive
works needed more space and the Christian Brook cemetery was destroyed) to visit the Stark and Gamble graves. The stone of Archibald
Stark ("a low slate headstone" Rowell, 1904) was found to be broken.
They took a piece home.

The next day Jennie was sent by her mother to return it. Even so
small a piece as she could carry caused Mrs. Osborne to remember
the incident always. Was Herrick right, in 1896, in asserting that the
remains of Archibald Stark, and presumably of Eleanor, though she
never had a stone (his buried 136 years, hers ten years less) were actually removed after the second interment, to "Stark Park", time "a year
or two since"? If not, and only his broken stone was moved, their dust
is mingled with the clear sand just north of the old stone of their son,
Samuel, the one spoken of as having a "bullet hole" in it, but which is
nothing more than a hole due to spalling of the soft material. Potter
in printing six inscriptions on the stones recently removed, (in his and
Rowell's time) from Christian Brook, made four mistakes!

Archibald's name (with incorrect dates) is on the monument in
Stark Park but there is no "marker" (as is the case of the 26 others)
with his name nor one with that of Eleanor (the "Eleanor Coombs"
being that of the general's daughter). If the Archibald stone was ever
moved from the Valley cemetery to Stark Park it became lost when
the desecration occurred. It may be, like that of Molly and the others,
a dozen or more in all, subject to possible discovery and retrieval. The
ground to the west of the present high fence slopes off, down steeply,
showing the necessity of much filling and grading.

When John Stark was 20 years of age the Treaty of Aix-la-Chapelle
brought its temporary peace and the border settlements of New
Hampshire enjoyed comparative freedom from Indian incursions.
From that year, 1748, the English settlements grew steadily, especially
across the Appalachians. In 1753 Governor Dinwiddie of Virginia sent
George Washington into the edge of the Ohio country, in the following year with an armed force. It was the small beginning of a struggle
that was to bring about the emergence of many a man of spirit and
ability. By the experience gained and the strong habits of life then
formed such men became leaders years later in the larger struggle
when the yoke of Great Britain was thrown off by the colonies.

John Stark's short trips as a pilot in 1753 and 1754 opened for
him a vista which he was to follow the whole course of his adventur-

ous life. An enlistment in one of the three companies locally forming was almost inevitable. The one chosen was that headed by his friend, Robert Rogers. It was a natural selection, influenced by the association of their respective fathers in the acquisition and settlement of Starkstown (Dunbarton) and by the appeal that scouting had for the young woodsman who had already seen enough of the life to realise he was fitted for it.

A condensed account should precede the story of their exploits in the war about to open. Stark's relations with Rogers can now be better understood because of the constantly widening knowledge of the latter, confirming Parkman's early judgment of his true character. From Allan Nevins (1914, the Caxton Club) to Burt G. Loescher, (1942, the *History of Rogers Rangers*, Vol.1) documentary evidence is now complete. But few items show Rogers between March, 17 53 (the Lovewell-Page-Talford expedition, Stark "Scout" Rogers one of the men) and the Summer of 1755.

In this period the smuggling and counterfeiting began and, perhaps, ended. Rogers had undertaken to raise 20 men for Major Joseph Frye of Massachusetts toward the quota of the Bay Colony, "taking the King's pay for it", Frye later contended (Prov. Pap. N. H. VI. 3 64). In the following month, February, 1755, Rogers was tried on a counterfeiting charge. The case was so important it was before a bench of three Justices of the Peace, Joseph Blanchard of Dunstable (Nashua), John Goffe of Derryfield and Matthew Thornton of Merrimack. Thornton became one of New Hampshire's three "Signers" of the Declaration of Independence.

The trial was at Rumford (Concord) and as the result of it, Rogers with 15 others were bound over to the Superior Court, to sit at Portsmouth on Feb. 12th, 1756. A transcript of the incriminating evidence, including the examination of Rogers was, in the usual way, sent to the appeal court. Some of the records are in the archive room of the New Hampshire Historical Society. Unfortunately, what the Provincial Court at Portsmouth did about it cannot be found. Rogers was there. Probably thoroughly frightened but with the outward plausibility and the cool effrontery which he could always assume, Rogers himself seems to have found a way out.

At any rate he was permitted to switch the would-be soldiers he had 'listed for Massachusetts over to the quota that Governor Wentworth was raising for New Hampshire, by methods not too squeamish, if accepting "King's evidence" from Rogers is any indication. It was not a time to be particular about personal records, of men who were needed, men of stamina, to go into the wilderness to fight the Indians and the French. Parkman (*Montcalm and Wolfe*) more than hints that smuggling was one of the early exploits of Rogers and that during his illicit intercourse with the French in Canada he acquired a smattering of the language. At more than one dangerous juncture Rogers in the future found the knowledge serving him well.

In April, after getting his freedom at Portsmouth, Rogers barely escaped the toils again. His dupe or confederate, Carty Gilman of Exeter, tried to swallow Rogers' incriminating letter (but did not succeed for it is still a loathsome court exhibit) when he was found with counterfeit bills and gave up that he had had dealings with Rogers. The Provincial authorities and all the Justices for Rockingham County were, of course, fully cognizant of these and other works of the strapping young man of 25 with the enormous nose, his distinguishing feature, if we may believe the somewhat doubtful and unconfirmed evidence of his only portrait done in London by an unknown hand in later years. If his nose was any bigger than two of Gilbert Stuart's of Washington, it would have been a monstrosity, and probably just escaped that misfortune.

Among the strange and perhaps true stories of Rogers and Stark one is to be found in William Little's *History of Weare, N. H.* (1888) which records how Rogers, Stark and one Samuel Orr of Goffstown were hunting on the Asquamchumauke River near Mount Moosilauke. The year must be inferred, probably about 1753. It was a rainy day in camp, three Indians called, departing shortly before night. Rogers slipped away, Stark and Orr not thinking much of his absence. About midnight he returned and carelessly threw down three bloody scalps. As Little has it; "Stark reproved him for killing these Indians in time of peace. 'Oh, damn it' said Rogers 'there'll be war before another year'". True or false the story illustrates a significant difference between Rogers and Stark.

How Robert Rogers' name had been connected with counterfeiting, and perhaps smuggling, could not have escaped the notice of Archibald Stark and his sons, located as they were where the traffic along the river passed their very door. John Stark could have remained with no illusions as to the course of Rogers. The unstable moral poise exhibited at times through Rogers' career, never seemed to sway the canny and observant Stark. The free gossip of every hamlet in the county ran in every ear, some of it, arrant hearsay but a good deal of it true, backed by the assertions of trustworthy men.

In the following year counterfeiting was again prevalent. The printing of the bills themselves was a simple business. Many a country yokel was deceived by more intelligent men who had yielded to cupidity. Utterers from the Bay colony were continually corrupting overwilling listeners in New Hampshire in a get-rich-quick circulation of the forged notes.

For the full story of Rogers' counterfeiting trial see Loescher's *Hist. Rogers Rangers*, and Provincial Court files, Concord, *Boston Newsletter*, Apr. 1, 1756, and State Papers (N.H.) VI. 364. John Stark gave testimony relative to Rogers' asseveration that he would have nothing further to do with the men who offered to buy oxen with counterfeit money. Rogers on the stand admitted taking a "20 pd. bill" from the man "to pasture his horse", but strongly denied other dealings.

That John Stark was not debased at this time by his association with Rogers must have been due to the strong fibre of the man's inherent morals. While this resistance was going on unconsciously, the reserved man learned to become bolder and the venturesome one become wary, a process in Nature in compensations where forces were constantly interacting. Stark's stability of character, due in part to Scotch caution, received some rude shocks (and became tougher thereby) for in the years to come Rogers and Stark were thrown together intimately. Often beneath the stars in the fastnesses of some unbroken wilderness, lying side by side, confidences were exchanged.

On the shores of Lake George on summer nights of Sylvester beauty, and by the camp fires in the dead of winter in the snows of mountain passes, John Stark learned to know Robert Rogers. From Rogers' own narratives it appears that more than once Stark helped him out of a bad situation. When Rogers, in the same accounts, deviated from the rules of scouting that he himself drew up, endangering himself and his men, it is noticeable that Stark was not with him. The time came when Stark's make-up sufficed to direct him on a true and honest course, while John's own brother, William Stark, went the way of Robers. Both became Tories and worse, as the records will show in due course.

As to the three companies enlisted and organised locally, Potter's history of Manchester states that one was that of Capt. John Goffe, another that of Capt. John Moore and the third, in spite of the Carty Gilman affair, that of Robert Rogers, all being of Derryfield and vicinity:

> Noah Johnson of Dunstable and John Stark of Derryfield were lieutenants in Rogers' company, which, as it was principally

employed in scouting and ranging the woods was called "The Rangers". This was the nucleus of the afterwards celebrated battalion known as "Rogers Rangers".

The roll has not been preserved but the company of about 50 men had Abraham Perry as the ensign and Hugh Stirling as Clerk, the latter brother-in-law of Stark he having married John's sister, Isabel. Stirling did not remain a Ranger very long. Later, when he was able, Johnson, a much older man who had seen service in Lovewell's war, was let out in favour of Robert's brother, Richard Rogers.

The ambitious plans of Commander-in-Chief Shirley (who was also Governor of the Massachusetts Bay colony), embraced three objects, his own expedition against the forts on the great lakes, General Braddock's advance westward in Pennsylvania and the assembling of a large force under Gen. William Johnson (afterward Sir William) to attack Crown Point, that thorn in the flesh of the New Englanders and of the settlers along the Hudson. The New England regiment of Col. Blanchard was slow in getting under way. It was rendezvoused at the fort at Stevens town (Salisbury) and Captain Rogers' company was sent on in advance, to the Coös meadows.

There a small fort was built at the junction of the Ammonoosuc with the Connecticut and the men were vigorously employed in constructing light *batteaux*. Ignorance in high places expected the force to reach Lake Champlain in that manner. The idea corrected, the troops went by way of "No. 4" and crossed the wilderness, now Vermont, reaching Albany on August 12, 1755.

There the New Hampshire force was assimilated at the "flats", river bottoms just above Albany, with the men of Johnson's army from Massachusetts, Connecticut, Rhode Island and from the Mohawk and Hudson. Stark soon learned that William Johnson had remarkable influence with Indians, but may with others have doubted Johnson's ability in a military way, seeing, as Parkman remarked, that he "knew nothing of war." But able and energetic Johnson was not the only man to head several thousand men with no more adequate training than himself. Another was his second in command', Phineas Lyman of Connecticut, lawyer, a brave and vigorous raw soldier.

In the commissary line there had been poor co-operation and the New Hampshire men soon found themselves facing short rations. A private subscription was thought necessary for their relief. (Blanchard to Wentworth, Prov. Pap. N. H. VI. 429)

While at the "flats" just above Albany or at the camps across the river, John Stark had the opportunity to renew his acquaintance with the queer Dutch town. He was later to know it even better but, perhaps, to esteem it no more than he did on his release from Indian captivity. The place had grown and was destined to thrive in a material way from the profitable presence of one army after another. The Indians, whose impressions are indelible said that the storekeepers there and also those representing them who came to their villages to bargain for furs were "not men but devils". Nevertheless, the Indians were an asset in the hands of William Johnson and he was here now when Indians meant success or failure in the campaign.

Back home in New Hampshire in the Merrimack valley, the news of Braddock's defeat on July 9, 1755, was received with dismay. The 23rd of the month "was observed as a fast day throughout the Province" as Matthew Patten wrote in his *Diary*. It was deemed by Gov. Shirley too late and too far to carry out his design but he left a large garrison at Oswego.

When Gen. Johnson's army was marched northward to "the great carrying place", later Fort Lyman, later Fort Edward, it was Rogers' company that was ordered to remain behind to escort the provision trains. The alertness and mobility of the rangers were deemed the best procurable protection. It was already better passageway than the trails. To act as a garrison the New Hampshire regiment of Col. Blanchard, some 500 men, remained at Fort Lyman. How near they came being annihilated will be seen. On his arrival at the lake, Lac St. Sacrement, which Gen. Johnson proceeded to re-name "Lake George" in honour of the British King, the army prepared a flotilla for the journey to Lake Champlain.

Fort Lyman, on the level Hudson at the junction of a creek, had little merit in natural defence. Then and during the ensuing 25 years the stockades and minor earth-works, afforded no sense of security. The story of the first campaign against an enemy that John Stark was to have a part in is told, all too briefly, in the "Introduction" which Rogers wrote for his celebrated *Journals* his note books evidently not kept until the first of the narratives, Sept. 24th, 17 55. (*Vide Journals of Robert Rogers of the Rangers* by Robert Rogers; Leonaur 2005.)

On the 26th of August, 1755 he was employed to escort the provision wagons from Albany to the Carrying Place, so called, since Fort Edward. Here he waited upon the general to whom he had been recommended as a person well acquainted with the haunts and passes of the enemy and the Indian method of fighting and was by him dispatched on several scouts to the French posts. He was on one of these up Hudson River, on the 8th of September, when Lieut. General, the Baron Dieskau, was taken prisoner and the French and Indians under his command defeated, at the South end of Lake George, near Bloody Pond, so called, from that defeat. For this service General Johnson was created a baronet.

While General Johnson, who knew vastly more already about Indians than the stalwart captain before him, received Rogers, who was now in an unfamiliar country, though his 2nd. Lieutenant, Stark, was not wholly so, the latter, we may be sure had been left behind. Rogers, attired in some sort of a uniform seems to have favourably impressed Johnson "notwithstanding some insinuations have been made to his disadvantage" for, after the campaign was over, in October, he wrote that Rogers "is the most active man in our army" and that "his bravery and veracity stand very clear in my opinion". Parkman's thirty thrilling pages in *Montcalm and Wolfe* should be followed for the advance of Baron Dieskau down from Canada, along Wood Creek and a trail, till within 4 miles of Fort Lyman where lay Blanchard's 500 men on guard. (*Vide Musket & Tomahawk* by Francis Parkman; Leonaur 2007.)

The French general's Indian allies had no stomachs to face the cannon of a fort, so Dieskau turned his steps to Lake George. When within three miles of Johnson's camp, some of the latter's forces were found to be approaching to give battle. Hurriedly arranging an ambush Dieskau nearly wiped out the advancing troops killing Col. Williams and King Hendrick, the fat old Indian chief. Dieskau pressed on toward the lake to complete his victory but Johnson had intrenched behind trees hastily felled. The New England men did deadly work with their muskets. A few field pieces were placed and fired, creating terror among the Indians. Defending the position Johnson was wounded but Lyman, his second in command, successfully directed the fighting. Dieskau was severely wounded.

At Fort Lyman Col. Blanchard learned of the battle and courageously sent Captain Nathaniel Falsam ("Ensign Falsam of the New Hampshire regiment, wounded through the shoulder." William Johnson's Report to the Governors, Sept. 9, 1775) with about 80 men of the regiment together with 40 men of the New York forces under Capt. McGinnis. The latter was soon killed, but Folsom receiving his baptism of fire creditably, did good work against the retreating French, losing only six men. Johnson did not follow up his victory, due either to his own injuries or, as was suspected, to his unwillingness to let Lyman have greater credit.

As Rogers was on a scout "up Hudson River" at the time and we find no mention of Stark in any account, it must be assumed that Stark was with him and that the rangers knew nothing of the battle until their return to camp Lyman. Rogers was directed to remain and conduct scouting parties during the winter, beginning Sept. 23, 1755. A rough fort was built at the lake side and named Fort William Henry. The provincials, having been enlisted for short periods, were sent home, except some 600 retained for garrison duty at the two forts. In the *Journals* Rogers gives the stories of seven successive scoutings, made up of 4, 5, 40, 4, 30, 10 and 2 men respectively. He finally reported on Dec. 24th. at Fort William Henry and was directed to remain with that garrison. Of Stark's movements we see nothing in Rogers.

On October 6th, Johnson wrote to Gov. Wentworth "As Col. Blanchard is now obliged to return with his regiment" he proposed that Col. Symes and Captain Rogers with a few of their men should continue the work of scouting through the winter. Some 24 men stayed on at William Henry. It is probable that, on permission being given, the reduced Ranger company was partly reorganised, the Isle au Mouton ambuscade scout being the last under Blanchard, and that Stark returned to New Hampshire then. As Nov. 28th was the date of the appointment of Richard Rogers to be lieutenant, Stark's participation had probably ended.

Between Nov. 12 and December 19th Rogers conducted two scouts, reconnoitring Ticonderoga both times, finding the garrison large and very busy; three new barracks, four store houses, fifty tents and probably 500 men in all. Caleb Stark's note (1831) was in error as to time;

> This campaign passed without other occurence of note. In the Autumn the regiment was discharged and Lt. Stark returned home.

Rogers' account of his scouts indicates plainly the October-November termination, but Caleb didn't grasp the facts in the *Reminisences*.

Late in December, 1770, over 15 years after the event, John Stark was trying to help one of the old rangers. Who wrote the certificate, notable for direct and clear statement without an unnecessary word (but with a common grammatical error) is not known but it was signed by Captain Stark. (Vol. Ill, Indian, French and Rev. War papers, archive room, N.-H. Hist. Society)

This may certify whom it may concern that Peter Bowen of Salisbury was in the Provincial service in the year 1755 under the command of Major Rogers, who was then a captain, and that the gun of Charles McAuley was discharged accidentally being loaded with a ball which entered the head of said Peter near his right eye and blew same out, I being personally present and see the same. Dec. 24th, 1770.

John Stark, Lieut, to said Company.
The bearer hereof, Peter Bowen, has been under the care of Dr. Carter, (my deceased husband) and had the misfortune of losing his eyesight by a shot of a gun while in the province service. This account to the doctor amounted to upwards of £200 O. T. Attested by Ruth Fowler. Bouscowen, December 3rd, 1770.

Uneventful as the campaign had been it provided Lt. Stark with needed experience of large camps and the movement of troops, as well as more or less actual scouting.

At home the year 1756 opened inauspiciously for the Stark family. Archibald Stark had to give another note to Samuel Rankin, the innkeeper, this time for thirty-seven pounds. The former note of £57 was overdue, unpaid since 1748.

Counterfeiters were active in the Merrimack valley and on Feb. 3rd. Matthew Patten's diary told of his going down the river in search of the culprits;

Set out after midnight with Thomas McLaughlin and John Little to summon Aaron Quimby but mist of it he being absconded summond on Sabath day John Stark John Quig, Benj Smith & Wm. Moor to appear on Monday and Caleb Emery, Jun' on Monday to appear before Joseph Blanchard, Esq'.

What was done by Justice Blanchard after hearing these witnesses of what the counterfeiters were about is not seen but Patten gave in on the 8th. his account, "to Mr. Parker to carry to Court" (meaning the Superior Court) at Portsmouth. On the 4th. Patten had "rid all night" and had apprehended four men, whom he does not name. Though Aaron Quimby had "absconded" his name appears as one of the company of militia next to be enlisted. From time to time other counterfeiters and scares are found in the records but no further mention of Lt. Stark.

During February and March, while John Stark awaited the end of winter and his call to service, a poor and diffident young man about the homely tasks of the farm and saw mill, a study in contrasts is furnished material.

There entered Boston, only 60 miles away, by the road from New York, a showy cavalcade of five persons. The leader, an equestrian to claim the attention of every eye was no less than Col. George Washington, a tall and handsome man of 24, graced in all the courtly qualities of Virginia, a colony most like cultured England. At times by his side were Captains Mercer and Ashton, his aids. All were notably mounted and dressed in new and expensive uniforms. Behind were two negro servants "glittering in cream and scarlet and silver lace". The long journey of two months was to seek a favour of Governor Shirley, who welcomed Washington and granted his request. Capt. Dagworthy of Maryland had seen no reason to acknowledge any authority in Col. Washington of Virginia. Washington was determined to put him in his place; an early exhibition of his character.

The visitors saw little of the dark background of surviving Puritanism, were splendidly entertained and then headed their horses homeward. It was as commander-in-chief that Washington next saw Boston. Nineteen years were to pass before Stark and he were to meet. Never in their long association in wresting their diverse colonies from British rule were their characters and their modes of life to draw together. They were alike in unvarying patriotism, in all other essentials, poles apart.

In March 1756 General Shirley summoned Rogers to Boston for a conference. Washington had been and gone. It is doubtful if they were ever face to face but when during the Revolutionary war's early months Washington had to deal with Rogers, he made no mistake; he knew his man. Rogers in his *Journals* wrote;

> Leaving Ensign Noah Johnson, the command of my company I set out on the 17th. for Boston. On the 23rd, the general gave me a friendly reception and the next day a commission to recruit an independent company of rangers.

This was a feather in the cap of Rogers for it would take him out of the regiment of Col. Blanchard or any other. The ambitious captain "sold", as the present day has it, his project, as he did to most Britishers, though to but few Americans. We may presume that there were "red letter days" in Boston, sightseeing and the like, for the backwoods boy from the border town in New Hampshire. What Parkman said of William Johnson "a courtier in his rough way" may be applied to Rogers. He was to have a company of 60 privates, to be paid 3 shillings a day.

As captain he was to have his 10 shillings, his lieutenant, 7, his ensign, 4.

The instructions given Rogers by Shirley were predatory; at least Rogers recorded them thus; "to distress the French and their allies by sacking, burning and destroying." Shirley gave letters to the commanders at Fort Lyman and Fort Wm. Henry. While Rogers would be under the command of any superior officer the nature of his work would make his, a separate arm of the service. No roster of the new company is known but Potter says of the unit that it was "officered principally from Amoskeag and being enlisted from the New Hampshire regiment, most of the men were from this neighbourhood."

Between the time of his leaving Boston on March 24th. 1756, when he received his commission, and April 28th, when he left No. 4, the short gap suggests that Rogers looked to the selection of his junior officers. He would have no difficulty in securing the services of John Stark, to act as third in command, his second lieutenant. There would be time and inclination, so a visit to Starkstown would be natural, where his widowed mother kept the home place. It was somewhat remotely located in the south-east portion of the new town. In memory of the North of Ireland the farm had been named "Mountalona". On an Irish map of 1777 "Mounterlany Hills" are to be seen in Tyrone, not many miles south of the ancient city of Londonderry, the home of so many of the Scotch-Irish emigrants.

So, the Rogers family were of the hill country. Robert's sisters, Mary, Martha and Catherine were still unmarried. Daniel and Samuel, his elder brothers, had not left the farm, carrying it on while Robert ranged far and wide. He had already taken Richard with him and later James, still younger, went with Robert. Virgin forests nearly hemmed the clearings in. From rising ground, a little to the south there was visible the placid Merrimack above the falls. Behind a hill where the river disappeared was the hamlet, Derryfield, where the Starks lived. The City of Manchester now fills the view.

Scarcely ten years were to elapse before Robert Rogers, the boy brought up in the log cabin was to achieve fame and then a notoriety of more than doubtful cast. In London itself there was to be printed and be followed by acclaim sufficient to turn his head, his two books. One was the *Journals* dealing with his part in the French and Indian War. It became a chief source of information to historians and romance-historians. His note-books, if any, have not survived. His memory was doubtless remarkable, though it sometimes slipped. Perhaps his good mother, Mary McPhartridge, was better educated and more diligent than most pioneer mothers with their children, Eleanor Nichols Stark, for example.

Rogers continues the history of the rangers:

> When the company was completed part of it marched under the orders of Lieutenant Richard Rogers to Albany; with the remainder I passed through the woods to Number Four, a frontier town, greatly exposed. There I received orders to proceed to Crown Point, for which on the 28th of April we directed our course, through vast forests and over lofty mountains. The second day of the march Mr. John Stark, my second lieutenant became ill and was obliged to return to Fort Edward, with a guard of six men.

Split up into three parties the routes are not given in detail. There may have been a blazed trail for Robert, hardly one for John Stark, though his course may have anticipated the road up the Black River and over the mountains of Peru to Manchester, thence to Fort Lyman. To Albany Richard Rogers would have merely to descend the Connecticut and go over a road across the Berkshires. John Stark's course was hazardous. He was not long in making recovery from his sudden illness. His party was small enough, seven men in all, to be able to hide from roving bands of savages. His party was ever on the alert but if they were following a trail it was a matter of luck not to run into an ambush. Once there was imminent peril, for Rogers records it; Stark "discovered and eluded a scout of 400 Indians". Such a large party was probably in the region near the end of his journey, on the Hudson. But for Stark's unvarying caution his scalp might have been hung at St. Francis together with those of his companions, to be among the hundreds seen by Rogers when the village was burned and the inhabitants massacred by his men on Amherst's orders a few years later.

Rogers tells how he and his own party arrived at Lake Champlain, some four miles south of Crown Point (Ft. Frederic) at a place where there was an "unoccupied village". They saw 500 French go by. Rogers killed 23 cattle "whose tongues were of great service on our march". Then "each man taking a different route" they escaped French and Indians approaching, got in plain sight of Fort Ticonderoga (Carillon) and "reached Fort William Henry on the 11th day of May". The rangers thus began their series of exploits. They found that Richard Rogers had already been sent on a new scout.

The Bulletin of the Fort Ticonderoga Museum for July, 1942, published a translation of the journal of a French engineer, in rank a captain, one Gaspard-Joseph Chaussegros de Lere, covering a short period; May 8th. to July 2nd. 1756. De Lere was helping in the construction of the Fort at 'Ti" but set down in his daily account, in the accurate and painstaking way of his calling, many incidents, troop movements, casualties, accessions, departures, and the like.

The stories seem quite dependable and afford one of the few checks on the credibility of Rogers. In London in 1765 the latter was writing his books for the English market, based on memoranda in his *Journals*, Taken literally, and their form encourages that definite construction, we are able to see in one instance (the doings of May 21st, 1765) how long a time a diminutive Nemesis sometimes takes (in this case a matter of 186 years) in coming up, in order that Rogers might be brought to book. Under date, May 20, Rogers wrote;

> Was ordered by the general with a party of 11 men, to reconnoitre the French advanced guard. Viewing them next day from the summit of a mountain, their number appeared to be 300 men, who were then busy in fortifying their position with palisades. From the other side of the mountain we obtained a fine prospect of Ticonderoga and the French camp, which from the ground it occupied, I judged to contain 1000 men. This night was passed upon the mountain and early next morning we proceeded to the Indian Carrying path &c.

It was a near thing, how Rogers and his party of 11 men missed the most, important movement of the French at 'Ti" for weeks. Dated the 21st. the same day, Rogers scouted secretly first one side and then the other of "Mount Defiance", de Lere recorded how:

> At noon, M. de La Colombiere set out at the head of a party of 415 men to go and burn the boats of the enemy which are beneath the cannon at the fort of Ledius.

The junior officers are named, also the make-up of the troop units. At what hour of the day Rogers got his "fine prospect of Ticonderoga" is conjectural but it was probably, if we may credit the account, shortly after the flotilla, required in conveying the expeditionary force as far as the head of Champlain (now Whitehall), had passed, otherwise he could not have failed to discover the massing of boats and the troop movements, the bustle of the departures. As John Stark was probably not with Rogers on this small scout, it will not be necessary to show how the French task force returned on the 29th, bringing only four prisoners and three scalps.

One of the prisoners, a negro, told of the strength of the garrison at Fort William Henry, of Fontenay's disclosures of conditions at "Ti" and a good deal more, of interest to the student. Had the timing permitted, Rogers could have watched the boats of the French expedition for miles, going up the clay-mixed waters of Champlain, there in its narrowest stretches. In blissful ignorance of all this Rogers made his night camp on the mountain, possibly avoiding disclosure by not lighting a fire. Rogers' account, again taken up;

> Early next morning we proceeded to the Indian Carry path, leading from Lake George to Champlain. There an ambuscade was formed between the advanced guard and the Fort. About 6 o'clock 118 Frenchmen passed along the path without observing us; in a few minutes 22 others came the same way;—upon them we fired, killed six and took one prisoner; but the first party returning at the report of the guns, obliged us to retire in great haste. We reached Wm. Henry on the 23rd in safety with our prisoner who reported that 220 French and Indians were preparing to surprise the out parties at Fort Edward.

The French account, to be compared with that of Rogers of the same date, is;

> (de Lere)—At 9 o'clock of the morning there arrived 13 men of the Canadian militia who escaped from the portage where they were attacked by some 15 English as they say. It is true that M. deBeaujeu had ordered M. de Fortenay, cadet, to go there with 20 armed men, each one with an axe, to work on the portage trail. They left their arms at one end of the said portage with a sentry to guard them and came to the other end to work there. This portage is 3/4 of a league across. The English killed one man and scalped him after which they left more promptly than they had come without taking the trouble to follow the fleeing men; they could have captured these 20 men without firing a shot if they had wanted as they were all sitting in a circle smoking their pipes (calumet). There is still missing from this detail only the *sieur* Fontenay, and we are very anxious as to his fate.

Rogers succeeded, as he so often did, in capturing a prisoner from whom valuable information was to be obtained. DeLere mentions no detachment of a hundred men. Rogers may have dressed up the account, though the passage of troops between the fort and the advanced camp on Lake George would be a routine procedure. But for the purpose of comparison the discrepancy as to men killed is a serious one. DeLere recorded one man killed, and scalped. Rogers boasted of six killed. Both agree in one prisoner being taken by Rogers. This coincidence and other points make the date beyond question. The scalping of the killed Frenchman remains unexplained. A picket from the Fort was immediately sent to the scene. DeLere further stated that they remained out until 4:30 seeking to discover traces of the English (Rogers') party. Had the veracity of Rogers in his later life not been so thoroughly riddled, some reconcilement as to the six men killed, might be possible.

On Rogers' return to Fort William Henry he learned that Gen. Shirley had been superseded by Gen. Abercrombie. The latter reached Albany on June 25th. Rogers made a written report to him, recommending a greater ranger company. Soon after he went to Albany and there was ordered to organise an additional company. The command of it was given to Richard Rogers, Noah Johnson was made 1st. Lt. Nathaniel Abbott 2nd. Lt. and Caleb Page, Ensign. The latter was brother of Elizabeth Page who in due time became the wife of John Stark and achieve fame as "Molly Stark." Caleb was "the handsomest of the Pages." He was to die the following year, caught in ambush on one of the rangers' biggest scouts.

Rogers says of his own old ranger company:

John Stark my 2nd. lieut. was appointed my first, John McCurdy succeeded him and Jonathan Burbank was appointed ensign.

Having his brother taken care of, Stark's promotion was in order, though Richard Rogers was younger and of no previous experience and John Stark would have been of more value in the new corps. It is probable, however, that Robert Rogers had so learned to value John Stark that he depended on him. As it turned out some 8 months later a different decision might have cost him his life. But for his thriftily looking after his own family interests, the story of Robert Rogers might never have been written.

At Albany the English commander and the Colonial authorities were concentrating an army to attempt the reduction of Ticonderoga and the capture of Fort St. Frederick (Crown Point.). Rogers says that his brother's new company was "completed in 28 days and went on a scout up the Mohawk." Early in August, 1756, Robert Rogers with some of his men went on several scouts down the lakes. On one of these he detoured Ticonderoga by a route he had travelled before, in order to safely avoid that post.

A company of Stockbridge Indians was this year employed in His Majesty's service, officered by Indians commissioned by Gov. Shirley. Gen. Abercrombie was at a loss how to dispose of them; but was advised by Sir William Johnson to employ thirty privates and a lieutenant as scouts to scour the woods under the direction of the ranger officers. This party Lieut. Stark had strengthened with some of his own men and sent on a scout with particular directions, the day I returned from my last excursion.

It shows that Stark had enough authority to act in the absence of Rogers and that he was entrusted by the authorities with organisation and direction.

The Earl of Loudon arrived in Albany and assumed the chief command, Rogers rendering to him an account of his recent scouts and requesting permission:

To penetrate into Canada with the Indians and distress the inhabitants by burning their harvest (now nearly ripe) and destroying their cattle.

Accordingly, August 16 we embarked in whale boats in two detachments, Lieutenant Stark commanding one and myself the other. The next morning, we joined each other and proceeded to the place where our boats had been left July 7th, 20 miles North of Crown Point on the west side of Champlain. (The next day they made 20 miles also and at midnight discerned a schooner passing them, which they were unable to capture. After a short time further down the lake, without incident, they returned to) 8 miles North of Crown Point on the east shore. The 29th in the morning entered a village lying east of the fort and took prisoners, a man, his wife and daughter, (a pretty girl of fourteen) and with them we returned to Wm. Henry Sept. 22nd.

The Frenchman, two years at Crown Point, gave much information of value, detailed by Rogers, who was ordered by Lord Loudon to wait on Col. Burton at Saratoga. He was directed to scout down opposite Saratoga.

On this tour we apprehended 4 deserters from Ottway's regiment going over to the enemy, who were sent back to Fort Edward in the charge of Lt. Stark.

Under the direction of Col. Burton, the companies of Robert and Richard Rogers were utilised in scoutings, the Stockbridge Indians participating, "leaving the remainder of our rangers to serve as flankers to the parties convoying provisions to Fort Wm. Henry." It is probable that Stark was in charge of this work, Rogers going into several small scouts in much detail without mentioning Stark, the period embracing the greater part of September. On the 24th:

> Gen. Abercrombie ordered that three commissioned officers of the rangers with 20 privates each should reconnoitre Wood Creek, South Bay and Ticonderoga, who alternately kept up a continual scout for some time.

Normally Lt. Stark would have headed one of these parties, but is not mentioned. Rogers jumps to October 22nd. for his next item, then communicating the decision of Lord Loudon and Gen. Abercrombie at Fort Edward to do nothing further in the campaign, supposing the lakes would freeze, "as they generally do in December", Rogers added. The rangers were then ordered to proceed to "Ti" and bring in a prisoner. In graphic fashion Rogers describes the capture of one he deceived by first answering the sentry in French, who called out "*Qui estes vous?*"."I answered, 'Rogers' and led him from his post in great haste."

It was one of those instances when Rogers with animal quickness, one of his most valuable acquisitions, showed his outstanding value as a ranger. So, the name "Rogers" had for French and Indians alike a glamour that made him famous in every camp and feared on every expedition.

There was scouting about Fort Edward until on Nov. 19, 1756 when "Captain Abercrombie, *aide-de-camp* and nephew of the general, had the curiosity to accompany the expedition" down Lake George, getting a view of the French garrison (and nothing of more value) at Ticonderoga.

> He was delighted with the novelties of a scout and with the romantic and noble scenery through which we conducted him. He treated us handsomely on our return to Fort Edward, on the evening of the 25th.

Young Capt. James Abercrombie had in August previously, it seems, from another account than that of Rogers, been extremely critical of the rangers, saying that:

> Rogers undertook to go off with his company without orders and excused his action because of the unwillingness of his men

to stay behind when other parties were out.

After the scouting party he wrote of it;

> They even rebelled against their own officers. All I could do or
> say to the officers they could not prevent firing on our march.
> They slept one night near Ticonderoga and next morning a
> few of them were seen as they were about to capture a pris-
> oner. Capt. Stark who was with me set up the Indian hollow,
> upon that the whole party jumped up and yelled as if Hell had
> broke loose and all fell afiring at a few men running away. I did
> everything in my power to make them hold their tongues and
> behave as they ought to do. I even knocked several of them
> down and damned their officers for a set of scoundrels.
>
> A month later the rangers encamped on an island off Ft. Ed-
> ward and began a riot in an effort to rescue two of their num-
> ber who had been imprisoned by their own officers, cut down
> the whipping post, which was to them the chief emblem of the
> discipline they detested and dispersed only after Capt. Shepard
> confronted them with a firelock in their hands. After that they
> began to desert. . . . The rangers refused to take orders or to do
> any duty but that of scouting. If Webb is to be believed they
> were not above lying and sleeping on an island in Lake George
> one whole fortnight when they were supposed to be surveying
> the enemy positions.

And so, the rangers were like that? It would be worth a whole
picture show to see Lt. John Stark give the signal and start the fray by
clapping hand on mouth in the staccato and explosive Indian yell that
has come down to us from those times, probably unchanged, a yell
that strikes mock-terror to every boy's heart.

Yet young Abercrombie outdid himself in praise and polite com-
mendation a few months after the disastrous scout when Capt. Spikeman was killed and John Stark saved the expedition from complete
rout and disaster, he wrote Rogers:

> You cannot imagine how all ranks of people are pleased with
> your men's behaviour.
>
> I was so pleased with their appearance when I was out with
> them that I took it for granted that they would behave well
> whenever they met the enemy.

As to the rangers in another quarter, "Loudon had to bear with
their humours for he could not get along without them" (Pargellis in

36

Lord Loudon in North America.)

The summer had slipped away. After Montcalm had taken Oswego in August the French had little to fear, for from the St. Lawrence to the Mississippi, their communications were perfect. Parkman summed up. "Shirley's grand scheme for cutting New France in twain had come to wreck." The colonies, especially those of New England were in despair, their money and men had been wasted, heavy debts had accumulated. From Albany to Fort William Henry Abercrombie was able to count some 10,000 men. It was deemed by Abercrombie and Loudon too late to attack Ticonderoga. So, the season was allowed to close in idleness and inaction. Had the general's incapacity been recognised then, the great disaster of 1757 would have been averted.

Rogers records:

About this time his lordship drew off the main body of his troops from Fort Edward, to be quartered at Albany and New York. Both armies now retired to winter quarters. The rangers were stationed at Forts William Henry and Edward and were augmented by two new companies under Captains Hobbs and Spikeman. The two companies were posted at Fort William Henry and our two at Fort Edward. Capt. Richard Rogers was sent to New England for recruits. He waited upon the Boston Government to obtain pay for our services in the winter of 1755 but could obtain none, though Lord Loudoun generously supported the justice of our claim.

Rogers took seven pages in his *Journals* to describe and explain. The fact was that he walked the rangers into an ambush on January 21, 1757. Eight years after the event, in London, where he was trying to repair his fortunes and prestige, he wrote the principal account. Another is found in Parkman, who failed to give full credit to Stark, probably because Rogers understated the part. In 1831 Caleb Stark published a short and indifferent story, another in 1860, after Potter's *Manchester* (not being helped by any "family" narration) reprinted Rogers' *Journal* as to the battle. The locale of the night before the battle is probably, though this conclusion and that of Loescher (*History of Rogers Rangers*) must differ, up the steep valley where the reservoir for Ticonderoga is now located.

The locale of the battle itself is derived from a study of the actual ground, also from Rogers' own story and from conclusions as to the movements of the French, the element of time being of the utmost importance, along the bed of Trout Brook, above where it receives the "reservoir" stream. The theory that it was anywhere north of "Street Road" is not tenable. Compromises with descriptions and topography are required and the actual places can never be proven. Rogers' account began;

> Marched with Mr. Stark, my lieutenant, Ensign Page of Richard Rogers' company and 50 privates to Fort William Henry where we were employed in providing provisions, snow-shoes, &c. until the 17th. when being joined by Capt. Spikeman, Lt. Kennedy, Ensign Brewer and 14 men of his corps, together with Ensign James Rogers with 20 men of Hobb's company, with Mr. Baker, a volunteer of the 44th Reg. of the line, we proceeded down Lake George on the ice and at night encamped on the east side of the first narrows.

Spikeman's and Hobb's companies had come from Halifax, Robert's younger brother James being among the New Hampshire men. Brewer was from Massachusetts and later fought, or who had men who fought, at Bunker Hill. Ensign Page ("Molly Stark" was his sister) was out of Richard Rogers' company. Only 11 miles were counted up for the first day of travel. On snow-shoes it was slow progress for that usually fast accessory. The camp was under the lee of Shelving Rock mountain, opposite Tongue mountain and where the lake is filled with beautiful islands.

> Next morning some of our party who had become lame in consequence of the exertions of yesterday were sent back. This reduced our number to 74 men and officers. The 18th, camped 12 miles down the lake on the West side. The 19th, marched 3 miles down the lake, then took to the land with our snow-shoes, travelled 8 miles north west and encamped 3 miles from the lake. 20th, marched north west all day and encamped on the West side three miles from Lake Champlain.

> *Jan. 21st*, marched east to the lake, half way between Crown Point and Ticonderoga, where we discovered a sled passing from the latter to the former. Lt. Stark with 20 men was directed to head the sled while I with my party cut off its retreat, leaving Spikeman with the centre. Ten other sleds were discovered following down the lake and I endeavoured to give Mr. Stark notice of it before he showed himself upon the lake but could not. He sailed out and they hastily turned back toward Ticonderoga.

Rogers then pursued, took 7 prisoners, 3 sleds, 6 horses. The prisoners were separately examined, disclosing that there were some 500 in garrison at Crown Point with 350 at "Ti." Rogers adds:

> From this account of things and knowing that those who escaped would give immediate notice of us I gave orders to march with all expedition to the fires we had kindled the night before and prepare for battle, if offered, by drying our guns, it being a rainy day.

Rogers, whose 28 carefully written out rules for the guidance of the rangers he pompously published in his London book, no doubt greatly impressing his predisposed British audience, seems to have disregarded more than one of them. He proceeded to pay the penalty, as he did on other occasions, as when Israel Putnam was captured and nearly killed. Smoke from the fires of 70 men even in overcast weather could have been seen for some distance, so we must suppose that precaution was taken to camp off the beaten tracks of the red men and especially far from the direct route between the two forts. The guns were dried.

> We then marched single file, myself and Lt. Kennedy in front, Lt. Stark in the rear and Captain Spikeman in the centre. Ensigns Page and Rogers between the front and the centre and Mr. Brewer between the centre and rear, Sergeant Walker having command of a rear guard. In this manner we advanced half a mile over broken ground, passed a valley of fifteen rods breadth, when the front, having gained the summit of the opposite hill on the west side fell in with the enemy drawn up in the form of a crescent to surround us.

Drying their guns at the previous night's camping place had allowed ample time for the enemy at Ticonderoga to have found the trail of the northward journey and dispose the French and Indians for a perfect ambush, some little space in advance of Rogers, himself in the lead but carelessly, in the face of danger, walking into the trap. Caleb Stark has a footnote;

> The late venerable Mr. Shute of Concord, N. H. remarked that Rogers did not act with his usual prudence. He states that after taking the sleds, a council of war advised to return by a different rout, from that by which the party came, which was the usual practice of the rangers and on this occasion would have enabled them to escape the hazards of a battle. Rogers, however, said in regard to the enemy that they would not *dare* to pursue him

and took the same rout back.

In 1756 Rogers printed his rules, two of them being as follows;

No. 2. In your return take a different rout from that by which you went out.

No. 5. If the ground will admit send a man in front and one on each flank, to give notice of the enemy, his number, &c.

It is not surprising that Shute reported the strain of *braggadocio* in Rogers. That day the intrepid leader was careless to the point of rashness. There may have been more than the usual inward fortification; it was rainy. Caleb Stark, grandson of the general, knew Mr. Shute well, their homes being but a few miles apart. Rogers' account is resumed and he wrote that:

They were immediately saluted with a volley of 200 shot at a distance of five yards from the nearest and thirty yards from the rear of the party. This fire took place about two o'clock p.m. and proved fatal to Lt. Kennedy and Mr. Gardner, a volunteer, besides wounding several and myself in the head. I ordered my men to retire to the opposite hill where Lieut. Stark and Mr. Brewer had made a stand with forty men to cover our retreat. We were closely pursued Capt. Spikeman and others were killed and several made prisoners. Lieut. Stark repulsed them by a brisk fire from the hill, killing a number and affording us an opportunity to post ourselves to advantage.

Mr. Stark then took a position in the centre with Ensign Rogers, Sergeants Walker and Phillips acting as reserves, to protect our flanks and watch the enemy's motions. Soon after we had thus formed for battle the enemy attempted to flank us but the reserve bravely attacked them giving the first fire which stopped several from retreating to the main body. We were then pushed closely in front, but having the advantage of the ground and being sheltered by large trees, we maintained a continual fire upon them, which killed a number and compelled the others to retire upon the main body. They attempted to flank us once more but were again gallantly repulsed by our reserve. In this affair Mr. Baker was killed.

We kept up a constant fire till sunset, when I received a shot through my wrist, which disabled me from loading my gun. The action, however, continued till darkness prevented our seeing each other. Our men gallantly held their position till the fire of the enemy ceased and he retired.

Caleb Stark (1831) after a preliminary, went on:

A most bloody and desperate action ensued, perhaps according to numbers, one more sanguinary was not fought during the war. Major Rogers was wounded, Capt. Spikeman was killed and the command devolved upon Lt. Stark who by his prudence and firmness secured the wounded and drew off the detachment in such order as to keep the enemy at bay. They reached Lake George at 6 a.m.

In another footnote Caleb Stark comments;

Stilson Eastman of Concord, N. H. who was one of Stark's Rangers in this action states that on receipt of his second wound, Rogers thought of ordering a retreat as the only safety of the party. Lieut. Stark who was then almost the only officer fit for duty declared he would shoot the first man who fled, said he had a good position and would fight the enemy until dark and then retreat, and that in such a course consisted their only safety. While he was speaking a ball broke the lock of his gun; at the same time, observing a Frenchman fall, he sprang forward, seized his gun, returned to his place and continued the action. Eastman stated that Stark's courage and prudence saved the party and that to the bravery and skill of William and John Stark, the rangers were indebted for much of their success and celebrity in the campaigns against the French. The late Col. Webster of Plymouth made a similar statement.

In 1860 Caleb Stark added a number of lines of anecdote which he doubtless got from his father, Major Caleb.

General Stark stated in after times that he was never conscious of taking the life of an individual except in this action. While the rangers were defending their position on the crest of the hill, he observed that several balls struck near him from a certain direction. In a moment afterward he discovered an Indian stretched at full length upon a rock behind a large tree. His gun was soon ready and he saw the Indian rising for another shot at him. His *fusee* was instantly levelled, discharged, and the savage rolled from the rock into the snow, pierced by the bullet through the head

(Footnote) He was at this period twenty-eight years of age. He had been an expert and successful hunter and was well known to have been one of the best marksmen of his time; and the most savage animals in his native forests the catamounts, bears, wolves and wildcats in numerous instances, felt the effects of his unerring aim.

Rogers made a point of the following;

> The enemy during this action practised several stratagems to induce us to submit; sometimes assuring us that they had a reinforcement at hand, which would cut us to pieces without mercy and that it was a pity that so many brave men should be lost; that in case of surrender we should be treated with compassion; calling me by name they assured me of their friendship and esteem; but the brave men who fought by my side, were neither to be dismayed by their threats, nor flattered by their professions and determined to conquer or die with arms in their hands.

Incidentally the foregoing paragraph is only one of many in Rogers' book, printed in London in 1765, going to show that the narrative was actually written by one having the command of perfect English only the facts being told off by Rogers, from memory and his memoranda. The utter impossibility of Rogers himself, a raw country boy brought up in a frontier town in New Hampshire, entirely devoid of school facilities, penning an excellent relation, replete with the amenities of the cultivated life of England did not seem to occur to Parkman (who may not have known of the deprivations Rogers suffered in his youth) for the great historian observed:

> His style is direct, simple, without boasting, and, to all appearances without exaggeration.

Nevins' words "He may have been in school" are on the favourable side, though the few log houses in the wilderness of Dunbarton are not historically credited with even an itinerant schoolmaster. Sir William Johnson, (*Journals*, 1767) probably told the truth in indicating that the services of one Nathaniel Potter (and see Kenneth Roberts) were necessary and that he had been employed "because Rogers was so illiterate as to require someone to do business for him." Nevertheless, Rogers had great ability in picking up knowledge and his grade of intelligence was superior. He knew what he was about but a loose screw in his moral make-up made his actions unpredictable.

His account concludes with "six wounded men" but as relief was limited to "the sleigh" it is likely that Rogers made an unconscious exaggeration.

After the action we had a great number so severely wounded that they could not travel without assistance; but as we were near to the French garrison, it was thought best to take advantage of the night and retreat, which we did, keeping up the spirits of the wounded as well as possible, and reached Lake George six miles south of the French advanced guard next morning.

The place was probably Cook's Bay, the route having been by Trout Brook during the night. It was a comparatively level if difficult trail, often followed both by Indians and white men. Rogers finishes the account;

Our wounded men were now exhausted and could march no farther. Lieutenant Stark then volunteered with Thomas Burnside and another, to proceed to Fort William Henry and procure sleighs for the wounded. They reached the Fort that night and next morning the sleigh arrived though the distance was nearly forty miles. Lieut. Buckley of Hobbs' corps of rangers came out with fifteen men and met us at the first narrows of Lake George (The narrows at Tongue Mountain) Our party of forty-eight effective and six wounded men, arrived with the prisoners at William Henry the same evening, being the 23rd of January, 1757.

To this Caleb Stark's footnote is pertinent;

He travelled a distance of forty miles through the wilderness on snow-shoes and with great fatigue reached the fort on the evening of the same day when the party above named was immediately dispatched to the assistance of Rogers and his wounded men. The snow was four feet deep upon a level.

The amazing fortitude of John Stark was put to the test. It was after a night of mental distress and muscular toil, following the intensest nerve strain during a battle the day before. Lake George is about 30½ miles long in a straight line. Deducting about six miles at the north end (where the party of 54 men waited, exhausted) the distance "as the crow flies" of about 25 miles actually means little, for the route followed must have been considerably lengthened, though perhaps not to 40 miles, in seeking better going where the snow was wholly or partly blown off the surface of the ice and in avoiding the deep slush due to recent rains. It was an almost superhuman task for the three men. Stark himself and his companions were not called upon, and probably did not go, when the sled for the wounded was pulled and pushed to the point indicated, because fresh rangers were available at the fort.

Rogers thought the enemy numbered 250; heard that those killed or who had died of their wounds numbered 116, but Vaudreuil, the principal French source, gave, according to Parkman, only 89 regulars with 90 Canadians and Indians. Vaudreuil, with his usual inaccuracy, wrote that of the English some 40 were killed and that only three reached Fort William Henry alive. What was done about the killed at the scene of the fight may be imagined, but the Indians would scalp them all.

Necessarily left where he fell was young Caleb Page, townsman of Rogers and friend of Stark. He had married his young wife, Hannah Carleton, less than two years before (Haverhill record). It was a tale of anguish for Lt. Stark to tell his future father-in-law, Caleb Page in Dunbarton. In the rude house, that preceded the mansion there, the grewsome story, Elizabeth, then 20 years of age, would hear from the lips of her future husband, who was to make her known to posterity as "Molly Stark".

To his immediate superior, Major Sparks, at Fort Edward, he told his losses. His report was followed by one to Aide-de-Camp Abercrombie at Albany, recommending:

> Such officers as were most deserving to fill the vacancies occasioned by the late action, as follows; Lieut. Stark to be Captain of Spikeman's corps, and Sergeant Joshua Martin to be ensign of Richard Rogers' Company.

The response was:

> The general received your report by Major Sparks. He returns to you and your men thanks for your good behaviour. . . . We sent an express to Boston, recommending your brother James for lieutenant of Spikeman's company. Please send the name of the officers you recommend for your own company and your recommendation shall be duly regarded. You cannot imagine how all ranks of people are pleased with your men's behaviour When Gen. Abercrombie receives his lordship's instructions respecting the rangers, I shall send you notice of it. In the meantime, I hope you'll get the better of your wound.

The letter revealed no intentions as to Stark, though Rogers asserts his favouring him for captain. The wording of the report has never become known.

My wound growing worse I repaired to Albany for medical

aid, and there received from Gen. Abercrombie the following instructions.

These, (no doubt after conferences with Rogers), involved cutting down the pay of some rangers, making them all on the same basis and if those cut down did not wish to serve they could resign; "you are at liberty to discharge them" was the general's phrase. The four companies of 100 each were to be completed as soon as possible and brought to Fort Edward. The date was Feb. 26th, 1757.

Rogers was probably informed of the reason for the prompt action ordered as to the rangers. Lord Loudon had his plans made for the taking of Louisburg. It was a laudable ambition, quite the strategic move for the control of North America by the British. But Loudon was a weak and leisurely organiser and his chief aid, Abercrombie, was no better. It is well known that had the expedition arrived a month earlier at Halifax, assuming that the British fleet could have met the place and date, Louisburg must have fallen. As John Stark was not fated to go, the story will be abridged, to include one of the most surprising episodes of his life, nevertheless.

The willingness of Rogers to have the pay of some of his most experienced and best men cut down was, probably, never known to them, but came directly as orders from headquarters. Rogers, always intent on retaining the ascendancy, capitalized in the increasing numbers of Ranger companies, keeping his prestige and his leadership, showing his extreme cleverness. His choice in having John Stark head Spikeman's company must have been prompted by recognition of Stark's outstanding efficiency, by his long friendship with him and, last and not least, in unacknowledged gratitude in redeeming the rangers' reputation and probably saving the life of its chief. In a few months Robert Rogers was again to show his fairness to him and the corps, in a striking way. For the time being, Stark, who as senior lieutenant had frequently to attend to many details for Rogers, thus gaining experience and confidence in handling all the rangers' life and operations, assumed the usual duties of captain of a separate co. He was succeeded by John McCurdy, a veteran, as 1st lt. of Rogers' own company.

It may have been that Jonathan Brewer, ensign in Spikeman's company had aspired to become captain, though that would have been contrary to the ethics of the corps, as shown by custom. No outbreak resulted and perhaps none was imminent but shortly a series of events presented an opportunity to Brewer and he made use of it, though he gained nothing but temporary prominence and satisfaction, at Stark's expense.

Somehow at Albany, though taking the smallpox was always a hit or miss matter, Rogers acquired the disease, entering this in his *Journal*:

March 5th, I suffered with the smallpox which confined me till the 15th of April, during which time my officers were recruiting according to the instructions.

At New York headquarters, plans for the expedition were being advanced. New Hampshire raised a regiment; Major John Goffe of Derryfield with a surprising number of recruits (all named by Potter,) marching toward New York, crossing to Flushing bay. On April 22nd, Rogers was to:

Inform Col. Gage (later to be Governor of Massachusetts and commander in chief at Boston during the siege) that it is Lord Loudon's order that the two companies at Wm. Henry and your own at Fort Edward, proceed immediately to Albany and embark for this place.

Rogers had endured rather more than the usual period with the disease, perhaps aggravated by the condition of his system due to his wound, which may have suffered an infection. His exact whereabouts is not always clear.

Loudon, Abercrombie, and Rogers, occupied with the proposed expedition, overlooked the possibility that the French on Lake Champlain might take occasion to make a surprise attack on the light garrison at Fort William Henry. The force had been much depleted, only 346 effectives. There were no less than 128 invalids, showing the inroads of disease and old casualties. Not being a participant, and while he was at Albany confined with the small-pox, Rogers has an indifferent account. Capt. Stark had been obliged to send to New England five of the best officers under orders to recruit. The ice and snow restricting activities out-of-doors, life in the fort and huts had settled down into a dull routine.

But something arose to excite the watchfulness and apprehension of the head of the rangers, Capt. John Stark. Parkman (1884) calls the story of Caleb Stark (1860) "a curious mixture of truth and error". After one of his finest descriptions of Nature in that season and place, Parkman tells the story of the advance of Rigaud and his force of 1600, mostly Canadians and Indians, and their discomfiture when their planned surprise came to naught through the vigilance of the garrison, it being, Parkman was satisfied, the 19th, before daybreak.

His notes refer to all the Loudon papers and the French sources. Loescher (*History of Rogers Rangers*, San Francisco, 1946) does not disagree but says that Eyre's Regulars were not drunk when Rigaud appeared but had a "bad hangover"; likely enough but which does not detract from Stark's forethoughtfulness. Rigaud had been given every possible accoutrement, food supply and clothing (provision for 12 days) and at Ticonderoga a week had been spent making 300 short scaling ladders.

Whether rangers or British soldiers it is certain that watchmen were on the alert during the night between the eighteenth and nineteenth, and that towards one in the morning they heard a sound of axes far down the lake, followed by the faint glow of a distant fire. The inference was plain that an enemy was there and that the necessity of warming himself had overcome his caution. Then all was still for some two hours, when, listening in the pitchy darkness, the watchers heard the steps of a great body of men approaching on the ice, which at the time was bare of snow. The garrison were at their posts and all the cannon on that side of the lake vomited grape and round shot in the direction of the sound, which thereafter was heard no more. (*Montcalm & Wolfe.*)

Parkman indicates that the story (Caleb Stark, *Memoir*, 1860):

May be doubted, for without counting the English soldiers of the garrison, who had no special call to be drunk that day, the fort was in no danger till twenty-four hours thereafter, when the revellers had had time to rally from their pious carouse.

But 346 effective men against 1600 well equipped attackers with scaling ladders, would have had little chance of successful defence had John Stark's precautions, time element to the contrary notwithstanding, not been taken, and the garrison or a part of it, been asleep, as in the dead of a long winter they would have been. Sound narrative or not, Potter's description, closely followed, in substance and in point of time, by Caleb Stark, may justifiably be included:

Many of the troops under Major Eyre, who held the fort, were Irish and the company of rangers then in the fort were, many of them, of Amoskeag and of that class of men known as "Scotch Irish" who, though of Ireland, were yet not Irish nor particularly in love with Irish customs but had no objection to uniting in a celebration in honor of St. Patrick. This company was under the command of Capt. John Stark of Amoskeag, a son of a Scotch Irishman.

His knowledge of Irish customs doubtless saved the fortress. The garrison had determined to celebrate St. Patrick's Day which is the 17th of March. Stark upon the alert, determined that the rangers at least should be sober and commanded the sutler, Samuel Blodgett of Amoskeag, to deliver no rum to the rangers without a written order from him and he refused all solicitations for orders under the pretence of a lame hand.

Thus, on the night of the 17th of March the rangers were ready for any emergency while the rest of the garrison were in the greatest excitement from deep potations in honor of St. Patrick and his wife Shelah. The French leaders aware of the character of the troops in the English forces laid their plans to attack it on St. Patrick's night, supposing that amid a bacchanalian carousal it could readily be surprised. Accordingly, on the night of the 17th of March the French crossed the crackling ice of Lake George with their scaling ladders confident of easy success in escalading the fortress from which sounds of deep debauch were wafted upon the air.

They advanced near the fort in silence prepared to adjust their ladders when a flash struck their eyes and the rattling of small arms and the booming of cannon filled their astonished ears while their ranks were thinned and broken by a shower of shot from well directed musketry and cannon from the walls of the fort. They retreated astonished but not disheartened. The foresight and prompt action of Stark saved the fortress. The crackling of the ice under the heavy tread of the French soldiery fell upon the practised ears of the rangers and gave them timely notice of the approach of the foe. . . . They were suffered to approach within half musket shot when the terrific fire was opened upon them.

At this time 1st Lt. Stark was a captain but did not know it until March 24th. His commission was dated Feb. 24th but was not signed by Lord Loudon (in Virginia) until March 8th, 1757.

Loudon's *Report* to the Minister, Pitt, paid the garrison and rangers a fitting tribute, says Loescher, in giving his authorities, greater in number and scope than were available to Parkman:

I cannot enough on this occasion commend every officer who

had either the defence of the forts or the command of the regt's. for the alertness and the activity with which each behaved in their different stations as well as the behaviour of the men; those in the fort determined to defend it to the last, and the sick crawled out to the ramparts. (Loudon, Apr. 25, 1757-L03467)

It was very handsome of Loudon, of course, but it does not seem that he mentioned the two senior officers, Major Eyre and Captain Stark it was usually that way, "The old Army game". Gage received the report, giving all the facts, at Albany, as Abercrombie had gone to New York and Loudon had gone to Philadelphia. Had Rigaud been successful in taking a British stronghold, with Rogers and his superiors all away, some explanations would have been in order. At the critical moment Stark's precautions and Eyre's complete support of him, saved the fort and Britain's repute.

Loescher found that Stark's men numbered but 60 though they included two good ensigns, Jonathan Brewer and James Rogers, (brother of Robert) and that the rangers were in their picketed fort on the east side of the main work until Major Eyre ordered them into Fort William Henry and "the Regulars were roused from heavy sleep and hushed into silence as they took their places along the ramparts with Rogers' Rangers who had reluctantly abandoned their picketted village." The following morning, Sunday, Eyre ordered Stark to make a reconnaissance of the enemy's camp a mile away and found them forming a column of their men, two abreast and a mile and a half long on the ice.

Rigaud now sent Chevalier Mercer under a flag of truce to Major Eyre asking him to surrender. In spite of the sight of Rigaud's numerous force before his fort, the valiant Eyre flatly refused to surrender even on good terms. A general assault was now expected and when the news reached the sick rangers and regulars below the ramparts, who were suffering mostly from scurvy, those that could walk or crawl bravely made their way to a firing position on the ramparts. (Loescher's *Rogers Rangers.*)

But nothing resulted until nightfall when Rigaud burned the few lake boats in dry-dock nearby and also the ranger's huts, which contained all their personal belongings. In spite of a sortie by Stark and a few men, 17 ranger huts were thus destroyed, three of their men were wounded and Stark "was touched by a bullet, for the only time in his adventurous life" (Parkman). Caleb Stark presented a copy of his 1831 book to Lt. John A. Winslow, annotating it :

Respecting the night attack on March 16, 1757, the ball produced a slight contusion but did not draw blood.

In another place Caleb wrote that "it was a spent bullet". The date was carelessly set down.

On the 22nd most of the ice-bound flotilla had been destroyed but rum from the ranger's storehouse was saved when "part of the sallying party maintained a covering fire" (Loescher). The Johnson papers show that Munro relieved the garrison and Eyre arrived at Albany on April 2nd but the rangers had to remain at the Fort. Rigaud lost 14 men killed and his three wounded were captured. The defenders lost no men and had but seven wounded.

About this time Rogers, who usually sent some cadets on scouts to educate them, took into his own company William Stark, who, of course, he knew well from Starkstown associations. Hugh Stirling, brother-in-law of the Starks, was also taken in with four other men, all to be given commissions, "if they proved capable".

To make sure that the enemy had withdrawn from the country Capt. Stark was sent on a scout to Ticonderoga. He returned and reported that all was quiet and inactive. (Gage to Loudon from Albany, April 16th, 1757). Shortly thereafter McCurdy made a similar scout toward Crown Point with 13 men. But a courier from Fort William Henry was sent to order him to return at once and march to Albany. When the two companies, Stark's and Rogers' (McCurdy in command) reached the vicinity of New York the sloops they came down the river on were searched for smallpox suspects.

Capt. John Stark was found to have taken the disease and was hospitalised, just where is not shown. A new company of rangers had been recruited in New Hampshire, but not by Rogers. Its captain was John Shepherd, James Neal, 1st Lt., Samuel Gilman, 2nd Lt. Loudon commissioned Shepherd Feb. 25th. The company went across New Hampshire to "No. 4" on the Connecticut, which feared an attack, but was soon ordered to New York, reaching Long Island (Flushing Bay) and camped with Col. Meserve's company. Four transports were set aside to convey the Ranger Companies, that for Stark's company being the brig *Betsey*, Rogers' was to go in the *Sheffield*, Bulkley's in the *Snow Tartar* and Shepherd's in the *Delight*.

A Portsmouth, N.H. surgeon was obtained for the Louisburg campaign and on May 6th Dr. Ammi Cutter and Col. Meserve waited on Lord Loudon in New York. The sum £10 covered the cost of his medicine chest. Cutter was kept busy eliminating the victims of the prevailing scourge. Shore leave for the rangers was limited in an effort to stop gambling. There was some robbery and once a loose woman was drummed out of camp. Bathing was finally forbidden as sharks attacked the soldiers. Delays were many and it was not until June 18th (the 20th according to Parkman) that the big fleet of transports left Sandy Hook, 100 sail (Rogers' *Journals*). What Rogers was doing between April 15th and June 18th (or 20th) and where he was, do not appear of record, evidencing the large gaps in his narratives.

Just before sailing time Lieutenant Brewer, under circumstances not clear, took summary action against his captain and superior officer and confined him, either in his quarters or a pest house, until the expedition had sailed. It is to be supposed that Brewer, having a taste of command during Stark's illness, wished to prevent his captain from going, so as to retain the command during the coming campaign at Louisburg. Presumably Stark considered himself fit to go. His period of danger, in giving the disease to others, was undoubtedly over, but perhaps not so much so but what Brewer had a semblance of right and duty.

As soon as he was out of custody Stark used the very first packet to convey a letter that, we may be sure, blistered and crackled with rage, to the ranger commander, Robert Rogers. The expedition reached the port of Halifax on July 1st and there waited the delayed arrival of the ships of war under the command of Admiral Holbourne, which came straggling in until the 10th of July.

Stark's story of his dastardly treatment by Brewer roused Rogers' sense of justice and he supported Stark, arrested Brewer and called for a court martial. The presiding officer of the tribunal was one day to be an antagonist of both parties, Lt. Col. Thomas Gage, when in 1775 he was governor and commander-in-chief at Boston. Brewer was convicted of "confining his captain illegally" and was sentenced to be cashiered. Lord Loudon approved the sentence "but in consideration of his former good service His Lordship pardons him" (Court Martial, July 21st LO 3576) Brewer continued to have charge of the Ranger Company; his title "Captain-Lieutenant", without incident.

Lord Loudon had, in his *Journal*, some time back, entered a memorandum that Brewer was to be given a company when available. He probably had little interest in the affair. Rogers, however, recognised that such an infraction of discipline should follow its strict legal course, for the good of the corps. Stark's letter to him would be one of the most interesting of all of Stark's correspondence. In it the true significance of the act should be discernible for Stark would not mince matters. If the records of court-martial are still preserved in London the papers may yet turn up. The Loudon *Orders and Journals*, now in the Huntington Library, do not include it.

Stark missed a short sea trip and never in his life had one. As far as military experience was concerned, he was no loser. More delays occurred in Halifax, thousands of troops were put through endless exercises and training. While drilling, vegetables were planted for the troops. Louisburg was reconnoitred and it was resolved to proceed, until, on the 4th of August, word came that three fleets of the French Navy were anchored in the harbour of Louisburg, 22 ships of the line besides frigates.

The garrison comprised 7000 men and Louisburg was the strongest fortress in America! As Parkman concluded "Success was now hopeless and the costly enterprise was at once abandoned". Loudon with his troops sailed back for New York, but Holbourne, with a few more ships sailed for Louisburg and dared the French to come out. A terrible gale followed, almost destroying the British fleet.

What became of Stark? Having no command and with no superior in the land, he was left to his own devices. A little record remains to indicate that he was in Marblehead, Massachusetts, on July 21st, 1757 (the same day that Brewer was being tried by Gage's court-martial) for a receipt was signed in Stark's pocket-book, by his brother-in-law, Hugh Stirling, for wages received.

When Rogers and his rangers reached New York, Brewer was tactfully sent recruiting, presumably in his native state, Massachusetts. About this time promotion for Brewer was envisaged, as enabling the two officers to be retained in the service, heads of separate Ranger companies. It is not known that Brewer apologised to Stark, though the ethics of military life would require it. Stark was not the man to forget, though he could forgive. Future records show nothing as to their relationships. The time came, however, when they both became heroes in the Battle of Bunker Hill and the alembic of patriotism fired them in a common cause.

When the long winter was over it became certain to Montcalm at Montreal that Loudon had taken his best troops, and many of Rogers' Rangers, to Halifax, and thus offered him a rare opportunity. Montcalm, therefore, proceeded to put his French troops in order, gathered his supplies and rounded up his Indian allies. Thousands of Canadians were requisitioned. The Indians came from far and near, so many and so lacking in restraint that they became unmanageable from the very first. One day they seized 18 head of cattle, butchered them, had a great feast and made themselves mad with the brandy the French were obliged to supply.

At the foot of Lake George, Montcalm, small, keen-eyed, gesticulating, harangued the representatives of no less than 41 tribes of Indians. Some of the latter had caught a small inexperienced party of New Jersey troops sent to reconnoitre by Col. Parker from Fort William Henry. When a priest remonstrated on finding parts of one of them being boiled in a kettle, the Indians invited him to partake.

There being insufficient water transportation for all of the 8000 men, Levis was started off along an old Mohawk trail by the side of the lake, with 2500 troops.

One of the tragedies of history was in the making. Loudon, thinking only of his Louisburg project, had withdrawn too many defenders from Fort William Henry and Fort Edward. They were only 14 miles apart with a good road between. At Fort Lyman, (Fort Edward) General Webb, in command of both outposts, had some 2600 men, though Rogers says 6000, while at the head of the lake Col. Munro had only 2200, not all effective soldiers. Even superior strategists might disagree as to what should have been done when Montcalm's army was discovered coming up; any choice being perilous.

After Montcalm began the assaults on Fort William Henry, Col. Munro firmly refused to surrender even in the face of overwhelming odds. He sent urgent appeals to Gen. Webb. Not until after days of cannonading, which Webb could plainly hear, did he suggest to Munro that he give up. Montcalm intercepted the note and kept it for days.

As Stark is not involved in the story, it may be shortened. The surrender took place on August 9th, 1757 and was to be, as all the world knows "with all the honours of war" and with a firm guaranty by Montcalm in person, of full protection from the Indians. The frightful slaughter that ensued is a familiar story. Montcalm, whose reputation suffered in the affair of Oswego, has been bitterly censored by historians. "One of the blackest incidents in the history of our country" (Fiske). Of the New Hampshire force of 200, over 80 were either massacred or taken prisoners. Of Samuel Blodgett, one of the sutlers, Potter noted:

> Escaping from the *mêlée*, he ran to the shore of the lake and secreted himself under a *batteau*. Here he tarried until he thought all risk was at an end. When leaving his hiding place, he was discovered by some prowling savages and stripped of every vestige of clothing. In this plight he escaped his captors by running

into the woods and got safely to Fort Edward."

Blodgett was a friend of John Stark. He was to die of old age, a famous man locally, who, under great difficulties and discouragements, built canals below Amoskeag falls. The water-power of the Merrimack encouraged cotton manufacturing. The city of Manchester resulted.

Parkman's account of the whole affair is one of his most vivid and eloquent (*Montcalm & Wolfe*). After almost frantic efforts Montcalm finally secured order and days later, making no effort to capture Fort Edward, being satisfied with his signal success, he allowed the harassed British and Americans to make their way to Fort Edward. The Indians, taking 200 prisoners and their plunder, made for Montreal. Montcalm proceeded to destroy the fort and barracks, throwing on the timbers and fittings of the latter, the dead bodies that filled the casements, and then fired the mass.

The mighty funeral pyre blazed all night. Then on the sixteenth, the army re-embarked. The din of ten thousand combatants, the rage, the terror, the agony were gone; and no living thing was left but the wolves that gathered from the mountains to feast upon the dead.

September 14th, 1757, Stark's company of rangers arrived in Albany with other ranger companies to go to Fort Edward where Gen. Webb still commanded. It is presumed that Capt. Stark was with his company but no record remains.

In October a small scout was described in the diary of Joshua Goodenough. At night, two days out, howling of wolves was heard, a gun being discharged at a distance frequently. At daybreak the scouts investigated, saw five Indians lying in blankets around a fire. One moved when a wolf tugged at his blankets. The scouts prepared to fire, but, advancing, they found all the Indians had died of smallpox, the last one firing his gun as long as he could. The rangers made a quick getaway.

Lord Loudon hurried back from Nova Scotia, arriving at New York on the last day of August. Gen. Webb, in command at Fort Edward, remained in fear of an attack by the French until the large numbers of militia, coming in haste, made camps all around the fort, the reinforcements being sufficient to dispel the danger. Montcalm was back in Canada. It was at this time that Brigadier, Lord Howe, went with Rogers on one of his scouts;

Lord Howe accompanied us on one of those scouts, being desirous of learning our methods of marching, ambushing, and retreating; and on our return expressed his good opinion of us very generously.

The short, intimate and good-behaviour association of Rogers with George Augustus Scrope, Viscount Howe, then 33, not too old for enthusiasm, not too young for wide experience, taught him something of the character of the famous Ranger. After many desertions the militia was discharged and went home. Loudon visited the Fort on December 1st, 1757 and returned to Albany leaving Col. Haviland in charge, with a strong garrison. The rangers were quartered on an island in the Hudson near the fort.

Rogers was well enough to go on a large scout, ordered by Col. Haviland, beginning December 17th. He took 150 men to reconnoitre Carillon "and if possible, take a prisoner". The start was in a heavy snow storm. The site of Fort William Henry was viewed "a deserted mass of ruin". They cleared away the snow under one of the mounds of the old fort and camped. After the scout at Ticonderoga had been accomplished Rogers returned on December 27th to Fort Edward.

Rogers then went to New York on orders to confer with Lord Loudon "upon the subject of augmenting the rangers". Rogers prints his instructions for bringing up the companies to five additional, four from New England, one made up of Indians, each company to have 100 privates, a captain, two lieutenants, one ensign, four sergeants.

The officers are to receive British pay, that is, the same as officers of the like rank in the line.

The men were to bring their own arms, good blankets and warm clothing "the same to be uniform in each company". All were to be at the fort by the 15th of March next, instructions dated Jan. 11th, 1758. Rogers indicates the levies were completed by the 4th of March but four of the companies went to Louisburg to join Gen. Amherst "and the other remained with me".

The operations of 1757 and 1758 merged imperceptibly. A large force of British Regulars, some Connecticut Provincials under Capt. Israel Putnam, and other troops were kept, practically under arms, in the fort at Fort Edward. On the island in the river the rangers were quartered. Rogers went to Abercrombie, then to Loudon, after he had failed to get humane treatment of his revolting and disorderly rangers by Lt. Col. Wm. Haviland, the rigid and intolerant commandant. Rogers had reluctantly complied with Haviland's order that whippings of rangers should be the punishment of infractions. The men, confined in ramshackle quarters, the best they could make themselves, quite inadequate against the rigors of a northern winter, became restive.

The whippings were excessive, 800 and 500 lashes. After 300 were administered the men would be horribly mutilated, their backs raw. An incipient mutiny was barely checked. The men cut down the whipping post on the island. Haviland was obdurate, determined to discipline some of Rogers' men, deciding one must hang, to bring about a cowing of the rest. The situation resulted in Haviland becoming hated as no post commander had ever been. After Rogers had stood up for his corps with Lord Loudon at New York, Gen. Abercrombie being an intermediary at Albany, those superiors of Haviland sensibly viewed the indispensability of the rangers as the main consideration.

Rogers was allowed to discharge a few of the chief actors but the whole situation was a menace to the future and the reputation of "Rogers' Rangers", Capt. Stark was in and about the island most of the time, but appears to have had no prominence in the disturbances. After recovering from an illness during the turn of the year (1757-1758) Rogers made important plans for the capture of Ticonderoga and Crown Point by the rangers.

He saw Lord Loudon on Jan. 9th, and had his ideas checkmated, without divining that Loudon himself wanted Rogers to do nothing to interfere with his own schemes of taking the French strongholds. There is little doubt that Loudon's selfish ambition prevented a good measure of success, had Rogers received permission and been granted the necessary supplies for a large scout, over the snows to the northern posts in surprise attacks on the insufficient winter garrisons of the French.

During this period Robert Rogers was doing some of his best work. His address and resourcefulness, his patience and leadership were never so conspicuous. Double-crossed by Loudon, by Abercrombie, but not Howe as far as known, Rogers contended daily with the local authority, Haviland, who, to spite Rogers used the ranger company of Putnam, Connecticut's contribution, a unit camped not on Rogers' island but separately, near the British. On Jan. 25 when Rogers had reached his headquarters, back from his trip south, he sent Lt. Phillips to Lake George to see if it was frozen enough to bear troops. It was. On the 28th a large convoy of provisions and artillery shells arrived by sleighs from Albany.

A few days later Rogers sent Capt. John Stark with a party to the first narrows of Lake George to test the condition of the lake. While Stark was gone Fort Edward had a bitter surprise attack by a large French party under the Ranger, Langy De Montegron, as intrepid a leader as Rogers himself. Coming by Wood Creek from "Ti", Langy's party of 100, Regulars, Canadians and Indians, laid an ambush near Fort Edward, where British regulars and Connecticut Provincials were gathering firewood.

The men had been allowed out with almost no protection and without snow shoes. Driven into the deep snow the men were helpless. The results were 13 killed, 4 wounded, five prisoners, some scalps taken. Rogers, somewhat belatedly got 140 rangers together but could not overtake Langy. Rogers tried a shortcut to head off the Frenchman and in doing so met with Capt. Stark and his party at Half-way Brook. They combined and crossed over to South Bay, but Langy had passed.

Loudon reluctantly gave up a plan he had to lead an expedition during the winter against Ticonderoga, leaving it for execution to Abercrombie and Lord Howe. Rogers and Stark bent their energies in preparations, Howe getting his order from Loudon on Feb. 1st, 1758. An engineer, Lt. Leslie, was sent up to test the lake route, with some light sledges, 30 in number, leaving on Feb. 11th with Capt. Stark and two subalterns and 40 rangers on snow shoes. The snow was too deep and the weather too severe and 40 men too few to make a solid path but Leslie and Stark and 10 rangers went on to Lake George. The snow was found to be four or five feet deep.

Shortly a few sleighs and horses reached the lake and found it safe. The parties then returned and Leslie reported to Lord Howe and Abercrombie at Albany. Instead of adopting Rogers' plan of a flying Ranger unit of 400 men with snowshoes, it was foolishly considered that light field pieces should form a part of the attacking force. Snow shoes, however, being short, they were feverishly constructed at Fort Edward. The story is clear from Loudon's diaries and other sources.

In a curious vellum-bound old account book, now owned and kept in safe-deposit by Wm. S. B. Hopkins, Esq. of Worcester, Mass., a descendant of the Stinsons of Dunbarton, some entries by John Stark place him in Albany at various times during the winter, 1757-1758. He was not home at all. His brother, Capt. William, was (on January 14th on furlough in New Hampshire) informed by Rogers of his appointment and urging the enlistments that he, William, and other officers were to secure in the augmentation of the Ranger force. No time was to be lost and Rogers went to his own expense in sending two men to New Hampshire on horseback.

It is evident that John Stark during January and February was second only to Rogers in importance. The items in the account book show Stark's presence in Albany at various times. An entry in Matthew Patten's diary referred to men of Stark's company, probably fresh enlistments, rather than to Stark's presence, March 1, 1758 "Muster of Capt. Stark's men at Thomas Hall's tavern" (later East Manchester). As early as Dec. 12, 1757 the account book speaks;

> This day received of Capt. John Stark thirty dollars for Samuel McLarney (?) per me, William Stark.

Also:

> Received from Capt. Stark one hundred and fifty dollars by order of Capt. John Shepard. Samuel Shepard.

The entries might be interpreted as made by Capt. William on his way to New Hampshire but for the fact that, in accordance with custom, the entries were written on pages of the book, not on separate bits of paper. Isaac Temple receipted for "my paye to the 25 Febrery". Ranger recruits receipted for pay on March 8th, the 9th and the 10th and Samuel Gilman receipted for "a sword that he brought to me", meaning Capt. Stark. Andrew Miller (or McMullen) received from Capt. Stark £63 "which I promise to be accountable to him at Fort Edward." J. Roorback receipted for 22 shillings, 6 pence, an amount which Nicholas Williams owed one Annatze Vischer; but the most interesting and important items are without date:

> Memorandum of what bills I have left at Albany. Received of Capt. Christy two bills one of 140 & 1 of 150 which is £290. Drawd two orders upon Gen. Abercrombie one in favour of Capt. Dow for £15, the other in favour of William Frossy (?) for £100.

What with the history of the scouts and the now fugitive hints of his pocket-book, it is clear that Capt. John Stark was on the road between Fort Edward and Albany several times during the winter and was of some importance over periods of weeks in personnel work of the new and old ranger companies. It is to be noted that Stark probably had, during this formative period, more than casual contacts with Lord Howe, who was a man who mixed freely with all classes, endeavouring to learn the business of soldiering in strange environments.

These meetings would lend more significance to the statements by Caleb Stark (1831 and 1860) of the high esteem Stark held Lord Howe in and that the association of the two men was not limited to the brief meetings when the Abercrombie expedition was on its way from Fort William Henry down Lake George and the consultation Howe held with Stark at Sabbath Day Point on the eve of the fateful battle. That John Stark was the trusted confidant of Rogers and the only man in the entire corps whom he could depend on in every respect, is clear. It is probably true also that Stark was "in the know" as to plans and the ways and means necessary, in spite of the secrecy attending such matters.

Due to his various assignments, John Stark was not called upon to go upon the most disastrous scout in the history of Rogers' Rangers. The story really begins with the action of Haviland in sending out the. favoured one, Capt. Putnam, ("One Putnam", Rogers called the man who was to become the celebrated Revolutionary War General) on a large scout to Ticonderoga to take a prisoner. His decision followed immediately after word came from headquarters that the Howe expedition had been abandoned and that all the stores accumulated for it, were to be sent back to Albany. It was not intended that Putnam should fight the enemy but return with information, upon which Haviland intended, and publicly disclosed, his plans to have Rogers go out with a huge scout of 400 rangers.

This general knowledge among the men of Putnam's party was unfortunate. Putnam returned safely on March 6th. (a few days before incoming rangers were receipting Stark's pocketbook in Albany) but had lost a man, who was picked up by the French. Rogers, after his fatal scout, blamed Haviland for the disclosure of plans which ought to have been perfected with the upmost secrecy. There is, however, nothing to show that the French actually knew. On March 10th, after two minor incidents, Rogers got his orders to take 180 rangers, including officers, but he could pick his men.

As the affair did not include John Stark, the account may be shortened. Rogers' reluctance to go against the very active French at Ticonderoga and Crown Point, is disclosed in his *Journals*, but not a word remains of any Haviland record. Loescher gives the personnel in detail, all being volunteers, none ordered to go. The expedition, fitted out hastily, camped at the first narrows of Lake George on March 11th, 1758. Rogers, due to his small force, was cautious.

Reaching the vicinity of Trout Brook, Rogers made two divisions of his force, laying an ambush to capture a daily patrol of the French. On sighting about 100 of the enemy, chiefly Indians, the rangers dropped their packs to fight. The encounter was quick and bloody, the rangers winning, and proceeded to scalp about 40 Indians, a thrifty move that cost them plenty later. Word coming to DeHebecourt, commander at "Ti", he organised with a force of about 300 men to go after Rogers.

Rogers assumed, as he admitted, that he had defeated the whole enemy force. He soon encountered the main body who were out to get him. A truly desperate situation immediately developed. The rangers fought with great bravery and in the best traditions of woodland warfare but were greatly outnumbered and the decimation of their force at the very first clash was fatal. To make the situation worse Langy's men joined the fighting. After a long fight, retreats following rallies, the Indians infuriated by brandy and vengeful on discovering so many of their tribesmen scalped by the rangers, pushed Rogers' force against the west side of Bald Mountain, later to become famous as "Rogers' Rock" on the Lake George side.

After a fierce attack from three sides Rogers gave the order to scatter, every man for himself. Lt. Phillips accepted the offer of quarter and good treatment. Most of his men were tied to trees immediately and slowly hacked to pieces. Phillips escaped, cutting his cords. Rogers climbed the side of the hill, saw before and below him the ice-covered lake at the foot of the smooth mass of solid rock. The prospect appalled him but the man's cunning sufficed. He turned his snow-shoes around and made back tracks until he found a ravine, which he descended while the Indians looked in vain for him on the open top. In due time a legend resulted, that he had slid down the rock-face in its winter dress of ice, to the lake below.

Of the apocryphal story the *Journals* say nothing, Rogers merely stating "I now retreated with the remainder of my party in the best possible manner" which discredits spectacular feats. In extreme cold Rogers and some of the fugitives gathered and remained the night without food or fire, sending an appeal to Haviland for assistance for the wounded. It was Captain John Stark who responded, finding only 52 survivors of whom 8 were badly wounded. Of his scouting force Rogers had lost 124 men on the battlefield. The disaster was long remembered in the homes of New Hampshire.

Rogers made fair progress up the frozen surface of the lake, and records:

In the morning we proceeded up the lake and at Hoop Island, six miles North of William Henry met Captain John Stark coming to our relief bringing with him provisions, blankets and sleighs. We encamped on the island, passed the night with good fires and on the evening of the next day arrived at Fort Edward.

It was March 15, 1758. Rogers enumerated his casualties; in his own company, 36 privates killed with Lt. Moore and Serg. Parnell. In Shepard's company, 16 privates and two sergeants killed. In the company of his brother, James Rogers, who was not present, only ensign McDonald killed. In Capt. Stark's Co. 14 privates and 2 sergeants killed. In Capt. Bulkley's Co. 47 privates killed or missing, including the Captain himself, Lt. Pottinger and Ensign White. In Capt. Wm. Stark's Co. only Ensign Ross killed and in Capt. Brewer's Co. Lt. Campbell killed. Wm. Stark and Brewer did not accompany the scout. The distressing result detracted from the prestige that had been built up by the exploits of Rogers' Rangers. Yet the famous corps was not without acclaim for their ability in fighting against odds of two to one, for their killing of so many Indians.

Lord Howe, now in command at Albany (incidentally enjoying the hospitality of Philip Schuyler and his wife, the acknowledged heads of society there) was apprised of the result. What Haviland thought is not known, though the enterprise he sponsored and so niggardly supplied, could not have resounded to his credit or have enhanced his reputation among the rangers, or even his own rank and file.

Rogers, received by Lord Howe, was given permission to journey to New York to lay before Abercrombie, successor of Lord Loudon, his plans. He learned that 4 of the 5 new companies were destined for Louisburg and claimed the raising of them had been at his own charge. Everything had gone wrong with him, yet the hardy young man looked forward especially to being made major of his corps and thus command an independent battalion. Forgetting Stark and other able captains, Abercrombie wrote of Rogers that the rangers "without him would be good for nothing". To keep an implied promise Rogers received on April 6, 1758 his coveted commission. About this time something was going on which Rogers did not understand;

About the middle of May a flag of truce was sent to Ticonderoga on Col. Schuyler's account, which put a stop to all offensive scouts until its return.

Apparently, nothing resulted. Capt. John Stark was in Albany. The old account book shows; (on May 8th):

Received of Capt. John Stark the whole of my pay of a lt. in Capt. John Shepard's Company of rangers from the 24th of Oc–

tober to the 24th of February; Samuel Gilman (signature partly rubbed out, not crossed out).

On the 23rd of May; "Archibald Stark to cash ten dolars". On May 20th, James Moore receipted for money. It was while Rogers was in New York, without doubt, that Capt. Stark was favoured, though the issuance of a commission to his brother, Archibald, was delayed until April 28th. No doubt competency was at the base of appointments as Lieutenant and Captain but John Stark could urge Rogers that a little nepotism should not stand in the way of Archibald's advancement. In view of his record in that respect Rogers could have no material objection. So, Abercrombie as "Colonel of His Majesty's 44th Regiment of Foot" signed the document, which may still be seen, a veritable relic of "The Old French War", in the *Stark Papers* (Vol. 1, 1743-1779) in the New Hampshire Historical Society.

A decision was reached at Albany during the conferences, to learn more of the enemy's strength and situation. Four trips were planned for the rangers, Captain Stark to go as far as "Ti" on the west side of Lake George, Captain Jacob, the Indian, to go there by the east side, Captain Shepard to take a route between the lakes, presumably on the ridge of the high hills dividing those waters, while Rogers was to go by whatever route he should decide upon, as far as Crown Point. Each party had orders to take some prisoners. Stark returned on May 8th, with six, Jacob with ten and seven scalps. Rogers gives his own route day by day. On May 5 "killed a Frenchman and took three prisoners"; one of the latter giving valuable information as to the enemy. Large scouting parties were kept out continually until Lord Howe's arrival at Fort Edward with one half of the army. It was a good beginning but not enough as Howe wished to know definitely the geography of Ticonderoga and what could be observed of the enemy.

> His lordship immediately ordered me to take 50 men and my whale-boats, which were carried over to Lake George in waggons, and proceed to Ticonderoga, to obtain at all events a plan of the north end with all possible accuracy.

So directed, Rogers on the 30th made the plan and while at some distance from his men they were attacked, Capt. Jacob's Indians suffering, and inflicting some losses. Rogers' dates conflict but he soon after went to Half-way brook and met Lord Howe; "gave an account of my scout and the plans he has requested". Then Rogers did another characteristic thing; he asked and received permission to visit "his Excellency Major Gen. Abercrombie at Fort Edward". The latter promptly ordered Rogers back to Lord Howe "with all the rangers, amounting to 600 men, and proceed with him to the lake". The rangers camped 400 yards to the west of where Fort Wm. Henry had stood, presumably where the village of Caldwell now stands. From June 28th till July 5th Abercrombie massed his forces at the head of the lake.

The great army of nearly 16,000 men, regulars, colonials, rangers and a few Indians (Sir Wm. Johnson arrived the day of the battle with 450 more) embarked in boats of every description. Even Rogers wrote; "It afforded a splendid military show". The scene in magnitude and import was never again equalled. The 900 *batteaux*, 135 whale boats and the artillery flat-boats completely hid the surface of the lake for three miles from the starting place. Parkman, as usual, outrivalled all in his description;

> The spectacle was superb, the brightness of the summer day; the romantic beauty of the scenery; the sheen and sparkle of those crystal waters; the countless islets tufted with pine, birch and fir; the bordered mountains with their green summits and sunny crags; the flash of oars and the glitter of weapons; the banners, the varied uniforms and the notes of the bugle, trumpet, bagpipe and drum, answered and prolonged by a hundred woodland echoes.

Lord Howe ate his evening meal with Capt. John Stark. It was one of the high spots in the latter's life. From about five in the afternoon until ten at night the more forward portion of the great flotilla rested at Sabbath Day Point. It was to await the slower boats though Rogers says the halt was "to refresh". Two-thirds of the journey having been accomplished the immediate steps ahead were considered anew. For some reason it was to Capt. Stark that Lord Howe turned when he wanted to be certain.

His acquaintance with the erect and energetic scout had not been extensive but he had, no doubt, marked him well. The moment was serious enough. Having crossed the ocean to effect the capture of the French fortress and from thence advance into Canada, Lord Howe, on whom the hopes of Britain were pinned, though the command had for certain reasons been given to Abercrombie, eagerly sought every aid. It is regrettable that we have only one account, Caleb Stark's in 1831, though it is to be noted that Parkman, who selected his incidents with care, and, be it also noted, for their illustrative and even picturesque effect, adopted the family account.

The evening before this fatal battle, Captain Stark had a long conversation with Lord Howe, resting upon a bear skin (his lordship's camp bed) respecting the mode of attack and position of the fort. They supped together and orders were given to the rangers to carry the bridge between Lake George and the plains of Ticonderoga at an early hour in the morning.

On the dusky bank from which more than half of the whole lake could be seen, were camp fires accentuating the gathering gloom. The light faded from the tops of the mountains across the beautiful water. The scene was an indescribable *mêlée* of boats, soldiers, officers, regulars from across the sea, colonial troops, and rangers in their nondescript garb, mingling for the time without order to partake of food and have relaxation. There were two figures somewhat apart, for a respectful distance would be kept by his *aides*, permitting Lord How to have a private conference with Captain Stark.

It was plain and hard fare that they enjoyed as they sat on bear skins and the like while England's gallant son extended his courtesies to the tanned and coarsely dressed woodsman. A servant or two brought the food, members of Howe's official family were about. Between the principals was, no doubt, Rogers' plan. What became of it has never become known. As Howe had ordered it, he probably kept it and that night as his bear skin cushioned his last slumbers on earth, it was probably by his side. In what manner should the attack on the fort be made on the morrow? Howe's intentions, formed while with Stark, and after further consideration, may have been modified or completely set aside when Howe talked with his chief, Abercrombie, this is to be presumed since the arrangements adopted could not have been worse.

There was one point upon which Capt. Stark was not in position to give the best information. It was surely an engineer's business, and not within a Ranger's knowledge, to conjecture if the long cannon then resting on the flat-bottoms, could with a heavy powder charge send round shot down into the fortification, if the brasses and their carriages could be, separately, hauled up the long, yet comparatively easy slope from the foot of Lake George to the top of Sugar Hill.

But even engineers and ballistic experts of that day were sceptical, as may be seen in the *Revolutionary War Chapters*. An almost bloodless victory could have been obtained by Abercrombie and Howe over the French, who must have evacuated their fortress, commanded as it was from a height of 772 feet above Lake Champlain (U.S. Survey). Montcalm was not without some fear of this possibility.

Howe, with the instincts of a born commander, discussed the point with John Stark. Else in what way could the curious foot-note in Caleb Stark's 1831 book have come about? Either the idea was not considered feasible of accomplishment or else such an attempt was vetoed by Abercrombie, who, confident in the numerical superiority of his army or from plain rashness and impatience, decided not to wait for results from a slow and doubtful experiment. So, the solitary height was not visited, covered with the dense growth of forest trees, that distinguishes it to this day.

> The importance of occupying the mountain which overlooked and commanded the works of Ticonderoga did not escape the military eye of Howe. But the attempt to transport cannon to the summit (800 feet) was considered in those days a task which nothing short of miraculous aid could accomplish. Abercrombie, therefore, confident of success, from the number, discipline and valour of his troops waived an opportunity of reducing the place without loss. Gen. Burgoyne afterward acted a more prudent and military part. He took possession of this mountain, drew up his cannon in the greatest secrecy in the night, by using large brass tackles and from the summit shew (sic) himself to the astonished Americans on the morning of July, 5, 1777. The immediate evacuation of the post and the disastrous retreat of St. Clair were the consequences.

The profound study of all source material, nearly as complete in Parkman's day as in ours, is evident in his unusually long account of the battle, some 20 pages (*Montcalm and Wolfe*) from the landing of the troops on July 6th. 1758 during the forenoon, until their ignominious retreat late on the afternoon of the 8th. Even Parkman was unable to reconcile conflicting data. His compromises, however, were woven invisibly into the best story of the whole affair ever printed. It has the advantage of French material, sometimes lacking in American histories.

The chieftains, Abercrombie and Howe, were strangers in a strange land. Their training and experiences were not adaptable to the new surroundings or methods of fighting, though Howe set himself to master everything needful. How much his wonderful personality and initiative were negatived by Abercrombie can never be known. Howe's death in the first moments of combat was the beginning of disaster.

The decision to get at the French by entering the woods and following down the left bank of the stream which flows from Lake George into Lake Champlain was not faulty. Landing at the "French advanced post", found abandoned, would provide a short and smooth way, long cleared by the enemy in years of occupation of Fort Ticonderoga, to the bridge, or bridges (accounts are not definite) at the falls where the saw mill was located on the left bank. But Montcalm was holding that bridgehead with nearly half his whole force and to cross the rushing stream after the bridge should be destroyed, would be impossible.

Rogers with 700 hardy and trained rangers should have been given the responsibility for the safe conduct of the army of 15,000 men through the two mile stretch of woods, having only the fordable Trout brook to cross to approach near enough to the enemy's defence position a half mile from the fort itself. A man of greater generalship than Rogers was needed, for his force of character ran in minor adventures. In many cases he was a "yes" man taking orders against a judgment that should have been given exercise, especially by a leader of quick sensibilities like Lord Howe.

But in the usual way the strict precedents of British military procedure were adhered to and the rangers were treated as an arm of the service, as skirmishers or as protectors of flanks and the like. In the case at hand a tenuous but expeditious passage for a strong column (not four) could have been cleared in a few hours, though days could have been allowed if necessary. This, even though Abercrombie had been erroneously informed that Montcalm had 6,000 men and was shortly to be reinforced. But the safe and deliberate processes of an Amherst found no forerunner in the present undertaking. The course of events proceeded rapidly. Rogers gives this;

> At daylight his lordship, Col. Bradstreet and myself proceeded within a quarter of a mile of the Landing place and perceived a small detachment of the enemy in possession of it. Whereupon his lordship returned to assist in landing the army, intending to march by land to Ticonderoga. At 12 o'clock the landing was effected and the rangers posted on the left wing. I was ordered by General Abercrombie to gain the summit of the mountain which bore north one mile from the landing place and the saw mill and to take possession of a rising ground on the side of the enemy, there to wait for further orders.

In Rogers' *Journals* of 1765 one must be on guard against forget fullness, intentional omissions and misleading statements, for the *Journals*, as printed, are as ingratiating in some respects as was the man himself in his personal contacts. It was too late for reconnoitring if that was the object of an order to climb a mountain, which must have been Cook's, (972 feet above Lake George; U. S. Survey) or else the easterly summit of the "Three Brothers", (668 feet) but neither could be a mile north of both the landing place and the saw mill, two and a half miles apart. Rogers indicates he did not literally follow his orders, which as time was important, were foolish;

> After a fatiguing march of one hour I reached the place whither I was ordered and posted my men to the best advantage, being within a quarter of a mile of where the Marquis de Montcalm was posted with 1,500 men, as my scouts ascertained. At 12 o'clock Colonels Lyman and Fitch of the Provincials took post in my rear. While I was informing them of the enemy's position a sharp fire commenced in the rear of Lyman's regiment.

Rogers and his men were on familiar ground. The nature of the woods was well known to them. The two Provincial regiments had evidently come direct through the woods from the landing place and had made excellent progress. There was no preparation for the army, no way, or ways, cleared for the British regulars, who were, for some reasons better known in the 18th century than in this, formed into four columns, which perhaps meant three or four abreast each.

The sharp fire was from a party of French under Langy and Trepezec. They were trying to get to Montcalm. They had been posted near "Rogers' Rock" to observe the movements of the British and Americans. Mostly French there were some Indians, the whole about 350. Their progress was slow and uncertain, beating their way northerly. When they thought themselves near the rapids which for a long distance precede the falls, they turned easterly and ran into Lyman's men, a contact they would have avoided if possible.

There was no help for it, firing began at once, the French were nearly cut to pieces, some few escaping. During the hottest of the firing Lord Howe, much too far in advance for a commanding general, was instantly killed. The confusion was intensified and all progress arrested. Abercrombie's army, already out of formation and floundering, was without leadership.

To those familiar with the aspects of an Adirondack forest, much of which remains to this day as the Creator made it, Parkman's description of the scene suggests an exaggeration of the physical facts, the novelist in him writing;

> The forest was extremely dense and heavy and so obstructed with undergrowth that it was impossible to see more than a few yards in any direction, while the ground was encumbered with fallen trees in every stage of decay. The ranks were broken and the men struggled on in dampness and shade, under a canopy of boughs that the sun could scarcely pierce.

> The difficulty increased when advancing about a mile they came upon undulating and broken ground. They were now not far from the upper rapids of the outlet. The guides became bewildered in the maze of trunks and boughs, the marching columns were confused and fell in one upon the other. They were in the strange situation of an army lost in the woods.

The first movement of this, the 6th of July, ended when the army "was needlessly kept under arms all night and in the morning was ordered back to the landing place from whence it came" (Parkman). On the afternoon of the 6th, Montcalm after consulting with his general officers, decided to withdraw from the bridge at the saw mill, first destroying the bridge. This action, when discovered, changed the approach from the woods route down the outlet's left bank, to the short course across level ground, Abercrombie's decision coming the forenoon of the 7th. The intention of the 6th was a march without encumber merit; artillery and baggage left at the landing place. The intention of the 6th was the same, even though the bridgehead crossing might have been disputed in force and with cannon.

About noon of the 7th Bradstreet, unopposed, threw across a temporary structure, near the old one, and sent word the way was open. Meanwhile all day long the French were feverishly felling trees, piling up breastworks (8 or 9 ft. high) at the edge of moderately high ground half a mile from the Fort, where the French command judged, after much indecision, the terrain would support the best defence. Not content with the wall of solid logs the ground in front of it was left with the loppings and smaller trunks and branches, all disposed so cleverly as to make a maze of obstructions to entangle assailants while being shot down. Hundreds of sharpened boughs were disposed so as to form an abbatis. As evening fell the huge work was nearly finished.

Where was Captain John Stark? Parkman does not mention him. He is found in no account except one of the "family", which Parkman did not see fit to adopt. Caleb Stark's incident is found in two places, 1831 and 1860, the former in a foot-note, referring to the usual duties of rangers;

On this occasion they cleared the way to the saw mills. The bridge between Lake George and the plains of Ticonderoga was forced by Capt. Stark at the head of 200 rangers, which left the passage for the army to advance to the attack.

The other is in the *Memoir* of Gen. Stark, the words directly following the story of the interview with Lord Howe at Sabbath Day Point (which Parkman did adopt) as though the plan to "carry the bridge at an early hour in the morning" was immediately achieved;

Accordingly, they advanced and on approaching the bridge Major Rogers, who was at their head, perceiving a party of French and Indians prepared to dispute their passage, halted for a few minutes, which pushed the rear upon the front. Stark, not knowing the cause rushed forward saying that 'it was no time for delay' pushed boldly on to the bridge and in a few moments the enemy fled, leaving a clear passage for the army.

Parkman's researches failed to discover historical mention of this incident and the present investigation is likewise barren. Yet the strength and reliability of Stark traditions makes it likely that some such thing took place sometime before the battle. Major Stark, father of Caleb, was alive when the 1831 book was printed. The major's memory of his father's military actions has generally proven reliable, so the biographer is, perhaps, justified in going where the historian is more prudent. Rogers' story mentions Stark but once; in relating the events of the second day, July 7th;

At six o'clock I was ordered to the river running into the falls where I had been stationed the day before, there to halt on the west side with 450 men, while Capt. Stark with the remainder of the rangers proceeded with Captain Abercrombie and Mr. Clerk, the engineer, to reconnoitre the fort. They returned the same evening. The whole army passed the night under arms. At sunrise on the 8th Sir William Johnson arrived with 440 Indians. At seven o'clock the rangers were ordered to march. A lieutenant of Capt. Stark led the advanced guard, which when within 300 yards of the intrenchments, was ambushed and fired upon by 200 French. &c.

For some reason Parkman does not mention Stark;

Clerk, chief engineer, was sent to reconnoitre the French works from Mt. Defiance; and came back with the report that from what he could see, they might be carried by assault. Then, without waiting to bring up his cannon, Abercrombie prepared to storm the lines.

In 1856 Potter (*History of Manchester*) had had the advantage of being old enough to have heard much from aged sons and daughters of Gen. Stark as to the latter's participation in the "Old French War". In 1860, having printed nothing before, Caleb Stark boldly copied Potter's matter;

> Major Rogers held the position with 450 men while Captain Stark with the remainder of the rangers (250) went with Captain Abercrombie and Colonel Clerk to reconnoitre the enemy's works. They returned in the evening, Col. Clerk reporting that the enemy's works were of little importance. Capt. Stark, however, was of a different opinion and did not hesitate to say that the French had formidable preparations for defence. Stark was but a provincial woodsman and Clerk a British engineer. The opinion of the former was unheeded, while, most unfortunately, the advice of the latter was followed.

It was not the first time that John Stark and Engineer Clerk viewed Ticonderoga. When Stark was in charge of the rangers on the scout when Capt. James Abercrombie later charged the corps with misbehaviour, Clerk was also along. After the fog cleared that morning the British officers and ten rangers went two miles to look at Ticonderoga fort. At dusk they saw it, distant 900 yards (one half mile) and saw 20 or 30 boats moored. This shows that they must have climbed up "Mt. Defiance" far enough to get the view. Clerk was probably not a highly trained engineer, or a ballistic expert. Had he been, his advice to Gen. Abercrombie might have been given and heeded, saving hundreds of lives.

Stark could have guided the observers far enough up the wooded slope to where they could not fail to observe the activity of the French at their new breast works though the devilish contrivances in front were either too small or too unfinished to show their defensive strength. Stark's duty was to find for the engineer and the large party of protecting rangers the best route. He had no responsibility except for that and a safe conduct. He would have had no standing before General Abercrombie in offering advice.

Overnight, in the French camps, the arrival of Levis with 450 men, was hailed. The defending forces were now about 3,600, only about a quarter of the attacking army. Nevertheless, it was fatefully illusive for Abercrombie, in his self-assurance, that there was no need of bringing up his heavy artillery for a softening up and for knocking down the new log ramparts.

If the student has Parkman, he will require Rogers for only a secondary interest. The latter points to the beginning of the real battle on the 8th as being "opened" by "a lieutenant of Captain Stark", indicating that Stark himself was otherwise employed. Parkman's seven pages of combat recital, begins:

> First came the rangers, the light infantry and Bradstreet's armed boatmen, who, emerging into the open space, began a spattering fire.

Provincial troops followed and then, in formation, the regulars, making the first attempts on the unique *chevaux de frise*. They never got any farther. After an hour it was found too awful. Yet, back at the saw mill, Abercrombie ordered a second attack and yet others. Parkman again excels;

> The scene was frightful; masses of infuriated men who could not go forward and would not go back; straining for an enemy they could not reach and firing on an enemy they could not see; caught in the entanglement of fallen trees; tripped by briers; stumbling over logs; tearing through boughs; shouting, yelling, cursing, and pelted all the while by bullets that killed them by scores, stretched them on the ground or hung them on jagged branches in strange attitudes of death.

Brave individual deeds there were and one nearly successful mass attack which Montcalm stopped with his reserves.

> The assault still continued, but in vain, and at six o'clock was another effort, equally fruitless.

Till early evening rangers and provincials kept up desultory firing to cover the collection of the wounded, while the regulars, "fell back in disorder to the Fall", where the last act was to set the saw mill on fire. On the morning of the 9th, there were signs of precipitate retreat, abandonment of stores, as far as the landing place, of the proud army of the 5th of July, 1758. Abercrombie's casualties were 1,944 officers and men. "A gallant army was sacrificed by the blunders of its chief" (Parkman). The French loss was 377. (*Vide Montcalm at the Battle of Carillon-Ticonderoga-July 8th, 1758*, by Maurice Sautai; Leonaur 2011.)

In addition to the bitterness of defeat and the loss of Ranger comrades, there was for John Stark a personal regret that was to become a sort of cherished bereavement, as it were. The young captain who had crowded so much experience into his thirty years was in reality nobody as yet, specifically only one of seven Ranger captains, though senior among them. But the flower of the British Army, Brigadier Lord Howe, had given him special notice and attention. The consultation on the eve of a great battle, accentuated the shock of a death with a bullet in his breast, as Howe fell fighting, perhaps not far from Stark, though nothing exists to show it. In 1860 Caleb had this;

> The regret of Capt. Stark for the fate of the gallant Lord Howe who thus fell at the age of 33, lasted his lifetime. He often remarked, however, during the Revolution, that he became more reconciled to his fate, since his talents, had he lived, might have been employed against the United States. He considered him the ablest commander under whom he ever served.

James Wolfe, hero of Quebec, wrote his father, August 7, 1758:

> The noblest Englishman that has appeared in my line and the best soldier in the British Army.

The great Pitt called Howe "a character of ancient times; a complete model of military virtue".

Parkman said:

> The young nobleman had the qualities of a leader of men. The army felt him from general to drummer boy. He was its soul. . . broke through the traditions of the service and gave it new shapes to suit the time and place.

Parkman then gave incidents illustrative. Such a man as Lord Howe would appeal to a man like Stark who well knew the ring of true metal from false. Mrs. Philip Schuyler, Howe's hostess at Albany, as Parkman commented, "loved him like a son, and, though not given to such effusion, embraced him with tears on the morning when he left her to lead his division to the lake." During the Revolutionary War, the happenings of those tragic days would be referred to by Mrs. Schuyler and General Stark. Lord Howe's body was brought to Albany, buried by Col. Schuyler in his own lot, until, with appropriate ceremonies, it was interred under St. Peter's Church. In the records the charges for the use of the pall are still shown.

The very day John Stark was making camp for the rangers at the head of Lake George, some 400 yards from the army of Lord Howe, an ailing man, far away in New Hampshire, feeling that his hour had come, was making his will. It was Archibald Stark and the day was June 22, 1758. The news did not reach his son, John until sometime after the battle and the retreat.

But after the defeated army had finished its entrenchments and the troops were relieved from exacting duties, probably shortly after the 9th of July, word of the loss of his parent could have reached him. A leave of absence would be granted readily. It may have been even later in the month, when the captain could have had the company of Capt. Shepard also of the rangers. Shepard reached New Hampshire on August 1st bringing money for Ruth Burbank, as her receipt still shows.

No hint of Archibald Stark's death is to be found in Caleb Stark, 1831. He seems to have been strangely ignorant of the career of his great-grandfather. The Probate records and those of lawsuits would, on examination, have afforded him the same information that now exists.

Of Captain John Stark's marriage there is the briefest mention. Evidently Caleb inferred that it was the cause of the furlough;

> After the close of this campaign, Capt. Stark returned home on furlough at which time he married Elizabeth Page, daughter of Capt. Page of Dunbarton.

His father's sudden death was the reason why Capt. Stark left the army at Lake George to return home. The marriage took place two weeks after the probate of the will. The union had probably been in contemplation for some time. As Capt. Stark was not the master of his movements the wedding was not delayed. The two families had known each other for some time, doubtless from 1752 when the Pages, of English descent, came to "Starkstown". Elizabeth a girl of 15, it is said, would sit by the spring nearby with a musket across her knees while water was taken for the house and barns, to guard against surprise by the savages. Elizabeth's sister Mary was about a year younger. Two brothers, Caleb and Jeremiah were older. In 1754 John Stark's brother William, married Mary, sister of another prominent settler of Starkstown, Capt. William Stinson, and was living in town.

In Rogers' accounts "Nothing material happened until the 8th of August." John Stark's lucky star was again in the ascendancy, for Rogers had one of his worst affairs. In one of his rash and bragging moments Rogers contended with Israel Putnam and others in target practice. It was near the site of Fort Ann. The large party of rangers and others were on a scout and, for the moment, had nothing to do.

The noise of the musket shots enabled some 500 French and Indians to discover Rogers' party. A terrific battle ensued. Putnam was tied and the Indians were about to burn him, but the French then getting the worst of it began to retreat, taking Putnam with them. The encounter is vividly narrated by Parkman and almost unbelievably exploited by Putnam's biographer.

Young Lieutenant, Archibald Stark, was old and experienced enough to serve on a court-martial. He was about 28. The diary of Lt. Edward Munro of Lexington, Mass. (N.E H-G Register, XV) for Sept. 1, 1758, gives;

> To march tomorrow morning with seven days provisions under Capt. Dalzell of the Light Infantry. Camp, Lake George, Sept. 3, 1758, Parole, Bratal, officers of the day, Col. Beckwith, Lt. Col. Handimand (*sic*). A court-martial to sit tomorrow to try such prisoners as may be brought before them. Capt. Noal, President, Lt. Stark, Lt. Babeston, Lt. Lyon, Lt. Foote, members. Three companies to be under arms tomorrow morning at guard mounting. A scouting party consisting of one sergeant and six members to go about six or seven miles to the Westward to Predee.

The campaign of 1758 had ended ingloriously and while some of the rangers remained on duty in the field there is nothing to show that Capt. John Stark returned to the vicinity of Lake George after his marriage, though Caleb Stark's "returned home on furlough" would invite such an inference. At home there was much onerous work for John. The estate of his father was insolvent and much involved and called for constant attention. Rogers would easily yield to any request of his senior captain for leave of absence until the next campaign should open.

By the children of Archibald there was no opposition to the full execution of the will, as far as the debts permitted. After they were paid there was little to be divided. The final terms were arrived at to the satisfaction of all, for John's equity was recognised without a contest. Both he and William took their full legal fees as executors. Custom did not run to any exceptions in that regard.

Of the long winter of 1758 9, Caleb Stark found nothing to record. Matthew Patten, however, had an interesting item;

> March 1, 1759, brought a load of hay from the little meadow and went to Thomas Hall's to the muster of Captain John Stark's men.

The make-up of the Ranger company is not given. The party made their way to Crown Point, without doubt. But Caleb Stark, quieting, as he thought, family traditions that were none of the happiest, saw fit to condense his grandfather's early military career, as follows;

In the following Spring he joined the army and was employed with 200 rangers in cutting a road from Ticonderoga to Charlestown, N.H. Under General Amherst he was present at the reduction of Ticonderoga and Crown Point. The conquest of Canada in 1760 put an end to military operations in North America; this circumstance together with the jealousies of the British officers induced him to quit the service. Gen. Amherst by an official letter assured him of his protection and that if inclined to re-enter the service he should not lose his rank by retiring. (*Vide The War for North America: The Struggle between France & Britain for a Continent, The Conquest of New France and The Fall of Canada* by George M. Wrong; Leonaur 2016.)

There was a great deal behind this hasty jumbling, two years into one.

When Capt. John Stark joined his chief, Rogers, is not certain but he was on the Hudson late in February. His services under General Jeffrey Amherst began.

Lord Jeffrey Amherst's career was set forth by Adams in 1896, Lawrence Shaw Mayo in 1916 and by J. C. Long in 1933. The operation against Louisburg the previous year redounded to his credit, as commander of 11,000 British troops and 500 Colonial militia, assisted by a huge fleet. But Fiske (*New France and New England*) gives most of the credit for the successful land operations, which made possible the proforma siege, to young Brigadier General James Wolfe and so it would seem, though not uniformly so to Amherst's biographers. William Stark, Capt. John's brother, was in the landings and early strategic work of Wolfe, if he may be believed in his assertions (letter to Gen. John Sullivan, Papers, I. 178-180).

To Amherst "grave, formal, cold, taciturn and reserved" in later life, as one who knew him then said, Fate was kind. The favour of Gen. Ligonier in a recommendation to Pitt, the minister, newly come to power, arrogant and ruthless, but a great soul, started the train of appointments, as commander against Louisburg. Part of Amherst's personality is revealed in the *Journal of Jeffry Amherst* (1931, Univ. of Chicago Press) edited by J. Clarence Webster of Shediac, N. B. who in 1927 had published a short journal of Jeffrey's younger brother, William, Lt. Colonel and Adjutant. Jeffrey's private life in England was no better or worse than men of his class. His military story is one showing intelligence, moderated by self-interest, settled purposes and willingness to undergo hardships. His delay in co-operating with Wolfe has been variously interpreted, the weight of evidence being adverse to him.

After he joined General Abercrombie, following the latter's defeat before Ticonderoga, at the latter's camp 45 miles above Albany, Amherst acquiesced in Abercrombie's plea that it was too late in the season (though Colonial leaders did not think so) to start all over against the French. Probably Amherst wanted to be better prepared and to add to, not run the risk of detracting from, his Louisburg glory. So, Amherst went back to New York and then to Halifax for winter quarters, where, with little astonishment he received word of his appointment as commander-in-chief "of all His Majesty's forces in North America".

He did not wait till spring to make his plans. Funds were lacking. The colonies themselves were heavily in debt, bled white by Lake George and Louisburg expenses. They were in no mood to become enthusiastic over one more Ticonderoga. Coming back, on his way to New York, Amherst sojourned with his friend, Gov. Pownal of Massachusetts, who in 1759, opened a new town for settlement, Amherst. Instead of dealing with the local civil and military authorities in the usual way Amherst began by inserting advertisements in newspapers, urging the public to respond to the need for troops.

His idea, to cut corners was "not to risk the delay in sending orders through regional channels" did not avail much. Amherst made the best of the social activities in New York until he could get near the source of operations, Albany. Rogers in the good English of his dressed-up printed *Journals* recorded the preparations in his field.

Rogers wrote Col. Townshend, deputy *aide-de-camp*, suggesting that he be allowed to go to New England, first stopping on the way to see the general. "But the general by no means approves of your leaving Fort Edward" was the cold reply. Rogers then proposed making up two new regiments of rangers and also three Indian companies. On Feb. 26th, Townshend wrote Rogers from New York:

> Your letter by Mr. Stark was yesterday received. (He added) The general approves of your raising the Indians. (but see Amherst's heated disavowal of Indian use when Pitt tried to pin it on him and had it pinned on himself a few years later) but does not agree to raising any more companies of rangers, &c.

As of this period Rogers prints five letters in full; he does not print this one and no copy is known.

Whether it was John Stark, his senior captain, or Lt. Archibald Stark, is not known but Rogers knew he ran no risk of disloyalty in John. As there is nothing in family accounts to show, it is possible that Amherst did not personally even see the messenger, so formal was headquarters staff work in those days, but if he missed an opportunity of getting first-hand information of the rangers, of the country of the coming operations, of Abercrombie's failure, it would have been because John Stark unlike Robert Rogers seldom pushed his way where he was not wanted. It is reasonably certain that the same messenger that brought the letter, took back the reply.

One reason why Rogers was not to visit New York was his being ordered to conduct one of Amherst's engineers, Lt. Brehme, to the vicinity of Ticonderoga for observations. On March 3rd. the big scouting party started out, some 358 men in all. Stark's name is not found in Rogers' account. There were long marches in the most intense cold. The whole of Lake George was traversed as well as South Bay, the upper portion of Champlain. "Two thirds of my detachment have frozen their feet" noted Rogers, but "Mr. Brehme is satisfied that he has done his business agreeably to his orders." On March 10, Fred Haldiman congratulated Rogers and advised that he was sending "twenty sleighs to transport your sick." When Rogers returned to Fort Edward, he received Townshend's reply, per "Mr. Stark" probably.

Early in March 1759 Amherst received the orders of his Minister, dated London December 29th, 1758. Pitt directed him to attack Canada, by way of Ticonderoga. He advised him that Gen. Wolfe had been directed to attack Quebec. After many weeks of slow organising Amherst advanced to Albany on the third of May, 1759. He found not a soldier from Connecticut and wrote the governor:

I had ground marked out on the hill for the Connecticut troops against they come.

The people locally seemed indifferent to the success of the campaign, for hardly a company reported for duty. The Council of Albany, wholly Dutch, backed Mayor Sybrant Gozen Van Schaick (in office from 1756 to 1761) in not interfering with the profits of the local storekeepers and taverners, in selling rum to soldiers. Constant violation of orders and much drunkenness prevailed. By the last week of May however, Amherst got his troops; from Connecticut 3640, from New York 2250, from Pennsylvania 2070, from New Jersey 928, from Virginia 800, from New Hampshire, 700, from Rhode Island 694 and from Massachusetts Bay 2740. New Hampshire also had regiments with Wolfe as had Massachusetts. With some 8,000, Amherst had an army.

When Amherst arrived at Fort Edward the first of June, he was nearly a month behind schedule. He sent General Thomas Gage on to Fort William Henry with a large part of his force, following himself on June 21st. Rogers wrote;

> I was directed to send Captain Stark with three companies to join Gen. Gage. I remained with the other three, &c.

It was not the first time Gage and Stark were associated. When Abercrombie met defeat the previous July, Gage had led the light infantry immediately behind the rangers. The camps at Fort William Henry were not far apart and while fraternising was not the common practice, there would be opportunities of becoming better acquainted with the British general whom Stark was one day to oppose in a memorable struggle, separated at the beginning only by the distance of Breed's Hill from Province House.

It was an aggregation of raw soldiers from several colonies brought together under the command of a British general who forgave few infractions of discipline. During a month of excessively rainy weather and heat, a fearsome and resentful condition of mind characterised the common soldiers. There were many desertions. Whippings and some hangings were thought necessary. Amherst's *Journal*, on Stark;

> (*June 13, 1759*) Captain Stark with his company of rangers will join the detachment from the 4-mile post.

> (*June 23*) Amherst noted that the fishing party got too far and that they were pursued by boats of the enemy, three in number. "I sent Captain Starks out with a party to secure their retreat & try to catch the enemy. Got up today 11 *batteaus* and 47 whale boats. (24th.) The party came in in the morning. Mr. Turnbal had joined them as he was coming to camp, for on finding himself cut off he thought 'twas best toward Ticonderoga and he and four men he had with him got into a little island where they intended to defend themselves."

By June 27th, organised fishing, to provide a welcome change of food, was reflected in the general and regimental orders. There was to be one boat for each battalion.

> (*June 27, 1759*) Capt. Stark will have a red flag in his *batteau*

and every *batteau* must be near enough to call to each other and to follow Captain Stark immediately as he knows where the covering party is located and will row in at the proper time. The fishermen will take their arms, which Captain Loring will deliver and great care must be taken that they are not too much crowded. Captain Stark will receive his orders when the whole is to return to Major Campbell.

So, it would appear that Major Allan Campbell of the Grenadiers had the duty of seeing that the fishermen under Captain Stark should be armed and, as they would be regulars and "Provincials", not rangers, it is likely they had arms from the British regimental depots. The bulletin of the Fort Ticonderoga Museum (January, 1942) contained a narrative made up from general orders, which shows that the original party had been fishing off Diamond Island, "distant fourteen miles from the army" and that Captain Stark's flotilla for fishing had the protection of a "covering party" consisting of no less than two companies of grenadiers, two of light infantry, some rangers and Indians. Three weeks later the whole army moved down the lake, water borne to the last cannon, for the grand attack on Fort Ticonderoga.

The scene had less than usual appeal to Parkman's brush. He devoted but a few pages to the fulfilment of Amherst's great enterprise.

As usual, the rangers led on the lake, though in their approach Gage's light troops covered the rear, the whole pulling off by daylight. The army remained in the boats all night ("Our wind and weather were very rough, with a disagreeable tumbling sea") but the debarkation was successfully accomplished after some 400 of the enemy were routed early the following morning (July 22, 1759). Rogers wrote:

> The general employed several provincial regiments to transport the cannon and stores across the carrying place.

The work of investment was carried on deliberately. Amherst is most unemotional in his own *Diary*. Rogers was given orders to cut the log-boom and chain. Several days were required to dig trenches and to bring up the heavy cannon. Bourlemaque, the brigadier in command, having his orders from Vaudreuil not to defend if attacked in force, made no serious attempt against the hosts of Amherst, who had double his number of men.

One night the French decamped leaving only some 400 under Hebecourt to keep up appearances. Watching the lake, though rangers were available, seems to have been indifferently done. During the one exchange of shots Col. Townshend was killed, the principal casualty. At dusk on the 26th, Hebecourt and his garrison escaped, three deserters reporting it to Amherst. Near midnight the northwest bastion of the fort was blown up, indicating the end of resistance. Early in the morning of July 27th a volunteer clambered into the fortress and took down from the great flag pole, the *fleur-de-lis* of the French kings. It had flown at Ticonderoga for the last time. A few days later Amherst was informed that he would have no further trouble, for Bourlemaque had followed his orders and had left the fort at Crown Point. Amherst moved in.

Amherst had promised Pitt that he would "make an irruption into Canada with the utmost vigour and dispatch". He did the reverse of this. Parkman does not spare him;

> Every motive public and private impelled Amherst to push to his (Wolfe's) relief, not counting costs or balancing risks too nicely. His industry was untiring, a great deal of useful work was done, but the essential task of making a diversion to aid the army of Wolfe was postponed.

Should Wolfe fail to capture Quebec from Montcalm, but survive? Parkman does not seem to have conjectured that Amherst may have speculated on such a possibility and have not been able to see a clear-cut future for himself, winner of Louisburg and of Ticonderoga. By slow motion he had profited by Abercrombie's failure. Amherst had not heard from Wolfe since June 9th, and the taking of Quebec had then appeared dubious. A latent talent for construction found exercise in Amherst's situation. He would make both "Ti" and Crown Point bulwarks of strength for King George. The only overland entrances into Canada had been mere trails; the invariable transportation for armies was by water.

Amherst had few vessels, did not bring over from Lake George the hundreds of small *batteaux*. He proceeded to repair the sawmill at "Ti" and was much annoyed by frequent break-downs of the gear, but it produced rough timber and lumber, so some sloops were constructed and other craft. He improved the condition of the troops, long dieted on salt pork and stale provisions. His interest in the good effects of "spruce beer" on the troops, shows in the *Diary*. He sent out unimportant scouting expeditions, explorations. He improved greatly the road between the two forts. Most constructive of all works, outside Crown Point itself, was the project for a military highway across the mountains to the Connecticut River.

In casting about for a leader, he found that Captain John Stark was the man for the job. The energetic captain was given 200 men. They were of the ranger service, hardy, most of them young farmers who, like himself, had helped clear their home lands, were accustomed to heavy work in fields and woods, acquiring muscles of steel. Rogers gives no details;

Captain Stark with 200 rangers was employed in cutting a road from Crown Point through the wilderness to No. 4.

Amherst in his *Journal* of August 8th (at Crown Point):

I ordered two scouts to St. Johns, sent 200 rangers to cut a road to open a communication from New England and New Hampshire to Crown Point.

It was evident that the way produced could have been not much more than a path, one impossible for teams or for cannon or their carriages for on September 9th there is Amherst's own entry;

Captain Stark returned with his party from No. 4. Fourteen of his men deserted, six left sick behind. He said that he had made the road and that there were no mountains or swamps to pass, as he came back it measured 77 miles. It may be much shortened.

With only 7% disloyal Stark can be credited with securing efficient service, his usual record, for when the woods were beginning to put on their Autumn glories and the home firesides were envisaged, the temptations to "cut it" and leave would appeal beyond resistance to a few. To Stark the decisions as to where the pathway should run would be difficult, his perplexities many, even though some portions, especially the beginnings and the endings, were full cart roads already and made up a fair proportion of the roundabout 77 miles, but in the great central wilderness of the Green Mountains there was neither path nor blazed trail. It is, however, known that the road started from Chimney Point, opposite Crown Point fortress, and ran through the level lands of the present town of Bridport through Shoreham, Sudbury and Pittsford. The end at the Connecticut River was described in Benjamin Hall's *History of Eastern Vermont* (1858);

It began at Wentworth's ferry, two miles above the fort at Charlestown and was laid out 26 miles in the course of the Black River as far as the present site of the town of Ludlow, where commenced a path which had been made before by Lt. Col. Hanks.

The officer, of course, was not Hanks but the then Major Zadoc

Hawke. In the next year, 1760, Col. John Goffe of Stark's own town, Derryfield, improved the Charlestown-to-Ludlow portion. In *Amherst*, (date of Oct. 26, 1759);

> I sent 250 men with proper tools under the command of Major Hawk to make the road to No. 4. Sent at the same time Lt. Small with 30 men with arms to give the Provincials papers from No. 4 to their homes and provisions or 4 pence per day for their march.

On Oct. 29th:

> I sent to Major Hawk's Party to kill them some fresh provisions.

On October 30th:

> It was very cold weather and frost.... I ordered the Provincials from Fort Edward and the Posts to join their Regiments at Crown Point that they may go home by No. 4.

Nov. 13th, Amherst noted:

> Lt. Small wrote that some of Major Hawk's party had deserted . ...The Provincials have got home in their heads & nothing can stop them or make them do an hour's work though the whole country depended on it, so I must send them all away.

The time of the year and the shortness of the workable period precluded much road making so that some further clearance of Stark's route must have been all that was accomplished by Major Hawke.

The whole story of this means for crossing the unbroken wilderness, settlements being only on the eastern and western areas of the mountains, has never been pieced together, materials lacking. Later during the Revolutionary war, the route was rough and dangerous. To those who now pass over it in vehicles of incredible swiftness, the perfect road does not suggest the difficulties that taxed the ingenuity of Stark and his men, to avoid swamps where horses and guns would bog down, to round hills to avoid the steeper grades and to pass the beautiful wooded mountains that still stand much as Stark and his men saw them in their day.

The enormous labour of cutting down the forest trees, of extracting the roots of the monarch pines, of rolling back the huge boulders, levelling here and filling in there, had to be left for the times of peace. But see Captain Stark, as he sits, a gallant figure on his active horse, watching the work his men could do, with axes and blasting powder. He picks his way every little while from one group to another. The intrepid future defender of Bunker Hill is there and the hero who risked defeat and won victory at Bennington. Between times does he think of his bride of a year ago with a peculiar interest? She is far away in her father's home. His bereaved mother in the loved homestead by the falls of the rushing river comes into his mind. He is only 31, as young as the country, but the future is clouded. He wheels his horse and goes to give directions somewhere and his reverie is over.

While John Stark was away during the month, between August 8th and September 9th., many hundreds of soldiers were acting as laborers under the urgent direction of Gen. Amherst himself, advised by engineers, in making a new fortress, near the old works, at Crown Point. Traces of the outlines are still to be seen, 200 years afterwards, even portions of the massive stone walls, the blocks of quarried stone, well mortared. The "Provincials", of course, included many of the needed artisans and had the sinewy strength for the hardest of hard work, which was distasteful to the British soldiers. The huge task went on slowly, the *Journal* full of items about it.

Capt. Kennedy had been sent with a flag of truce and the bearer of peace proposals from Amherst to the St. Francis Indians on the St. Lawrence. Incensed at Kennedy's capture and detention and the rejection of the overtures, Amherst decided to wipe out the tribe and all their works. Stark had returned from his arduous labours and was not sent with Major Rogers a few days later, (September 13th, 1759). Rogers devotes pages to the story, Parkman gives it equal prominence but Long in the most recent life of Amherst, avoids it for some reason. The diary merely says (Sept. 12th):

> As Capt. Kennedy's journey was now over I ordered a detachment of 220 chosen men under the command of Major Rogers to go and destroy the St. Francis Indian settlements and the French settlements on the south side of the river, not letting anyone but Major Rogers know what about or where he was going.

Rogers is more explicit, stating his instructions, including "take your revenge", but "no women or children should be killed or hurt." Stark, left as the senior captain of rangers, escaped an assignment which would have been distasteful to him and repugnant to his conception of handling Indians. During the absence of Rogers, he was needed by Amherst. The predatory exploit is well known, not only through the accessibility of source material but through numerous writers. In 1940 it became familiar to an audience of millions. It was filmed (at great expense at a locale in Northern Idaho) the screen being based on the historical novel *Northwest Passage* by Kenneth Roberts.

Stark was no molly-coddle and for ten years had fought the Indians relentlessly but he knew that their expeditions had been chiefly due to the crafty designs of the French and that they were always executed by the stimulation of brandy or rum. He had known too much of the better side of the Indian character to relish entering dark *wigwams*, hatchet in hand, to brain sleeping men, before firing their village. Amherst has several entries of how Rogers was doing; learned that the enemy had discovered and had destroyed the boats left by Rogers in Missisquoi Bay; that Rogers "thought of returning by No. 4", whereupon Amherst sent Lt. Stevens with supplies to Wells River. It was 'Very cold weather and frost" at Crown Point on October 30th.

> The barracks very slowly getting on. Lt. Stevens whom I had sent with provisions to meet Mr. Rogers, returned. Said there was no probability he would ever come back that way, but he should have waited longer.

The incredible hardships suffered by Rogers and his split-up parties are well known now as also Stevens' terrible mistake in destroying and not leaving the rations. On Nov. 5 Rogers sent his report to Amherst from No. 4, who replied on the 8th:

> Every step you have taken was well judged and deserves my approbation.

The account of one egregious liar, Thompson Maxwell, alleges the presence of Stark on the expedition ("chose Capt. Stark our leader") but it appears from the publications (HG. Reg. XXIV. 57, 1868, and XL, 1891) that the relators of the two stories got them at second hand and "from notes. . . .copied hastily". Maxwell's final reference to Stark was "70 of us under Gen. (*sic*) stark to No. 4" is not confirmed in the account of Rogers or anyone else. Parkman, a stickler for correctness, disposed of Maxwell thus (*Montcalm & Wolfe.*)

> There is another account, very short and unsatisfactory, by Thompson Maxwell, who says he was of the party, which is doubtful.

In July, 1778, Stark was writing Gates of his familiarity with the wild nature of the country Rogers came back through, to show the difficulties of any military enterprise. The letter negatives any assumption of Stark's presence at St. Francis at the time of its destruction. It refers to the journey Stark made as a captive;

I have once been across that country myself and in the year 1759 Major Rogers destroyed St. Francis but lost most of his party on their return by reason of the distance of the way and the badness of the country."

All of August, September, October and November Amherst continued his work at Crown Point and vicinity. On the very day, (September 13th) when Rogers was given his instructions as to St. Francis, Wolfe was paying the supreme sacrifice with his life, on the Plains of Abraham, unhelped by any troops of Gen. Amherst, but victorious nevertheless.

Amherst's boats, an armed brig, a sloop, a floating battery and other craft, were ready in October.

Capt. Stark is to man three whale boats with seven men each and to attend such directions as he shall receive from Capt. Loring (who was in charge of all floating equipment, on Amherst's staff.)

On the 10th of October, according to the *Journal*, Amherst's expedition toward Canada was begun by a start down Lake Champlain. There were "four columns" but bad weather and gales were encountered and when on the 18th word arrived that Quebec was captured by the British and that Wolfe had been killed, Amherst wrote that as Vaudreuil and the whole army would be at Montreal:

I shall decline my intended operations and get back to Crown Point where I hear works go on but slowly.

It was true that the season was far advanced and, in accordance with custom, campaigns would end with the advent of cold weather, so Amherst dilligently sought to complete the fort and barracks. On Oct. 31, it was;

Very hard frost. The mortar would not work in the morning. We must make the best of it we can and complete as much as I am able. Ordered a dram of rum to each man; 'twas very necessary.

It must be granted that Amherst stuck to his self-imposed task. On Nov. 22 is the last reference to John Stark.

It is time I should get the troops away but I must see the Forts first in a defensive state & cover for their garrisons, which two days more will accomplish. Captain Stark's could prevail only on 157 rangers to engage for the winter & next summer if wanted.

With the indication that Stark was fully in charge in Rogers' absence the next entry says:

I reduced the six companies of rangers to two. Shall keep the officers on pay in case they may be wanted.

This distinctly is the promise Stark referred to in 1760 in his letter to Amherst and is the best confirmation of Caleb Stark's 1831;

Gen. Amherst by an official letter assured him of his protection and that if inclined to re-enter the service, he should not lose his rank by retiring.

Though the world war between Great Britain, France, Spain and Portugal did not end until Feb. 10, 1763 with the Peace of Paris, that portion of it involving any extensive participation through the service of New Englanders, was over with the surrender of all Canada to the British on September 8, 1760. That event crowned, if it did not end, Amherst's American career.

There were several reasons or influences why Capt. John Stark had no part in the campaign of 1760, when Amherst took Montreal and compelled the cessation of French resistance in Canada. Stark, interested in his farms and his family, was with many Americans, becoming saturated with anti-British feelings, but mainly he was dilatory when Amherst was summary in the preparations for ranger participation.

The now available Amherst correspondence discloses Stark as more than willing to serve. The captain's pay was in itself a considerable incentive, going a long way to compensate the inescapable risks, even though a patriotic motive was supposedly the underlying one. With further promotions not in sight and noting the rigid framework of the British Army, Stark's enthusiasm may easily have worn itself out, leaving little more than the habit of going on campaigns. At the risk of drawing unsafe inferences the small amount of Stark material must be studied and amplified to the limit.

At home John Stark was going through the changeable New England winter but whether at his father-in-law's in Dunbarton or at the old house at the Falls, is not apparent. On January 1st, 1760, Squire Matthew Patten of Bedford probably went across the river. He was a great borrower and a slow payer. He entered in his diary "borrowed 25 Johannas or £45 sterling of Capt. John Stark." Months passed by. Stark probably heard little or nothing of what Major Robert Rogers was doing, but it was an active season for Rogers.

After his arrival, on December first, the previous year, at Crown Point he found that all the Ranger companies had been disbanded "except those of Captains Johnson and Tute." Some scouting was done. Then Rogers went to New York, met Amherst there and returned to Albany on Feb. 6th. Very shortly afterward on a small scout his party was attacked and he wrote "My own sleigh was taken at this time containing £1196, York currency, besides stores and necessaries".

On March 1st; "Captain Tute and six men went upon a scout and all were taken prisoners." Rogers received Amherst's letter (about March first) advising his intention to "Complete the companies of rangers which were on foot last campaign". At the moment Captain Waite was with Amherst and arranged to fill up his company from Massachusetts and Connecticut. He took with him money and beating orders. Amherst then wrote;

> I have also written Captain John Stark in New Hampshire and Captain Brewer in Massachusetts, enclosing to each beating orders for their respective Provinces. I send you a copy of their instructions, which are to send their men to Albany, as fast as recruited.

If Amherst's letter indicates anything it shows that he wanted and fully expected John Stark to continue as captain and that he put into his hands the recruiting credentials for his own and other ranger companies in New Hampshire. Stark received the letter but like most of the pre-Revolutionary correspondence of John Stark it has not survived.

Evidently John Stark did not recognise in Amherst's letter the importance of hurry. He knew that campaigns never got under way while snow was on frozen ground and also that large bodies move slowly. Amherst's letter was delayed in transmission; did not come by "express". It was through Rogers that Amherst conveyed his dismissal of the Stark brothers. The three letters, Amherst to John Stark, Amherst to Rogers, Rogers to John Stark have never been found but in the War Office, London, three illiterate letters remain (Vol. 34, No. 82, folios 114-115-116) of which photostats are in Converse Library, Amherst.

All dated April 12, 1760, they appear to be in the hand of Samuel Stark but are individually signed by each brother, all addressed to "Major General Jeffry Amherst, Commander in Chief of all His Majesty's forces in North America". All are couched in the servility of attitude toward high officialdom, characteristic of the times, but the bad spelling and inferior psychology add to the lameness of the excuses; Samuel's that he fell from his horse, was injured, hence the delay; William's, (at his worst) wanted to know "the cause of my bad fortune in this case." The letter came by express rider.

In this case it made a ticklish situation worse. John Stark was in no position to assume that Amherst was to repudiate his promise of pay, keeping the officers in pay from the end of the 1759 campaign, in order to retain their services, even if no money was advanced, as Stark may have heard as to Waite's getting with his beating orders. Indeed, Amherst may have forgotten his promises and certainly Rogers, in high favour, was no man to remind him. The beating orders for the New Hampshire Ranger companies was the important thing; Stark got them.

Whether the officers were to collect pay for the idle winter months could have been taken up later. It is hard to equitably assess delinquencies in conduct from the limited data surviving. The result was doubtless as much due to Rogers as to Amherst. Decisions, it seems, were being made (considering the slowness of campaign organisation in those times) with unexpected quickness; the Starks were dropped without notice, in a matter of days, not months. John Stark's letter was as follows;

I received your orders of the first of March and according to them I have sent copies to the (undecipherable) officers but did not receive them to the first of April and in five days afterward I received an order to deliver them up to Captain Rogers. I did expect to have had the honor to have seen the reduction of Canada inasmuch as I have been in every campaign since the commencement of the war and have set myself about no manner of business till I received orders to the contrary, in which I am sorry I behaved so ill that your Excellency discharged me without my knowledge.

But as your Excellency wrote to me if I changed my mind you would provide for me I beg I may not be forgotten and, as your Excellency told me at Crown Point, that the officers that went home have their pay till they received further orders I should be glad to know whether they might expect it as there is several of them that is not called for in the list I received of you. Lt. McMullen was at my house and told me he had enlisted forty men and he is not included in the number that is to serve.

John Stark may have heard about Capt. Waite getting money for expenses. Rogers was not standing in his own light to plead the cause of friend John, or of William, still less of Samuel Stark. Amherst's whole attitude was summary and impatient. He was depending on Rogers to expedite the assembling of ranger companies. On March 9th he wrote ordering that Lt. Solomon, the Indian of Stockbridge, be directed to raise a company. His intention as to William Stark is plain (Rogers to Amherst, March 15th):

I have sent Lt. McCormick of Capt. William Stark's corps, Lieutenants Fletcher and Holmes to recruit for my own and Capt. Johnston's company.

To Amherst, occupied with great affairs, the Stark letters conveyed the implication of an unfulfilled promise, of pay "till they received further notice", an absurd assumption for New England farmers to put up to him after their discharge. But his *Journal* now betrays him and shows his intention of 1759.

In spite of all his pushing, contrasting in a sinister way to the inaction of the previous year when Wolfe was expecting the royal order for help, Amherst was not able to accomplish the surrender of Canada, a not very hard undertaking, until Sept. 8th, 1760. On May 9th, in the Albany-Schenectady area he bewailed; "Not a Provincial yet come". On the 26th, Rogers was ordered with 300 men to surprise St. Johns and destroy the magazines at Chambly. Eventually a maximum of 800 rangers participated and when Vaudreuil's capitulation came "our troops took possession of the gates of Montreal". (Rogers)

Superficial evidences have led to a contrary belief, one from a petition (notably untrustworthy guides) to Congress in 1776:

When Canada surrendered to the British troops, I resigned my commission and returned to my family, laid up my sword in hopes never to have occasion to draw it again.

In view of his letter to Amherst of April 12, 1760, the inclusion of that sentence was not only unnecessary but misleading. Yet an historical error has Stark with Amherst's expedition down the St. Lawrence, starting at Oswego Aug. 10, 1760, and later with Rogers "near Detroit" to meet Pontiac. No doubt Augustus C. Buell ("Sir William Johnson" in *Historic Lives*, 1903) was paying too much attention to Judge Witherill's letter to "The venerable John Stark, Esq." written from Detroit May 26th, 1811, which even Caleb Stark saw fit to print in full in 1860). Witherill in turn had derived his belief from the vaporings of Maxwell (who, in another instance caused Parkman to discredit him);

I was much gratified by the feeling narration of this transaction by a man of the name of Maxwell, who served under you in that campaign, who while he related the events, frequently attempted to wipe away the encrusted tear from his furrowed cheeks, often exclaiming; 'Ah, is my old Captain Stark still living?'

Though official records fail to show John Stark anywhere in British service after 1759, the petition and Witherill have one more feeble prop in the "family" view, sliding over and covering up an unpleasant phase of John Stark's career, as it were, in Caleb Stark's 1831 and 1860 sentences:

The conquest of Canada in 1760 put an end to military operations in North America; this circumstance together with the jealousies of the British officers, induced him to quit the service. &c.

Caleb's excuses could be the petition's mis-statement. It is doubtful if his father (Major Caleb) ever told him of the Amherst-Stark-Rogers correspondence. His grandfather's letter, with those of his great-uncles, reposed in the Archives in London in a seclusion ending in very recent years.

His characteristic refusal to "toady", his sharing the feelings of his men had, no doubt, long before engendered an aversion, not to be wiped out by the gratification of Lord Howe's treatment of him. Young Abercrombie's excoriation (the "misbehaviour of the men" including Stark) the treatment of the rangers on the island at Fort Edward by Col. Haviland, the easy-going condescension of the British officers in all the campaigns toward "the provincials", even the officers of the rangers, rank for rank (though under British pay and, at the last at the same pay) did not disguise the British unwillingness to fraternise in the long intervals between battles.

The cheaply dressed, rough and ready, illiterate, poorly equipped, friends, neighbours and others in the ranger's dangerous service, always had the sympathy and understanding of John Stark. In the workings of a mind of his type a quick resentment would harden into an enduring antagonism to Amherst and spread to include all British officers, for the essence of good fellowship was seldom seen after Howe went. Passing in review his thoughts, time without number, would stress the exasperating attitudes of certain officers, their rigid adherence to class distinctions, the fine cloth and fit of the uniforms with gold plated buttons, heavy handsome overcoatings, no end of polished accoutrements.

This was to say nothing of the dandified majors and captains who had bought their places with unearned money, some of them young and all unwilling to learn. Their antipathy to dirty work did not endear them to the sturdy colonials who had to perform it. In promotions even Rogers got no higher than major, yet without the militia and especially the rangers, the campaigns of the British would have beggared description.

Captain John Stark

Archibald Stark was born at Glasgow, Scotland, in 1697, and received his education at the University of that city. At an early age he removed, with his father and family, to Londonderry, Ireland, where he married Eleanor Nichols, the daughter of a Scottish, emigrant.

In 1720 he embarked with a company of adventurers for New-Hampshire, whither a, considerable party of his countrymen had previously proceeded, to form a settlement. After a tedious voyage, during which all his children died, the emigrants arrived at Boston late in autumn. As many of them were ill with the smallpox they were not permitted to land, and were, in consequence, compelled to depart for the wilds of Maine. At a place called Sheepscot, near the site of the present town of Wiscasset, they endured their first trial of the horrors of a northern winter in the forests of New England.

In the course of the year following, after encountering and enduring many severe hardships and privations, they joined their Scottish friends, who had preceded them, at Nutfield, (now Londonderry, N. H.) then a wilderness, rendered hideous by the frequent incursions of hostile savages, who, at that period, and for many succeeding years, harassed the frontiers. His house in Londonderry having been burned in 1736, he, in consequence, removed to that portion of land on Merrimack River, then known as Harrytown, and settled upon a lot, which had been granted to Samuel Thaxter by the government of Massachusetts, a short distance above the Falls of Amoskeag.

There several of his friends soon afterward followed him, and the new location received the name of Derryfield. Several sons and daughters were born to him, after his arrival in America, to whom, at his fireside, he gave the best education his own acquirements and the circumstances of the times would permit. The historian of *Manchester* says:

> His education fitted him for the walks of civil life, yet, we find
> him a volunteer for the protection of the frontier against the rav-
> ages of the Indians in 1745; and for the protection of the people
> in his immediate neighbourhood, a fort was built at the outlet of
> Swager's, or Fort Brook, which, in compliment to his enterprise

in erecting and garrisoning the same, was called Stark's Fort.

His sons were William, John, Samuel, and Archibald, who all held commissions in the British service during the "seven years'" or "French war," and were distinguished for good conduct, coolness and bravery. William, the eldest, served with reputation on the northern frontiers, and, under General Wolfe, in the expeditions to Louisburgh and Quebec, where his courage and address rendered signal services. He afterward tarnished his well-earned fame by joining the British Army at New-York. In 1776 he obtained the rank of colonel of dragoons, but was soon afterward killed by a fall from his horse.

A stone, in the old burial ground at Manchester, bears this inscription:

HERE LYES THE BODY OF MR. ARCHIBALD STARK.
HE DEPARTED THIS LIFE JUNE 25TH,
1758, AGED 61 YEARS.

At this period hunting was the most agreeable and profitable occupation of the young men of New-Hampshire. They were accustomed, at certain seasons, to dwell in forest camps, at great distances from home, and thus became inured to hardships, and were early taught lessons of self-dependence. They were often, in the pursuit of their vocation, brought in contact with the native savages, from whom they obtained a knowledge of their language and customs, and became excellent marksmen.

Their occupation as hunters, in the wild forest, was admirably adapted to prepare these hardy woodsmen for the arduous services they were soon afterward called upon to render their country, in a war which engaged all the thoughts, fears and energies of New-England.

John Stark, the subject of this memoir, was born at Londonderry, in New-Hampshire, August 28th, 1728. He resided with his father until March, 1752, when, in company with his brother William, David Stinson, and Amos Eastman, he proceeded on a hunting expedition to Baker's River, in the township of Rumney, (now so called) but then a forest, without an inhabitant or name.

They constructed a camp in the woods of hemlock boughs and bark, in which they deposited the supplies of provision, ammunition, traps and necessaries which had been drawn hither on their Indian sleds, and commenced their operations. The game was abundant, and prior to the 28th day of April they had collected furs of the value of five hundred and sixty pounds sterling.

On that day they were interrupted by a scout of ten St. Francis Indians, commanded by a chief named Francis Titigaw. Signs of the enemy had been observed on the previous day, and the party had concluded to leave the hunting ground. John Stark, being the youngest of the party, was directed to collect the traps, and while thus engaged, at sunset, fell into the enemy's hands. While stooping to the water to take up a trap, the Indians suddenly sprang from their ambuscade. A sharp hissing sound, as of a snake, accompanied the movement. He looked up and found himself a prisoner, surrounded by savages, with guns pointed toward him, rendering escape impossible.

When interrogated by his captors in regard to his companions, he pointed in a contrary direction to the true position of their camp, and thus induced them to travel two miles out of their way. His friends, alarmed at his long absence, discharged several guns which discovered their position to the savages, who, proceeding a distance down the river, turned their encampment and formed an ambush to intercept their canoe. The hunters suspecting what had taken place, were proceeding down the river William Stark and Stinson in the canoe, and Eastman on the shore. Soon after daybreak, on the 29th of April, the latter fell into the ambuscade and was taken. The Indians then directed John to hail the boat, and bid the occupants to come on shore. He called to them, stated his own and Eastman's situation, and urged them to escape to the opposite shore.

Perceiving the boat turned from its course, a portion of the Indians rose and fired into it. At this critical instant, Stark had the daring temerity to strike up their guns; and when the remainder were about to fire, struck all the guns he could reach. One ball, however, pierced the canoe paddle in the hands of William Stark, and another killed Stinson. John then shouted to his brother to escape, as they had fired all their guns. He profited by the advice and made good his retreat.

★★★★★★

After the return of William Stark to the settlements, a party from Rumford (now Concord, N. H.) started for the scene of the disaster. They found the body of Stinson stripped and scalped, which they buried in the woods, near the place where he fell; and returned in safety, bringing home the paddle of the canoe pierced with a ball.

Baker's River is a small stream flowing into the Pemigewasset, and is so called from Captain Thomas Baker, of North-Hampton, Mass., who, in 1720, with a scouting party of thirty-four men, passed up Connecticut River, and crossed the heights of land to the Pemigewasset; where, at the junction of that river with the small stream above named, he destroyed a party of Indians, killing their chief, Wattanummon, with his own hand, himself and the *sachem* firing at each other at the same moment. He destroyed their *wigwams*, and the party, loading themselves with as much of the fur, collected by the enemy, as they could carry home, burned the remainder.—*Farmer's Hist. Coll.*

A considerable branch flows into Baker's River, from Stinson's pond, and is called Stinson's brook. The pond is four hundred rods long, and two hundred and eighty rods wide. Its name is probably derived from the circumstance that David Stinson was killed in its vicinity by the savages, April 29th, 1752.—*Hayward's Gaz.* (On a journey to the White Mountains we last year visited the place.)

******

Exasperated by this conduct of their prisoner, the Indians beat him severely; made prize of all the furs collected by the party, and proceeded to the place now occupied by the town of Haverhill, upon Connecticut River, where two of their party had been stationed to obtain and prepare provisions for the returning scout. There they tarried one night, and continued their route to the Upper Coös. From thence they dispatched three of their party, with Eastman, to St. Francis. The remainder of the Indians employed themselves, for some time, in hunting upon a small stream called John's River.

The prisoner was liberated during the day, but confined at night. While there, they allowed him to try his luck as a hunter. He succeeded in trapping one beaver, and shooting another; and received their skins as a present in compliment to his skill.

The Indians, with their captive, arrived at St. Francis on the 9th of June following, where he remained nearly five weeks. He was well treated by the tribe, and obtained a knowledge of their language and modes of warfare, which proved of great service to him in his subsequent military career. In July, Mr. Wheelwright, of Boston, and Captain Stevens, of Charlestown, N. H., who were the agents employed by Massachusetts to redeem her captives, arrived at Montreal.

Not finding the prisoners they expected to find, belonging to Massachusetts, they redeemed Stark and Eastman; and, returning by way of Albany, arrived at Derryfield in August following. The ransom of Stark was one hundred and three dollars, and that of his friend

Eastman sixty dollars. (Eastman was sold to a Frenchman.) These sums were *never repaid by the State*. Massachusetts, pursuing a more liberal policy, redeemed all her captives.

It may here be remarked, as a singular fact, that the scout which captured these prisoners accompanied the returning party to Albany, and there disposed of the furs taken from them without molestation.

When the prisoners arrived at St. Francis, they were compelled to undergo the ceremony of running the gauntlet. The young warriors of the tribe arranged themselves in two lines, each armed with a rod or club to strike the captive, as he passed them, singing some ditty which had been taught him for the occasion, and bearing in his hands a pole six or eight feet long, with the skin of some bird or animal attached to one end of it. Eastman advanced first, singing words which meant, "I'll beat all your young men." The latter, considering themselves insulted, beat him so severely with their rods that he fell exhausted as soon as he had passed the lines. (Stark stated that the first one who struck him was a youth, whom he knocked down; and that he did not see him again while he remained at the village.)

Stark followed, singing the words, "I'll kiss all your women," his pole being ornamented with a loon skin. After receiving a blow or two, he turned his pole right and left, dealing a blow at each turn, and made his way without much injury, his enemies making way for him to avoid the sweeping blows dealt by his pole. This feat pleased the old Indians, who enjoyed the sport at their young men's expense.

The principal portion of the labour and menial drudgery of Indians is performed by squaws and captives. They directed Stark to hoe corn. He at first carefully *hoed* the weeds, and *cut up* the corn; but finding his purpose of freeing himself from the labour not answered by this process, he boldly threw his hoe into the river, declaring that "it was the business of squaws, and not warriors, to hoe corn."

Instead of being enraged at this action, the Indians were pleased with his boldness, released him from his task, and called him "young chief." He was adopted by the *sachem*, and treated with kindness while he remained at the village. In the latter days of his life he often related, with much humour, the incidents of his captivity, observing that he had experienced more genuine kindness from the savages of St. Francis, than he ever knew prisoners of war to receive from more civilized nations.

Not daunted by this unfortunate enterprise, our adventurer repaired the next season to the River Androscoggin to pursue his vocation, and *raise means to discharge his redemption debt*. Upon this occasion he was very successful, and returned with a valuable lot of fur.

The reports of these prisoners, concerning the Coös Territory, induced the authorities of the province to dispatch a party to explore this hitherto unknown region. Colonel Love well, Major Talford and Captain Page were ordered to enlist a company for that service. They engaged Mr. Stark as their guide, and under his direction, on the 10th of March, 1753, their journey was commenced. In seven days, they reached Connecticut River at Piermont. There they passed one night; and, having made such observations as their time would allow, returned, reaching Concord on the thirteenth day from the time of their departure. An account of the proceedings of this surveying party, with the names of the company, is to be found in the *History of Manchester*.

In 1754 a report was current that the French were erecting a fort at the Upper Coös; and Captain Powers was dispatched by Governor Wentworth with thirty men and a flag of truce, to demand their authority for so doing. He applied to Mr. Stark to accompany him, who conducted the party to the Upper Coös, by way of the Little Ox-Bow, by the same route he had travelled two years before, as a captive to the Indians. Finding no French garrison there, the company returned, being, we believe, the first party of English adventurers who explored the Coös intervals, where are now located the flourishing towns of Haverhill and Newbury.

Mr. Stark had acquired so much reputation by these expeditions, that, upon the breaking out of the "seven years' war," he was commissioned by the governor as second lieutenant of Rogers' company of Rangers, attached to Blanchard's regiment. Captain Rogers, possessing a bold and adventurous spirit, soon mustered a band of rugged foresters, every man of whom, as a hunter, could hit the size of a dollar at a hundred yards' distance; could follow the trail of man or beast; endure the fatigues of long marches, the pangs of hunger, and the cold of winter nights, often passed without fire, shelter, or covering, other than their common clothing, a blanket, perhaps a bearskin, and the boughs of the pine or hemlock.

Their knowledge of Indian character, customs and manners, was accurate. They were principally recruited in the vicinity of Amoskeag Falls; where Rogers was accustomed to meet them at the annual fishing season; whom he knew to be accustomed to traveling in forests, and hunting, and upon whose courage and fidelity implicit confidence could be placed. They were men who could face, with equal resolution, the savage animals of their native woods, the mountain tempests, or engage in the combat of heroes.

In the summer of 1755, Rogers, with his command, was ordered to Coös to burn the intervals, preparatory to the erection of a fort. Before reaching their place of destination, a new order directed them to join their regiment, at Fort Edward, by way of Number Four. They reached headquarters in August, a short time before the provincial army, under the command of General Johnson, was attacked by the French and Indians, at the south end of Lake George, near Bloody pond, so named from the slaughter on this occasion.

The French were defeated with the loss of one thousand killed, wounded and prisoners, with all their baggage. Their general, the Baron Dieskau, was wounded and taken prisoner. General Johnson, was created a baronet; but the honours bestowed upon him were earned and deserved by General Lyman, who was the real hero of the battle of Lake George. After the enemy gave way, he urged a pursuit; but Johnson, having received a slight wound, became alarmed, and would not allow of it. In fact, he never commenced the erection of the fort, afterward called William Henry, until the rangers returned from a reconnoitring scout, with the information that the French were building a fortress at Ticonderoga. The campaign passed without any other occurrence worthy of notice. In autumn the regiment was discharged, and Lieutenant Stark returned home.

In the winter of 1756, the British commander at Fort Edward resolved to establish a permanent corps of rangers, to counteract the operations of the French and Indian scouts, which harassed the frontiers, and hung upon the wings of the army. Rogers was appointed to enlist and command the corps. He selected Stark again for his second lieutenant, (his own brother, Richard, being his first lieutenant) raised a company, and in April following reported himself and soldiers at Fort Edward.

Although no important military operations were at tempted during this campaign, the rangers were constantly on foot, watching the motions of the enemy at Crown Point and Ticonderoga, cutting off their convoys of supplies, and often making prisoners of sentinels at their posts. One of their parties brought in the scalp of a French sentinel, killed near the gate of Crown Point. The rangers sometimes used the scalping knife, in retaliation for the cruelties of the French and their savage allies. Rogers says:

> On one of our expeditions, my Lord Howe did me the honour to accompany me, being desirous, as he expressed himself, of learning our method of marching, ambushing, retreating, &c.;

97

and on our return expressed his opinion of us very generously.

George, Lord Viscount Howe, was at this time second in command of the British forces in the north.

In the autumn of 1756 the corps of rangers was reinforced by two companies from Halifax, which raised it to the force of three hundred, strong. These hardy woodsmen were familiar with all the practices of the French and Indian partisans, and, in many a fierce conflict, evinced their ability to contend with and defeat them upon their own terms, either of force or stratagem.

In January, 1757, a detachment of rangers marched from Fort William Henry to intercept supplies passing between Crown Point and Ticonderoga. They passed over Lake George, and turned the latter fortress, without being observed. They captured several sleds, and destroyed their loading. One sled, however, escaped, and was driven back to the fort.

Knowing that the garrison would immediately be notified of their presence in the vicinity, the party commenced their retreat homeward; when, at the distance of three miles from Ticonderoga, they were, in the afternoon of January 21st, suddenly attacked by a force of French and Indians, springing from concealment in their front. The strength of the enemy was in numbers more than double that of their own, and a sanguinary action ensued.

According to the numbers engaged, a more desperate and bloody encounter did not occur during the war. Rogers was twice wounded, Captain Spikeman killed, and the command devolved upon Lieutenant Stark, as senior officer; who, by his prudence and firmness, secured the wounded, and drew off the detachment in such order as to keep the enemy at bay. By marching all night, they reached Lake George at eight o'clock next morning. The wounded, who, during the night march, had kept up their spirits, were by that time so overcome with cold, fatigue, and loss of blood, that they could march no farther.

It became, therefore, necessary to forward a notice to the fort, that sleighs might be sent for them. Lieutenant Stark volunteered for this purpose, and, by undergoing extraordinary fatigues, reached Fort William Henry, distant forty miles, the next evening. (The snow was at this time four feet deep upon a level, and the journey was performed on snow-shoes.) Sleighs were immediately dispatched to bring in the wounded, who arrived at the fort on the evening of the 23rd of January.

General Stark stated, in after times, that he was never conscious of taking the life of an individual except in this action. While the rangers were defending their position on the crest of the hill, he observed that several balls struck near him from a certain direction. In a moment afterward he discovered an Indian stretched at full length upon a rock, behind a large tree. His gun was soon ready, and he saw the Indian rising for another shot at him. His *fusee* was instantly levelled, discharged, and the savage rolled from the rock into the snow, pierced by the bullet through the head.

★★★★★★

He was at this period twenty-eight years of age. He had been an expert and successful hunter, and was well known to be one of the best marksmen of his time; and the most savage animals of his native forests—the catamounts, bears, wolves and wild-cats—in numerous instances, felt the effects of his unerring aim.

★★★★★★

Rogers, after he received his second wound, advised a retreat; but Stark, now having the command, and being almost the only officer fit for duty, declared that he had a good position, and would fight the enemy until dark, and then retreat; that in such a course consisted their only safety; and that he would shoot the first man who fled. While speaking thus, a ball broke the lock of his gun; and, at the same moment, observing a Frenchman fall, he sprang forward, seized his gun, returned to his place, and continued the action. His decision, prudence and courage no doubt saved the party in the present instance, and afterward contributed much toward the attainment of that success and celebrity which distinguished the career of the rangers in the campaigns of the "seven years' war." So said many of his veteran comrades.

In the reorganisation of the corps, he was promoted to fill the vacancy occasioned by the death of Captain Spikeman. In March, 1757, while commander of the Rangers stationed at Fort William Henry, one of his eccentricities saved the garrison from surprise and capture.

At this time Fort Edward, on the Hudson, and Fort William Henry, at the south end of Lake George, were the two most northerly frontier posts of the British dominions in North America. They were situated fifteen miles apart. The latter fort was at this period occupied by an Irish regiment, and about one hundred and fifty rangers. The nearest French post was Ticonderoga, forty miles northward.

With the exception of the uneasiness occasioned by the smallpox, then among them, the garrison at Fort William Henry rested in confident security on the night of March 17, 1757.

While going his rounds, on the evening of the 16th, Captain Stark overheard a squad of his men, who were of the Scotch-Irish race, planning a celebration in honour of St. Patrick, for the next night. He afterward said he had then no presentiment of approaching danger, but disliked these wild Irish demonstrations. He therefore called for the ranger sutler, Samuel Blodget, and gave him directions to deliver the rangers their regular rations of grog until the evening of the 17th; and after that, no more, without a written order from himself.

On that evening he retired to his quarters, directing his orderly sergeant to say to all applicants for written orders that he was confined to his bunk with a lame right hand, and would not be disturbed. The Irish troops received an extra supply of rum on the night of the 16th, and commenced their carousal, which they carried on with unabated vigour through the night and during the ensuing day, in honour of St. Patrick, and his wife Shelah. They drank so freely that the officer of the day could find none of them fit for duty as sentinels; and the rangers, who were sober, supplied their places.

The rangers, seeing the Irish thus enjoying themselves, desired the same privilege. The sutler informed them of his orders, and the captain's quarters were beset to obtain a written order. The orderly refused to disturb his officer, as he was confined with a painfully lame right hand, and could not write. The soldiers felt somewhat cross, but bore their disappointment like philosophers.

At two o'clock on the morning of the 18th, a ranger sentinel on the ramparts observed a light upon the lake, and soon afterward became aware that a large force was advancing in the direction of the fortress.

Notice was instantly conveyed to the ranger captain. The lame hand was instantly restored to health, and he was among his soldiers. The commander of the post was quietly notified, and the rangers silently mustered upon the walls. The French Army, of more than twenty-five hundred men, with a large force of Indians in their rear, commanded by General, the Marquis Vaudreuil, advanced and halted within about thirty rods of the fort. A detachment of five hundred men immediately came forward with scaling ladders, thinking to carry the place by surprise.

They planted their ladders, and mounted; but as the foremost men were about placing their feet upon the ramparts, a deep, stern voice gave the word "fire." A volley of musketry was instantly poured, with fatal effect, upon the assailants, while the guns of the fortress opened with grape and canister upon the columns in the rear. The enemy were repulsed, and fell back, confused and mortified.

The expedition had been concerted with the hope of carrying

the fort by surprise, in consequence of the excesses which the French general knew would be committed by the adorers of St. Patrick, upon the anniversary of that worthy saint's birth. The roar of the guns dissipated the fumes of alcohol from the brains of the regulars; and the garrison was soon in condition for a vigorous defence. At daylight the French general sent a flag of truce by his lieutenant general of artillery, (he brought, however, no artillery on this occasion) and formally summoned the garrison to surrender. He stated that:

> They occupied territory belonging to his most Christian Majesty, the King of France. He offered them their lives, and the officers were to be allowed to retain their baggage and side arms; the troops were to march out with the honours of war. He suggested, however, that it would be well for them to bestow some presents upon the Indians, to keep them quiet; that if these terms were not accepted, a general assault would be made by their whole army, and if the fort was taken, no quarter would be given.

The messenger had been brought in blindfold, and after delivering his message was conducted to another apartment, while the council of war considered their answer. It was gallantly and unanimously resolved, by the officers, to bury themselves in its ruins, rather than surrender the fortress. The disastrous defeat of General Braddock, two years previously, was fresh in the memory of the soldiers. (*Vide Braddock's Campaign 1755: the Fort Duquesne Expedition During the French & Indian War* by Winthrop Sargent; Leonaur 2018.) They crowded around the commander's quarters, anxiously awaiting the council's decision. "Monongahela and revenge," were the words shouted by the men. The French officer was again brought before the council, where the colonel commanding gave him their answer, allowing him twenty minutes to regain the French Army.

In the course of the day a general attack was made upon the fort, with great obstinacy and perseverance, upon four different points, but was, at every position assailed, gallantly repulsed by its heroic defenders.

The enemy then burned a vessel on the stocks, set fire to the woodpiles and the rangers' summer huts, outside of the walls, and after a siege of five days retreated, carrying away most of their wounded. They concealed their loss in killed by cutting holes in the ice and throwing into the lake the bodies of the slain, after having, as report says, scalped them, to obtain the bounty then offered by both governments for the scalps of their enemies. Several wounded prisoners, who were brought in after the French had retreated, reported that their orders were, if the place was carried, to put every man, woman and child in it to death.

On the part of the garrison not a man was killed, and but few wounded. Captain Stark was struck by a spent ball, which produced a slight contusion, but drew no blood. It was not a wound, but was the only injury he ever received from an enemy's weapon during the whole course of his military career. Sometime after this affair, a few gentlemen from Nantucket, strangers to him, presented Captain Stark with a cane, made from the bone of a whale, headed with ivory, as a token of their admiration of his conduct in the defence of Fort William Henry. The cane is still in the possession of his family.

Thus, terminated the first siege of Fort William Henry, in March, 1757. In the month of August following, it was surrendered to the Marquis de Montcalm, after a siege of nine days, and entirely destroyed.

The cause of its capture was as follows: In 1757 the Earl of Loudoun was appointed commander-in-chief of the British forces in North America. He came to America with the hope of reaping a harvest of laurels, but gained none.

He drew off most of the forces from the north to Nova Scotia, threatened Louisburgh and Quebec, but effected nothing except a waste of time and treasure. He left a garrison of 4,000 men at Fort Edward, under the command of General Webb, an inefficient and imbecile officer, who suffered Fort William Henry to be besieged and reduced by the French, without making the slightest effort for its relief. General Wolfe, in his position, would have acted a bolder part, and no doubt have compelled the enemy to retreat. Sir William Johnson came to Fort Edward and urged General Webb to make a movement for the relief of the besieged fort. The troops were once paraded for that purpose; but Webb's courage failing him, they were ordered back to their quarters, and a message dispatched to Colonel Monroe, advising him to capitulate on the best terms he could obtain.

Captain Stark proceeded to New-York to join the eastern expedition, but was there attacked with the smallpox, and compelled to remain until the return of the armament. After his recovery he rejoined the army at Albany, in October, and passed the winter at Fort Edward.

In March, 1758, Lord Loudoun returned to England, having added nothing to his military reputation by his American campaign. The command of the British forces now devolved upon Major-General James Abercrombie, who resolved to attempt the reduction of Ticonderoga, Preparations were accordingly commenced to assemble for that purpose the most powerful armament ever mustered in America. In addition to a large force of disciplined regulars, numerous detachments of provincials were called out, and every preparation made to ensure success. Of this army, Lord Viscount Howe was second in command.

On the morning of July 5th the whole army (of 16,000 men) embarked in *bateaux* for Ticonderoga (on the waters of Lake George.) The order of march afforded a splendid military show. The regular troops occupied the centre, and the. provincials formed the wings. For the advanced guard, the light infantry flanked the right, and the rangers the left, of Bradstreet's *bateau* men.

The services of Captain Stark had long before this period attracted the notice of Lord Howe, by whom he had been treated with great kindness and respect. His lordship had accompanied the rangers on a scout; and had, on that occasion, been conducted to the summit of Mount Defiance, a mountain eight hundred feet in height, overlooking and commanding the works of Ticonderoga. He perceived, at that time, the advantage which a few pieces of heavy artillery, placed there in battery, would afford a besieging army over the garrison. But General Abercrombie, supposing his force of sufficient strength to carry the place by assault, brought no artillery with his army.

On the evening before the attack, Captain Stark had a long conversation with Lord Howe in his tent, seated with him upon the bearskins which composed his lordship's camp-bed, respecting the mode of attack, and the position of the fort. They supped together, and orders were given him for the rangers to carry the bridge, between Lake George and the plains of Ticonderoga, at an early hour in the morning.

On the morning of July 6th, they advanced at daylight; but on approaching the bridge, Rogers, who was with the front column, perceiving a body of French and Indians prepared to dispute the passage, halted a few moments, which caused the rear guard, which was advancing rapidly, to press upon the front. Stark, who led the rear column, not knowing the cause of the delay and confusion consequent upon the halting of the front column, rushed forward, exclaiming, "It is no time for delay;" and calling on the troops to follow, pushed boldly on to the bridge, where, after a contest of a few minutes, the enemy broke and fled, leaving a clear passage for the army.

The attacks upon the French lines were made on the 6th, 7th and 8th of July, and proved unsuccessful, partly through the overweening confidence of the commander-in-chief, in neglecting to bring up his artillery with the army, at the expense of 1,608 regulars, and 334 provincials killed, wounded and prisoners. The French force under Montcalm scarcely amounted to 3000 men, Indians included.

Of those who fell, none was more regretted than Lord Howe, who was mortally wounded in the action with the enemy's advanced guard. He had driven them in, but following up his success too closely, received a fatal wound. His fall checked the advance of the army, and paralyzed their efforts. Other attacks were made, but without success. On the evening of the 8th, the general ordered a retreat, directing the "corps of rangers to cover his rear." In general orders next day, he thanked the army for their good behaviour a compliment which his troops could not bestow upon their general. The following extract relates to transactions of the afternoon and evening of the 7th of July, 1758.

Major Rogers held the position with 450 men, while Captain Stark, with the remainder of the rangers, (250) went with Captain Abercrombie and Colonel Clerk to reconnoitre the enemy's works. They returned in the evening, Colonel Clerk reporting that the enemy's works were of little importance.

Captain Stark, however, was of a different opinion; and did not hesitate to say that the French had formidable preparations for defence. Stark was but a provincial woodsman, and Clerk a British engineer. The opinion of the former was unheeded, while, most unfortunately, the advice of the latter was followed. Early on the morning of the 8th, Abercrombie, relying upon the report of his engineer, as to the flimsy nature of the French defences, determined to commence the attack without bringing up his artillery. (*History of Manchester.*)

The regret of Captain Stark for the fate of the gallant Lord Howe, who thus fell at the age of thirty-three, lasted his lifetime. He often remarked, however, during the Revolution, that he became more reconciled to his fate, since his talents, had he lived, might have been employed against the United States. He considered him the ablest commander under whom he ever served. To his military services and private virtues the General Court of Massachusetts paid an honourable tribute, by causing a monument to be erected to his memory, in Westminster Abbey.

Until the close of the campaign the rangers were constantly employed in excursions to the French forts, and in pursuit of their flying parties. Returning home on furlough, Captain Stark was, on the 20th of August, 1758, married to Elizabeth, daughter of Captain Caleb Page, one of the original proprietors of Dunbarton, N. H.

In the spring of 1759, having enlisted a new company, he returned to Fort Edward, and was present under General Amherst, at the reduction of Ticonderoga and Crown Point. After the surrender of the latter fort, he was ordered by that general, with a force of two hundred rangers, to construct a road through the wilderness from Crown Point to Number Four, on Connecticut River.

The capitulation of Canada put an end, for the time, to military operations in America. This circumstance, together with the jealousies of the British officers, induced him to leave the service. General Amherst assured him, by an official letter, of his protection; and that, if he should be inclined to re-enter the service, he should not lose his rank by retiring. In the campaign of 1759, the name of Captain Stark is mentioned several times in general orders, as follows:

June 13, 1759. Captain Stark, with his company of rangers, will join the detachment from the 'four mile post.'

June 27. Captain Stark will have a red flag in his *bateau*; and every *bateau* must be near enough to call to each other, and ready to follow Captain Stark immediately, as he knows where the covering party is posted, and will row in at a proper time. The fishermen will take their arms, which Captain Loring will deliver; and great care must be taken that they are not too much crowded. Captain Stark will receive his orders when the whole is to return from Major Campbell.

According to the above order, a large detachment of rangers and other troops were sent out in *bateaux*, covered by a strong force on shore, that fresh fish might be procured for the use of the army, one *bateau* being allowed to each battalion.

October 10. Captain Stark is to man three whale boats, with seven men each, and to attend such directions as he shall receive from Captain Loring.

Copy of a Petition

TO THE GOVERNMENT OF NEW-HAMPSHIRE, IN 1754, AS ON FILE IN THE OFFICE OF THE SECRETARY OF STATE.

Amos Eastman, of Pennacook (Concord), and John Stark, of Starkstown (Dumbarton), both in the province of New Hampshire, of lawful age, testify and say "that on the 28th day of April,

1752, they were in company with William Stark, of Starkstown, and David Stinson, of Londonderry, on one of the branches of the Permigwasset River, about eighteen miles from Stevenstown (Salisbury); that on the same day, toward night, the Indians captivated the said John, and the next morning, soon after day break, captivated the said Amos; and fired upon David Stinson and William Stark; they killed and scalped the said David (the said William made his escape), and carried the deponents both to Canada; That the stuff the Indians took from the deponents and their company was of the value of five hundred and sixty pounds at least, old tenor, for which they have no restitution;

That the said Amos was sold to the French, and for his redemption paid sixty dollars to his master, besides all his expenses of getting home; that the said John purchased his redemption of the Indians, for which he paid one hundred and three dollars, besides his expenses in getting home; that there were ten Indians in the company who captivated the deponents, and lived at St. Francis. They often told the deponents it was not peace. One Francis Titigaw was the chief of the scout. There was in the scout one named Peer, a young *sagamore*, who belonged to St. Francis.

The deponents made oath to the preceding, May 23, 1754, before Joseph Blanchard, one of His Majesty's justices of the peace. In a memorial presented by John and William Stark to Governor Wentworth, in 1754, they say that they gave no offence to the Indians; that they had it in their power to destroy them, or defeat their enterprise; but esteeming it a time of peace with all the Indians who own themselves subjects of the French king, free from any expectation of any hostilities to be committed against them, they peace ably applied themselves to their own business, till ambushed by the Indians.

They killed, scalped and stripped David Stinson, one of their company, captivated the afore said John and Amos, and shot at the said William, who escaped; that they carried the said captives to Canada, and, at the same time, took the goods and effects of your memorialists and said David Stinson, in company, of the value of five hundred and sixty pounds at least, old tenor.

The government never refunded any portion of the above. In this respect Massachusetts adopted a more liberal policy, and redeemed all her captives from the Indians.

Captain Phinehas Stevens

To most of the pioneers who sought an abode in the wilds of America, the same circumstances will apply. Prior to the year 1760, the frontier settlers were at all times exposed to the incursions of hostile savages, who were continually on the watch for opportunities of laying waste their homesteads, and to slay or carry away as captives the inhabitants. Necessity, therefore, compelled them to become familiar with danger, and acquire a hardihood of character unknown to their posterity. Whether they attended public worship, or cultivated their lands, they departed from their fortified garrisons with arms in their hands, prepared for instant action, and worshipped or laboured with sentinels on the alert

In their warfare, the Indians preferred prisoners and plunder to scalps. Hence, few persons were slain by them, excepting those unable to travel, those who attempted to escape, and such as appeared too formidable for them to encounter with a hope of success. Of the latter class was Captain Stevens. He was athletic, hardy and resolute; ever ready to cultivate his acres, or arm in their defence, as well as for the protection of his countrymen. He was truly a martial husbandman—

Who, in the reaper's merry row
Or warrior rank could stand.

A man of self-acquired education, possessing deep penetration and intelligence, he was admirably fitted for the important public services, in the performance of which he was intrusted by the government.

He was the father and defender of the early settlements on the north-eastern frontiers of New-England, where he, like

The pastoral hero, assembled his hand,
To lead them to war at his monarch's command.

He was the son of Joseph and Prudence Stevens, and born on the 20th of February, 1706, at Sudbury, Massachusetts, from whence he removed with his father to Rutland, in the same State.

At the age of sixteen, accompanied by his three younger brothers, he was proceeding to a meadow where his father was engaged in making hay, when he fell into an Indian ambuscade. The enemy made him prisoner, slew two of his brothers, and were about to slay the youngest, then but four years of age. He succeeded, however, in making the savages understand, by signs, that if they would spare the life of his little brother, he would carry him on his back. He conveyed him in that manner to Canada. Such tragic events were not uncommon at that period. The captives were soon afterward redeemed.

He received several commissions from Governor Wentworth, of New-Hampshire, and Governor Shirley, of Massachusetts, and rendered important service in defending the frontiers.

In 1747, when Number Four was abandoned by its inhabitants, he was ordered to occupy the fort with thirty men. On the 4th of April, of that year, the garrison was attacked by more than four hundred French and Indians, commanded by Monsieur Debeline. The siege continued three days. Indian stratagem, French skill, and fire, applied to every combustible matter in the vicinity of the fort, produced not the desired effect. Its heroic defenders were not appalled, and would not capitulate. At length the enemy demanded a *parley*, and the commanders met outside of the fort. The Frenchman declared that he had seven hundred men, and depicted the horrid massacre which must ensue unless the post was surrendered.

"My men are not afraid to die," was Captain Stevens' noble answer. The attack was renewed, and continued with increased fury until the third day, when the enemy again called for a cessation of arms. They then proposed to depart if the garrison would sell them provisions sufficient to support them on their way back to Canada. Captain Stevens replied that he could not sell the supplies of the fort for money, but would give them five bushels of corn for every prisoner they would deliver up to him. Upon receiving this answer, the enemy discharged four or five guns at the fort, and departed.

This noble defence of a timber fort, by thirty-one persons, against a force of more than fourteen times their number, confirmed the high opinion already entertained both by the government and his fellow-citizens of the capacity and dauntless valour of our frontier hero. For his distinguished gallantry upon this occasion. Commodore Sir Charles Knowles presented him an elegant sword. From this circumstance the township, when its charter was granted by Governor Wentworth to Joseph Wells, Phinehas Stevens, and others, in 1762, obtained the name of Charlestown.

On two occasions (in 1749 and 1752), if not more, the Governor of Massachusetts employed Captain Stevens to proceed with flags of truce to Canada to negotiate the redemption of captives from the Indians. Of these expeditions he kept diaries, as we have reason to suppose he did of most of his transactions, as well in regard to the affairs of his farm, as of his proceedings in the public service. We have seen his journal of

1749, published in the *New-Hampshire Historical Collections*, and also his original journal of 1752, which was several years ago found at the bottom of an old chum in a garret in Charlestown. It was afterward lost at the burning of the Vermont State Capitol. The manuscript was written in a plain, legible hand. The language was concise and appropriate. His education, however obtained, must therefore have been superior to that of most of his New-England cotemporaries.

The journal of 1752 contained observations relative to his crops; mentioned the date when the first barrel of rum was brought to number four; detailed a journey to Portsmouth, and another with a flag of truce to Canada. It also contained a description of Montreal, Mr. Wheelwright, of Boston, was his colleague in this mission to Canada.

Captain Stevens died at Chenucoto, in Nova Scotia, April 6, 1756, while engaged in public service, in the fifty-first year of his age. He is the ancestor of many persons of high respectability in New-Hampshire and Vermont. His son, Colonel Samuel Stevens, was the first representative of Charlestown to the General Court. He was a councillor six years, and afterward register of probate until his death, November 17, 1823, at the age of 85 years. One daughter of Captain Stevens was born in the fort at Number Four, and married to Hon. John Hubbard, father of the late Hon. Henry Hubbard.

The president of the Vermont Historical and Antiquarian Societies, Colonel Henry Stevens, is the grandson of the hero of Number Four. Those societies are indebted to his laborious researches for a large portion of the valuable ancient documents and curiosities in their possession. The State of Vermont should also justly appreciate his exertions in procuring from Congress two of the most important trophies of a victory gained by the valour of the White and Green mountain boys, to adorn her capitol—the Bennington cannon.

He formerly resided at Barnet, Vt., but in 1858 removed to Burlington. As an industrious and scientific farmer, his experiments, his writings and addresses before the State and County agricultural societies, have obtained for him an extensive reputation.

His son, Henry Stevens, junior, was an assistant of Mr. Sparks while preparing those voluminous historical works which, while they reflect the highest honour upon that distinguished gentleman, also cast a brilliant light upon the achievements of the American revolution.

Since the foregoing was written, a communication has been received from Colonel H. Stevens, which we insert in his own words.

I find among my grandfather's old papers the following commissions:

To Phinehas Stevens, of No. Four so called, on ye east of Connecticut River. You, the said Phinehas Stevens to be lieut. of the foot company of militia, in the regiment whereof Josiah Willard, Esq., is Colonel.

B. Wentworth.

Dec. 13, *A. D.* 1743.

He was commissioned by Gov. W. Shirley, as lieut. in a company of volunteers, raised for the defence of the western frontiers, on the 26th day of October, *A. D.* 1744.

He was appointed captain of a company of volunteers, to be raised for his majesty's service against the French and Indians, January 9, 1745, by W. Shirley.

He was commissioned first lieut. of a company of soldiers raised for ye defence of ye western frontiers, for the protection of the inhabitants, whereof Josiah Willard, Jun'r, is Captain, 29th July, *A. D.* 1745, by W. Shirley.

The following commission I copy from the original, which is all written:

By His Excellency, the Governor.

Province of Massachusetts Bay.

These are to direct you forthwith to enlist sixty able bodied, effective volunteers to make up a marching company on the western frontiers. Twenty-five of which sixty men you may so enlist out of the standing company in those parts; taking effectual care, that, that enlistment be made with as much equality as may be, so as not much to weaken any particular party of those soldiers, and with the said company to scout during the summer season in such places where the Indian enemies hunt or dwell, keeping one half of your company at the garrison called Number Four, to guard and defend the inhabitants there, and to repel and destroy the enemy that may assault them; and upon return of the half that go out upon the march, the half just mentioned forthwith to march out and scout in the manner above said; and so interchangeably—one part to continue to do their duty at Number Four, and the other to be upon the march above said.

And you, the officer that shall command the said marching party, must keep exact journals of your marches, noting down all circumstances, and making such observations as may be useful hereafter. You must take care to keep an exact discipline among your men, punishing till immorality and profaneness, and suppressing all such disorders in your marches and encampments as may tend to disorder and expose you to the enemy.

Given under my hand, at Boston, the twenty-sixth day of April, 1746, in the nineteenth year of His Majesty's reign.

Wm. Shirley

To Captain Phinehas Stevens.

I find also one other commission, bearing date at Boston, 16th June, *A. D.* 1746.

Also, one other commission to Phinehas Stevens, "to be commander of the fort called Number Four, and the garrison there posted, or to be posted there, and to consist of the first company of soldiers in the said garrison." Dated the 25th of February, *A. D.* 1747. Wm. Shirley.

Also, one other commission: "You, the said Phinehas Stevens, to be captain of the garrison at the fort called Number Four." Dated at Boston, November 10, *A. D.* 1747. Wm. Shirley.

Also, a commission of captain of a company at Charlestown. Dated 26th April, 1754. B. Wentworth.

There were other commissions before and after the above, which I have not been able to recover.

I have a commission of Simon Stevens, as a lieutenant in John Stark's company, dated the 14th of January, 1758, signed "Loudoun."

Again, I have Simon Stevens' commission, as captain of a company of rangers, bearing date at Three Rivers, July 9, 1760. Signed, Jeff. Amherst.

Samuel Stevens was commissioned as a lieutenant by Jeffery Amherst, and had command of a party that went from Charlestown up Connecticut River to meet Robert Rogers with provisions, at the time he went to St. Francis, *A. D.* 1769.

Again, Enos Stevens (my father), was a lieutenant, *A. D.* 1756. I had his journal of an expedition up West River, and so on to Fort Massachusetts. His diary was burnt in the Vermont State House.

CHILDREN OF CAPTAIN PHINEHAS STEVENS.

Simon and Willard (twins), born February 4, 1735. (Simon died.)
Simon, 2nd, September 3, 1737; Enos, October 2, 1789; Mary,

111

March 28, 1742; Phinehas, July 31, 1744; Catharine, November 20, 1747. (The above named were born at Rutland, Massachusetts.)

Prudence, November—1750, Solomon, September 9, 1753—were born at Charlestown, N. H.

Dorothy, born October 31, 1755, at Deerfield, Mass. Died at Charlestown, September 10, 1758.

Enos Stevens, my father, married Sophia Grout, March 4, 1791. Of their ten children, only three are now (1877) living: *viz.*, Henry Stevens, Willard Stevens, of Barnet, Vt, and Sophia, wife of Jonathan Fitch Skinner, of Barton, Vermont.

Our friend, Colonel Henry Stevens, married Candace Salter, March 16, 1815. Of their eleven children, four sons and one daughter are now (1877) living.

Enos, the eldest, resides at Boston, Mass. Henry is now (1877) in London, agent for the trustees of the British Museum, literary agent for the Smithsonian Institute and several other American libraries; also, for several private American gentlemen.

Sophia Candace married her second husband, William Page, an artist, celebrated as the greatest colourist since the days of Titian, of whom, in that branch of the art, he has been a distinguished and successful imitator. He resides (1877) at Rome, in Italy.

Simon is a distinguished attorney and counsellor at law, in Lancaster, Pennsylvania.

Benjamin Franklin is now (1877) engaged at New York, assisting his brother Henry in purchasing and exchanging books for the British museum and other libraries.

Lieutenant George Stevens graduated at West-Point, in 1843, and was ordered to Fort Jessup. From thence he proceeded, with the army of occupation, to *Corpus Christi,* and was there attached to May's corps of dragoons. May, with his cavalry, cut their way through the Mexican field batteries, but on returning with five of his company, he found one battery still in operation. He rode up and demanded its surrender, with which demand General la Vega complied. Captain May placed him in charge of Lieutenant Stevens, who, with a sergeant, conveyed the Mexican general of artillery to the rear, and delivered him to General Taylor. After General la Vega recovered his baggage, he presented Lieutenant Stevens with several curiosities, bullets, cigars, &c., which his father now has in possession.

Lieutenant Stevens was drowned in passing the Rio Grande from Fort Brown to Metamoras. The cavalry were dismounted, and he proposed to take the lead on horseback, although advised by General Twiggs not to venture. However, he went on ahead. In passing the river the horses could ford part of the way, and three of the mounted dragoons followed to direct the foremost. When within sixty yards of the Mexican shore, the horses came into a whirlpool. About sixty of them were carried round and round, and Lieutenant Stevens became unhorsed. He kept above water for about sixty rods. Boats were put off from the shore, but could not reach him on account of the roughness of the water. He was recovered on the third day after, and buried on one side of the flag-staff of the fort. Major Brown lying upon its other side.

How sleep the brave who sink to rest,
By all their country's wishes blest!
Both for their country, and in danger's face,
Won chaplets which time's hand shall not erase;
Left her foes' cause, for memory stern and just,
To live, though valour's urn has claimed their dust.

Copy of a letter to Governor William Shirley, from Captain Phinehas Stevens, commander of the fort at Number Four, forty miles above Northfield, dated April 7, 1747:

Our dogs being very much disturbed, which gave us reason to think the enemy were about, occasioned us not to open the gate at the usual time; but one of our men, being desirous to know the certainty, ventured out privately, to set on the dogs, about nine o'clock in the morning, and went about twenty rods from the fort, firing off his gun, and saying choboy to the dogs. Whereupon the enemy, being within a few rods, immediately rose from behind a log and fired; but, through the goodness of God, the man got into the fort with only a slight wound. The enemy being then discovered, immediately arose from all their ambushments and attacked us on all sides.

The wind being high, and everything exceedingly dry, they set fire to all the old fences, and also to a log house, about forty rods distant from the fort, to the windward; so that, within a few minutes, we were entirely surrounded with fire—all which was performed with the most hideous shouting and firing from all quarters, which they continued in a very terrible manner until the next day at ten o'clock at night, without intermission, during which time we had no opportunity either to eat or sleep.

But, notwithstanding all their shoutings and threatenings, our men seemed not to be in the least daunted, but fought with great resolution, which doubtless gave the enemy reason to think we had determined to stand it out to the last degree.

The enemy had provided themselves with a sort of fortification, which they had determined to push before them, and bring fuel to the side of the fort in order to burn it down; but, instead of performing what they threatened, and seemed to be immediately going to undertake, they called to us and desired a cessation of arms until sunrise the next morning, which was granted; at which time they would come to a *parley*.

Accordingly, the French general, Debeline, came with about sixty of his men, with a flag of truce, and stuck it down within about twenty rods of the fort, in plain eight of the same, and said if we would send three men to him, he would send as many to us, to which we complied. The general sent in a French lieutenant, with a French soldier and an Indian.

Upon our men going to the *monsieur*, he made the following proposals: *viz.*, that, in case we would immediately resign up the fort, we should all have our lives, and liberty to put on all the clothes we had, and also to take a sufficient quantity of provisions to carry us to Montreal, and bind up our provisions and blankets, lay down our arms, and march out of the fort. Upon our men returning, he desired that the captain of the fort would meet him half way, and give an answer to the above proposal, which I did; and upon meeting the *monsieur*, he did not wait for me to give an answer, but went on in the following manner: *viz.*, that, what had been promised he was ready to perform; but, upon refusal, he would immediately set the fort on fire, and run over the top, for he had seven hundred men with him; and if we made any farther resistance, or should happen to kill one Indian, we might expect all to be put to the sword. 'The fort,' said he, 'I am resolved to have, or die. Now, do what you please; for I am as easy to have you fight, as give it up.'

I told the general that, in case of extremity, his proposal would do; but inasmuch as I was sent here by my master, the captain general, to defend this fort, it would not be consistent with my orders to give it up, unless I was better satisfied that he was able to perform what he had threatened; and, furthermore, I told him that it was poor encouragement to resign into the hands of an enemy, that, upon one of their number being killed, they would put all to the sword, when it was probable we had killed some of them already. 'Well,' said he, 'go into the fort and see whether your men dare fight any more or not, and give me an answer quick, for my men want to be fighting.'

Whereupon I came into the fort and called all the men together, and informed them what the French general said, and then put it to vote, which they chose, either to fight on or resign; and they voted to a man, to stand it out as long as they had life. Upon this, I returned the answer that we were determined to fight it out Upon which they gave a shout, and then fired, and so continued firing and shouting until daylight next morning.

About noon they called to us and said, good morning; and desired a cessation of arms for two hours, that they might come to a parley, which was granted. The general did not come himself, but sent two Indians, who came within about two rods of the fort and stuck down their flag, and desired that I would send out two men to them, which I did; and the Indians made the following proposals *viz.*, that, in case we would sell them provisions, they would leave, and not fight any more; and desired my answer, which was, that selling them provisions for money was contrary to the law of nations; but if they would send in a captive for every five bushels of corn, I would supply them. Upon the Indians returning the general this answer, four or five guns were fired against the, fort, and they withdrew, as we supposed, for we heard no more of them.

In all this time we had scarce opportunity to eat or sleep. The cessation of arms gave us no great matter of rest, for we suspected they did it to obtain an advantage against us. I believe men never were known to hold out with better resolution, for they did not seem to sit or lay still one moment. There were but thirty men in the fort, and although we had some thousands of guns fired at us, there were but two men slightly wounded: *viz.*, John Brown and Joseph Earl.

By the above account, you may form some idea of the distressed circumstances we were under, to have such an army of starved creatures around us, whose necessity obliged them to be the more earnest. They seemed every minute as if they were going to swallow us up, using all the threatening language they could invent, with shouting and firing, as if the heavens and earth were coming together.

But, notwithstanding all this, our courage held out to the last. We were informed by the French that came into the fort, that our captives were removed from Quebec to Montreal, which they say are three hundred in number, by reason of sickness that is at Quebec, and that they were well and in good health, except three who were left sick, and that about three captives had died which were said to be Dutchmen. They also informed us that John Norton had liberty to preach to the captives, and that they have some thousands of French and Indians out and coming against our frontier.

A very beautiful silver-hilted sword has been purchased by order and at the expense of the honourable Commodore Sir Charles Knowles, to be presented to Captain Stevens for his bravery in defence of the fort above mentioned.

The foregoing I copied from a Boston newspaper, with the note at the bottom in relation to the sword. This letter was addressed to His Excellency, Governor Shirley. I have to say that Captain Stevens received the sword, and it was kept, after grandfather's decease, by Colonel Samuel Stevens, of Charlestown. I have been told that Uncle Samuel took said sword to Northampton, to a goldsmith, to have it cleansed. The goldsmith left Northampton, and the sword was not returned.

Your friend,   Henry Stevens.

To Caleb Stark, Esq.

Addressed to Honourable Spencer Phipps, Lieutenant Governor of this Province (Massachusetts), and the Council, June 12, 1760.

The memorial of Phinehas Stevens, of Number Four, humbly sheweth:

That, upon his enlisting himself a volunteer in his majesty's service for the then intended expedition against Canada, he removed his family, viz.: his wife and six children, to Rutland, from Number Four, expecting himself soon to set out for Canada, on said expedition; and that, upon the delay of that expedition, he was, by direction from his excellency, the captain general, ordered to the frontiers of the province, and was constantly employed on the frontiers either in guarding stores to Fort Massachusetts or Number Four, or in keeping the fort at Number Four, till the said expedition was laid aside, and the Canada forces dismissed, in which time he defended the said fort, Number Four, from a vigorous attack of the enemy; and his other services, in that term, he humbly hopes were acceptable to the province, where he was at very great expense in supporting his family at a distance from his station; and as his expenses, so he humbly conceives, his constant labours and services for the province in that term, distinguish his case from that of most if not any of the officers who enlisted themselves for the Canada service. He therefore prays your honourable consideration of the premises, and that your honours would grant that he may be allowed the common allowance for a soldier, for subsistence during the said term; and your memorialist, as in duty bound, will ever pray.

Phinehas Stevens.

In the House of Representatives
June 13th, 1750.

Read, and ordered that the memorialist be allowed out of the public treasury the sum of ten pounds and eight shillings, in full consideration of the above named.

Sent up for concurrence,

D. Hubbard, Speaker.

In Council, June 18, 1750.

Read and concurred,

Sam'l Holbrook, Dep'ty Sec'y.

Consented to,

S. Phipps.

Colonel Robert Rogers

James Rogers was one of the early settlers of Londonderry, N. H. He afterward removed to the wilderness of the township now known as Dunbarton, where he was killed by mistake by a hunter, who was his intimate friend. The latter, in the dusk of the evening, perceiving a dark object at a distance, supposed it to be a bear, and fired through a thicket with fatal effect. The fur cap and dark clothing of Mr. Rogers occasioned the sad disaster. Mr. Hadley, in his notice of Dunbarton, gives the following account of this catastrophe:

Mr. Ebenezer Ayer, of Haverhill, Mass., a celebrated hunter of those times, came into these parts to pursue his usual avocation in quest of bears, deer, and other game. He had made a rude camp on Walnut hill, in Bow, near to Dunbarton line. He had been hunting all day, and came to his camp at evening, and it not being late, was still looking out for the approach of a bear. Mr. Rogers was an intimate friend of Ayer, and was coming to pay him a visit. He drew near to his camp; he was dressed entirely in black; and the dusk of the evening deceived the eye of the eager hunter. He took the fatal aim, and shot the man! He soon discovered his mistake, and with sorrowing heart stood over the bleeding form of his friend. Rogers did not long survive. He died before he reached his home. Ayer could never after relate the story of the sad event without shedding tears.

Robert Rogers, son of the above, was born at Londonderry, N. H. (or Methuen, Mass.), in 1727. He was from his youth inured, to the hardships of frontier life, from which circumstance he acquired a decision and boldness of character which served him in after years.

He was six feet in stature, well proportioned, and one of the most athletic men of his time—well known in all the trials of strength or activity among the young men of his vicinity, and for several miles around. He was endued with great presence of mind, intrepidity, perseverance, and possessed a plausible address.

In 1755 he was appointed by Governor Wentworth captain of a company of rangers. He afterward commanded that celebrated corps, with the rank of major, in the line of the army. With this corps—of which the most hardy and resolute young men New Hampshire and other provinces could produce, constituted the principal portion— he rendered important services on the northern frontiers, and in the Canadas, until the surrender of those provinces, in 1760, to the crown of Great Britain.

The enemy dreaded him and his daring followers with good reason. The rangers under his command were in their expeditions limited to no season. Summer or winter caused no difference or delay in their arduous duties. They made long and fatiguing marches in winter, upon snow-shoes, often encamping in the forest, without fire, to avoid discovery by the enemy, and with no other food than the game they had killed during their march. They penetrated into the enemy's country, and destroyed French settlements and Indian villages, sometimes at four hundred miles' distance. They were in truth the most formidable body of men ever employed in the early wars of America, and in every regular engagement proved themselves not inferior to British troops. To their savage and French foes, they were invincible.

After the year 1760, he served against the Cherokees in the south, under the orders of General Grant.

In 1765 he proceeded to England to prosecute his claims for services and money advanced during the northern campaigns of the "seven years' war." In 1766 he was appointed governor of Michilimackinac, where, sometime afterward, he was arrested and conveyed in irons to Quebec, charged with an intention to plunder the fort he commanded, and desert to the French. He managed to be acquitted of this charge and proceeded, in 1769, a second time to England, where he was presented to the king.

While in England at this time, the following characteristic anecdote is related of him.

A mail-coach, in which he was a passenger, was stopped by a highwayman on Hounslow Heath. The robber, thrusting a pistol through the coach window, demanded the purses and watches of the occupants. While others were taking out their valuables, the bold American ranger suddenly seized the man by the collar, by main strength drew him through the coach window, and ordered the coachman to drive on. The captive was an old offender, for whose apprehension a reward of fifty pounds sterling had been offered by the government.

While at a social party of British officers in England, of similar spirits, it was agreed by the company that whoever of them should relate the greatest falsehood, or the most improbable story, should have his bill paid by the others. When his turn came, Rogers stated that:

His father was shot in the woods of America by a hunter, who mistook him for a bear; that his mother was followed by a hunter, who mistook her tracks in the snow, on a stormy day, for those of a wolf; and that he, when a boy, had carried on his back birch brooms for sale to Rumford, ten miles distant from his father's house, following a path through the woods only marked by spotted trees.

The company admitted that Rogers had related the greatest falsehood, and the most improbable story, when he had narrated nothing but the truth.

Rogers returned to America in 1775, where, had he not been suspected of being hostile to the revolutionary movement, he might perhaps have obtained an important command, and rendered signal services. He had seen more arduous and difficult service than most of the continental officers. He visited New Hampshire, came to Cambridge and Medford, then occupied by continental troops. At the latter place he had an interview with Colonel Stark, who had been his second in command in the ranger service. Washington suspected him to be a British spy, and prohibited his entering the American camp. He also visited Congress, but his fidelity being considered doubtful, received no appointment.

He obtained, in 1776, the rank of colonel from the British general at New York, and raised a corps known as the "Queen's Rangers," with which, for a time, he was a scourge to the people in the vicinity of Long-Island Sound. In October, 1776, he made an attack upon an American outpost near Maroneck, of which a Hartford, (Conn.) paper states the following particulars:

> On Monday last (October 21st) a party of Tories (100), some of whom came from Long-Island, under the command of the infamous Major Rogers, made an attack upon an advanced party of our men, when a smart engagement ensued, in which the enemy were totally routed. About twenty were killed on the spot, and thirty-six taken prisoners, who were safely lodged in the goal at White Plains. Their gallant commander, with his usual bravery, left his men in time of action, and made his escape.

He came very near being made prisoner. Soon after this affair, he went to England, and the command of the "Queen's Rangers" devolved upon the noted Colonel Simcoe. In 1778 he was proscribed by the legislature of New Hampshire, who also granted his wife (a Miss Brown, of Portsmouth) a divorce. She afterward married Captain John Roach.

His son, Arthur, resided with his mother, and at her decease inherited the property at Concord. He died at Portsmouth, in August, 1841, leaving two sons and one daughter, then occupying respectable positions in the West Indies. His eldest son, Robert, now a respectable farmer in Derry, is the only survivor of a family of eight children. For other particulars respecting Colonel Rogers, see the *History of Manchester*, from which several of the foregoing statements were obtained.

The following account of his services during the "seven years' war" in North America, contains the substance of his journal, published in Loudon in 1765, with information in regard to the same subject obtained from other sources.

Account of the Services of Colonel Robert Rogers.

In 1755 an expedition was organised for the purpose of reducing Crown Point, a post from which had for several years been fitted out most of the Indian scouts which had harassed the English frontier settlements. Troops were accordingly raised in New England, New York, and New Jersey. Albany was designated as the place of rendezvous, and Major General Johnson appointed commander.

Captain Robert Rogers, with a commission from Governor Wentworth, raised a company of rangers in New Hampshire on account of that province, and made several excursions to the north-western frontiers to prevent inroads from the enemy. On the 26th of August, 1755, he was employed in escorting provision wagons from Albany to the carrying place, since called Fort Edward. At this time, he waited upon General Johnson, to whom he had been recommended as a person well acquainted with the haunts and passes of the enemy, and the Indian methods of fighting. He was by him dispatched on several scouts to the French posts. He was on one of these up the Hudson, on the 8th of September, when General Dieskan was taken prisoner, and his army routed at the south end of Lake George. Johnson's army was composed principally of the troops raised by the above-named province for the Crown Point expedition. With the exception of those who were with Rogers on his scout, the remainder of the rangers were engaged in this action.

September 24, 1755. General Johnson ordered Rogers to reconnoitre Crown Point, and, if practicable, to secure a prisoner. He embarked, with four men, and proceeding down Lake George twenty-five miles, landed on the west shore. There leaving his boat in charge of two men, he proceeded with the other two, and on the 29th obtained a view of Crown Point. A large body of Indians were observed about the fort, who, from their irregular firing, were supposed to be shooting at marks—a diversion of which Indians are very fond. At night the party crept through the French guards into a small village, south of the fort, and passed through it to an eminence at the south-west, where it was ascertained that the enemy were erecting a battery, having already thrown up an entrenchment on that side of the fort. The next day, having gained an eminence a short distance from the former, an encampment was discovered, extending from the fort south-east to a windmill, at thirty yards distance, containing about five hundred men. Finding no opportunity to obtain a captive, and that they had been observed, the scout retreated on the first of October.

On the route homeward they passed within two miles of Ticonderoga, from which a large smoke was noticed, and the discharge of a number of small arms heard; but, as their provisions were expended, they could not remain to ascertain the enemy's force. On the second they reached the place where their boat had been left in charge of two men, who, to their surprise, had departed, leaving no provisions behind. This hastened their return to camp, where they arrived on the fourth, not a little fatigued and distressed with hunger and cold.

October 7th. General Johnson ordered Rogers to embark with five men to reconnoitre Ticonderoga. He proceeded at night to a point of land on the west shore of the lake, where he landed, concealed his canoe, and leaving two men in charge of it, arrived at Ticonderoga point at noon. Here were about two thousand men, who had thrown up an intrenchment, and prepared a large quantity of hewn timber in the adjacent woods. He tarried there a second night, and in the morning saw the enemy lay the foundation of a fort, on the point which commands the pass from Lake George to Lake Champlain, and the entrance to South bay or Wood Creek.

Having made what discoveries he could, on his return he found a large advanced guard of the enemy posted at the north end of Lake George, near the outlet to Lake Champlain. While viewing these troops, a bark canoe, containing nine Indians and a Frenchman, was observed passing up the lake. He kept in sight of them until they passed the point where his boat and men had been left. They informed him that the party had landed on an island, six miles south of them, near the middle of the lake. In a short time, they put off from the island, and steered directly toward their place of concealment. At the distance of one hundred yards, the party gave them a salute, which reduced their number to four. (Each marksman hit his man.) The party then took boat and pursued them down the lake until they were relieved by two other canoes, upon which the rangers retreated toward the camp at Lake George, where they arrived on the 10th of October.

October 15. Rogers embarked with forty men, in five boats, with orders to ascertain the force of the enemy's advanced guard, and if possible to decoy the whole or part of them into an ambush. The exertions of the party were indefatigable for several days, but to no purpose, and on the 19th they returned to camp.

October 21. Rogers embarked for Crown Point, with four men, in quest of a prisoner; at night they landed on the west shore, twenty-five miles from the English camp, and marching the remainder of the way, on the 26th came in sight of the fort. In the evening they approached nearer, and next morning were within three hundred yards of it. The men lay concealed in a thicket of willows, while Rogers crept nearer, and concealed himself behind a large pine log by holding bushes in his hand. Soon afterward the soldiers came out in such numbers that the party could not unite without discovery. About 10 o'clock a man came out alone, and advanced toward the ambush. Rogers sprang over the log and offered him quarter, which he refused, making a pass at him with his dirk. This he avoided, and presented his *fusee* to his breast; but he pressed forward with resolution, which compelled Rogers to shoot him. This alarmed the enemy, and the party retreated to the mountain. They returned, October 30th, in safety to camp.

November 4. Rogers embarked for the enemy's advanced guard, with thirty men in four *batteaux*, each mounting two wall-pieces, and next morning arrived within half a mile of their position, where the party landed, and concealed their boats. Four spies were sent out, who returned next evening, reporting that the enemy had no works around them, but lay entirely open to assault. Notice was immediately sent to the general, requesting a sufficient force to attack them; but, notwithstanding his earnestness and activity, the force did not arrive until the party were compelled to retreat. On their retreat they met the reinforcement, and turned again toward the French. Two men, sent out next evening to see if their sentinels were on the alert, were fired upon, and so hotly pursued that the whole party was discovered.

They obtained the first notice of this from two large canoes, containing thirty men, which were supposed to have come out at the same time with another party by land, to place the English between two fires. To prevent this Rogers embarked with Lieutenant McCurdy and fourteen men, in two boats, leaving the remainder of the party on shore, under the command of Captain Putnam. (Afterwards General Putnam.) To decoy the French within reach of the wall-pieces, they steered as if intending to pass them, which answered the purpose meditated. The enemy boldly headed them, and when within one hundred yards the guns were discharged, which killed several men, and put the boats to flight. They were pursued, and driven so near to the land party that they were again galled by the wall-pieces. Several of the enemy were thrown overboard, and their canoes rendered very leaky.

At this time Rogers discovered their land party, and notified his men on shore, who immediately embarked without receiving much injury from the sharp fire which the French for some time kept up in their rear. The enemy were pursued upon the water with diligence, and the wall-pieces again discharged. They were followed to their landing, where they were received, and covered by two hundred men, whom a discharge from the wall-pieces compelled to retire. They were greatly superior in numbers, and it was deemed most prudent to return to camp, which was reached on the 8th of November.

November 12. Rogers proceeded, with twelve men, to ascertain the enemy's strength and condition at Ticonderoga, and on the 14th came in sight of that fort The enemy had erected three new barracks, and four storehouses in the fort, between which and the water, they had eighty *batteaux* hauled up on the beach. They had fifty tents near the fort, and appeared busily employed in strengthening their works. Their object being attained, the party returned to camp on the 19th of November.

December 19. After a month's repose, Rogers embarked, with two men, once more to reconnoitre the French at Ticonderoga. On the way a fire was observed on an island near the fort, which was supposed to have been kindled by the enemy. This obliged the party to lay by and act like fishermen, to deceive the enemy, until night came on, when they gained the west shore, fifteen miles north of the English camp. Concealing the boat, the march was pursued by land on the 20th, and at noon on the 21st the party reached the fort. The enemy were still engaged in their works, and had mounted four pieces of cannon on the south-east bastion; two on the northwest, toward the woods; and two on the south bastion. They mustered about five hundred men. Several attempts were made to take a prisoner by waylaying their paths, but they passed along in too large parties.

At night the scout approached near the fort, but were driven, by the severity of the cold, to seek shelter in one of the enemy's evacuated huts. Before daybreak, a light snow fell, which obliged the rangers to hasten homeward with all speed, lest the enemy, discovering their tracks, should pursue. They reached their canoe in safety, although almost overcome with cold, hunger and fatigue. They had the good fortune to kill a deer, with which being refreshed, on the 24th they returned to Fort William Henry, which during the year had been erected at the south end of Lake George.

About this time General Sir William Johnson proceeded to Albany to meet the commissioner from the several governments whose troops he had commanded, (New Hampshire excepted.) These persons were empowered, with the consent of a council of war, to garrison Forts William Henry and Edward, for the winter, with the troops then in service. A regiment was therefore organised, to which Massachusetts furnished a colonel, Connecticut a lieutenant colonel, and New York a major. The general and the commissioners judged it most prudent to leave one company of rangers under the command of Captain Rogers, to make excursions to the enemy's forts during the winter.

January 14, 1756. Rogers marched, with sixteen men, toward the French forts. They proceeded down the lake on skates until they halted, for refreshments, near the falls between Lakes George and Champlain. At night the march was renewed, and at daybreak on the 16th an ambush was formed on the east shore of Lake Champlain, within gunshot of the path by which the enemy passed from one fort to the other. At sunrise two sledges, laden with fresh beef, were intercepted, with their drivers. Their loading was destroyed; and on the 17th, with their prisoners, the party returned to Fort William Henry.

January 26. Colonel Glasier ordered Rogers, with a party of fifty men, to discover the strength of the. enemy at Crown Point. On the 2nd of February they arrived within a mile of the fortress, and ascended a steep mountain, the summit of which afforded a full prospect, and an opportunity for taking a plan of the works. In the evening they retired to a small village, half a mile south of the fort, and formed an ambush on each side of the road from that to the village. Next morning a Frenchman fell into their hands, and soon after two more men appeared, but took alarm before they could be seized, and fled to the fort. Finding themselves discovered by this accident, they set fire to the houses and barns of the village, containing large quantities of grain, and killed fifty head of cattle. They then retired, leaving the whole village in flames, and with their prisoner reached headquarters on the 6th of February.

February 29. By order of Colonel Glasier, Rogers marched, with fifty-six men, down the west side of Lake George, proceeding northward until the 5th of March, when he steered east to Lake Champlain, about six miles north of Crown Point, where, from intelligence received from the Indians, he expected to find inhabited villages. There he attempted to cross the lake, but the ice was too weak. On the 7th he returned, and passing round the bay west of Crown Point, at night entered the cleared land, among the houses and barns of the French.

Here the party lay in ambush, expecting laborers to attend the cattle, and clean the grain with which the barns were filled. They remained there all night, and the next day until dark, when they set fire to the village and retired. Returning, they reconnoitred Ticonderoga, and the advanced guard on Lake George, approaching so near to the fort as to see the sentinels on the ramparts; and, after obtaining all the information desired of their works, strength and situation, on the 14th of March they returned to camp.

The next day Captain Rogers received a letter from Mr. William Alexander, (afterwards known as Lord Stirling, and a major general in the United States revolutionary army), secretary of Governor Shirley, who last year commanded at Oswego, and who, upon the decease of General Braddock, had succeeded to the chief command of His Majesty's forces in North America, stating that, upon General Johnson's recommendation, he was invited to wait upon the governor at Boston, where he was preparing for the next campaign. Thither he repaired, leaving his company in command of Ensign Noah Johnson.

On the 23rd the general gave Captain Rogers a friendly reception, and a commission to recruit an independent corps of rangers. It was ordered that it should consist of sixty privates, at 3s. (York currency) per day; an ensign, at 5s.; a lieutenant, at 7s.; and a captain, at 10s. Each man was to be allowed ten Spanish dollars toward providing clothing, arms and blankets. The company was to be raised immediately. None were to be enlisted but such men as were accustomed to travelling and hunting, and in whose courage and fidelity the most implicit confidence could be placed. They were moreover to be subject to military discipline and the articles of war. The rendezvous was appointed at Albany, whence to proceed to Lake George, and:

> From time to time to use their best endeavours to distress the
> French and their allies by sacking, burning and destroying their
> houses, barns, barracks, canoes, *batteaux*, &c., and by killing their
> cattle of every kind; and at all times to endeavour to waylay, attack and destroy their convoys of provisions by land and water,
> in any part of the country where they could be found.

With these instructions, he received letters to the commanding officers of Forts William Henry and Edward, directing them to forward the service with which he was charged.

When the company was completed, a part of it marched, under the orders of Lieutenant Richard Rogers, to Albany. With the remainder Captain Rogers passed through the woods to Number Four, a frontier town greatly exposed. There he received orders to proceed to Crown Point, for which, on the 28th of April, his course was directed, through vast forests and over lofty mountains. On the second day of the march Mr. John Stark, his second lieutenant, became ill, and was obliged to return with a guard of six men.

May 5. Captain Rogers reached Lake Champlain, four miles from Crown Point, with nine men. They concealed their packs, and entered a village on the east side, two miles from the fort, but found no inhabitants. They waited the whole day following, opposite the Point, for some party to cross the lake. Nothing however appeared, excepting five bunded men, in *batteaux*, coming up the lake from St. Johns. They kept their stations until ten o'clock next day; but finding no opportunity to trepan the enemy, they killed twenty-three head of cattle, whose tongues were of great service on the march. They now discovered eleven canoes, manned by French and Indians, crossing the lake directly toward them. It was then judged most prudent to disperse, each man taking a different route, and looking out for himself

This course put their pursuers at fault; and the party, assembling at the place where their packs had been left, made a raft, and crossed to the western shore. They obtained a view of the old Indian carrying-place, near Ticonderoga, and reached Fort William Henry on the 14th of May. Mr. Stark and his party reached Fort Edward three days before, having, on their way, discovered and eluded a scout of four hundred Indians. Lieutenant Rogers had arrived some days before, and was then on a scout.

May 20. Rogers was ordered, with eleven men, to reconnoitre the French advanced guard. When viewed next day from the summit of a mountain, their numbers appeared about three hundred, who were busy in fortifying their position with palisades. From the other side of the mountain the party obtained a fine prospect of Ticonderoga and the French camp, which, from the ground occupied, was judged to contain one thousand men. This night was passed upon the mountain, and early next morning the party proceeded to the Indian carrying-path, where an ambuscade was formed between the advanced guard and the fort. About 6 o'clock one hundred and eighteen French-men passed along the path without observing them; in a few minutes twenty-two others came along the same way. Upon this party they fired, killed six, and took one prisoner. The first party returning at the report of the guns, obliged them to retire in great haste.

On the twenty-third they reached Fort William Henry in safety with the prisoner, who reported that two hundred and twenty French and Indians were preparing to surprise the out parties at Fort Edward. This information occasioned Rogers a march, with seventy-eight men, to join a detachment of Colonel Bayley's regiment, and scour the woods as far as South bay, to intercept the enemy; but they could not be found.

June 12. According to orders, in the evening Rogers embarked, with twenty-six men, to visit the French advanced guard. A severe thunder storm compelled the party to land ten miles from their own fort, and spend the night. At sunrise they heard the discharge of about twenty small arms, on the opposite shore, which was supposed to proceed from the enemy cleaning their guns after the rain. The party embarked in the evening, and early on the morning of the 16th drew up their *batteaux* four miles from the advanced guard, and lay in ambush, by a path leading to the mountain, to surprise the enemy who went there daily in parties to view the lake. They soon afterward discovered that the advanced parties had evacuated their position, and demolished their works. They then approached very, near Ticonderoga, and viewed their works from an eminence, judging the garrison to consist of three thousand men. The party returned to their fort on the 18th, excepting one man who strayed away and did not return until the 23rd, then almost famished for want of food. About this time the general increased the force of the ranger company to seventy men, and sent them six whale-boats from Albany, with orders to proceed to Lake Champlain, to cut off the supplies and flying parties of the enemy.

June 28. Rogers, with fifty men, embarked in five whale-boats, and proceeded to an island in Lake George. The next day they passed over to the main land, and carried their boats six miles over a mountain to South bay, where they arrived on the 3rd of July. The evening following, they embarked, and proceeded down the bay till they came within six miles of the French fort. There the boats were concealed. The next evening, they embarked again, and passed the fort undiscovered, although so near as to hear the sentinel's watchword. They judged, from the number of fires, that the enemy had two thousand men in his camp. Five miles farther down they lay by all day, concealing their boats. Here several *batteaux* were seen passing by up and down the lake.

At night they put off with the design of passing Crown Point, but afterward, considering it imprudent, on account of the clearness of the night, they lay concealed through the next day, during which a hundred boats passed by them. Seven boats came near their place of concealment, and would have landed there, but the officer insisted, in their hearing, that he would go a hundred and fifty yards farther, where they landed, and dined in the rangers' sight, without discovering them. At nine o'clock at night the latter re-embarked, passed the fort, and concealed their boats ten miles north of it.

July 7. Thirty boats and a schooner of forty tons burthen passed by toward Canada. In the evening they proceeded fifteen miles farther down, and dispatched a scout, who soon brought intelligence that a schooner lay at anchor one mile distant. The rangers lightened their packs, and prepared to board her; but were prevented by two lighters coming up the lake, whose crews intended to land where they were posted. These were fired upon, hailed, and offered quarter, if they would come on shore; but they pushed for the other side, whither they were pursued and intercepted. Their crews consisted of twelve men, three of whom were killed by the fire, and two wounded; one in such a manner that he soon died.

Both vessels were sunk, and the cargoes, consisting of wheat and flour, wine and brandy, were destroyed, except a few casks of the latter, which were carefully concealed. (A good thought for a soldier.) The prisoners stated that they were a portion of five hundred men, the remainder of whom were not far behind on their passage. This report hastened the return of the scout; which, on the 16th of July, returned to the garrison with their prisoners.

The latter reported that a large force of regulars and militia were assembling at Chamblee, destined for Carillon, (of this fortress, Ticonderoga was the Indian name, and Carillon the French name; each signifying "the meeting of waters"), and that large quantities of provisions were on the way; that a new general, with two veteran regiments, had arrived from France; that there was no design against the English forts on this side, but that a party of three hundred French and twenty Indians had already set out, to intercept the provision convoys between Albany and Lake George; that sixty *livres* was the reward for an English scalp, and prisoners were sold in Canada at fifty crowns each; that the prospect of a harvest was very encouraging, but that the smallpox had made dreadful havoc among the inhabitants.

Upon his return from this expedition. Captain Rogers learned that General Shirley had been superseded in command by Major General Abercrombie, who arrived at Albany, June 25th, with two regiments of regular troops from England. He forwarded to him the report of the last scout, and recommended the augmentation of the corps of rangers. Soon afterward he waited upon him at headquarters, and received orders to raise a new company, the command of which was given to his brother, Richard Rogers. Of this company Noah Johnson was appointed first lieutenant, Nathaniel Abbot second, and Caleb Page ensign. Of his own company John Stark was appointed first lieutenant, John McCurdy second, and Jonathan Burbank ensign.

August 2. Captain Robert Rogers, by order of General Abercrombie, embarked, with twenty-five men in a lighter, from Fort William Henry, to reconnoitre Ticonderoga and Crown Point. Captain Learned, with sixty provincials, was ordered by General Winslow to proceed as far as the French advanced guard, but not being acquainted with the country, he placed himself under Rogers' command. The latter landed about fifteen miles down Lake George, and on the 4th encamped one mile from the advanced guard. On the morning of the 5th the whole party mustered, and gained the summit of a hill west of the enemy, from which they discovered two advanced posts; one on the west side, half a mile south of Lake Champlain; and the other on the east side, opposite the former, at the old Indian carrying-place. They supposed four hundred men were on the east, and two hundred on the west side.

After deliberating upon the situation of the enemy, it was deemed imprudent to remain there any longer. Captain Learned returned to camp, while the rangers went down toward Ticonderoga. They passed that post, and proceeded toward Crown Point, on the west side of the lake, where they discovered several *batteaux*, with troops bound for Carillon. They then proceeded to the place where they had burned the village, as before stated, where they observed a party of the enemy sally out, driving horses and cattle to feed.

August 7. They ambushed the road to intercept those who should come to drive in the cattle; but no one appearing, they approached within half a mile of the fort, and were discovered by two Frenchmen before they were in their power. This caused a retreat, during which they killed forty head of cattle. August 10th, they reached headquarters.

A company of Stockbridge Indians was this year employed in His Majesty's service, officered by Indians commissioned by General Shirley. General Abercrombie was at a loss how to dispose of them; but Sir William Johnson advised him to employ thirty privates (the remainder were sent to Saratoga, to serve under Colonel Burton), and a lieutenant as scouts, to scour the woods, under the direction of ranger officers. This party Lieutenant Stark had strengthened with some of his own men, and sent on a scout, with particular directions, the day before the party above named returned. (Captain Jacobs, with his Indians, returned a few days after, with four French scalps, taken on the east shore of the lake, nearly opposite Ticonderoga.)

About this time the Earl of Loudoun had arrived at Albany, and assumed the command in chief. Rogers sent him an account of the Indian scout before mentioned, requesting permission to penetrate into Canada with these Indians, and distress the inhabitants, by burning their harvest (now nearly ripe), and destroying their cattle.

Accordingly, August 16, a party embarked, in whaleboats, in two detachments—one commanded by Lieutenant Stark, and the other by Captain Robert Rogers. The next morning the detachments fell in with eight Mohawks, who had left Fort William Henry the day previous. The whole party then proceeded to the place where the boats had been left, July 7, twenty miles north of Crown Point, on the west shore of the lake, arriving there on the 24th. Embarking again at night, they steered down the lake toward St. John's, and the next day proceeded twenty miles.

At midnight a schooner was seen standing up the lake, with a fair wind, toward Crown Point. She passed so swiftly that they could not board her, as was intended. On the 26th they landed, and the Mohawks departed to join a party of their brethren, then on a scout On the 27th the rangers ambushed a point of land to intercept the enemy's *batteaux*, which might pass up and down; but not finding any, they returned up the lake, and landed on the east shore, eight miles north of Crown Point. On the morning of the 29th they entered a French village, east of the fort, and made prisoners of a man, his wife, and daughter, a girl of fourteen, and returned to the garrison September 22.

The Frenchman stated that he was a native of Vaisac, in the province of Guienne, France. He had been in Canada fifteen years; in the colony's service six years; and two years at Crown Point; which fort was garrisoned by only three hundred men, and those mostly inhabitants of the adjacent villages; that four thousand men occupied Ticonderoga, fifteen hundred of them being regular troops, who had plenty of stores and provisions; that he was never at Carillon or the advanced guard, but had heard there were only fifteen men at the latter place; that six hundred Indians were at Carillon, and six hundred more expected; that twelve hundred men had reached Quebec, on their way to Carillon; that the last eighteen hundred were commanded by Monsieur Scipio de la Masure.

Also, that Ticonderoga was well supplied with cannon, mortars, shells, shot, &c.; that the garrison expected a reinforcement in two or three days, having sent boats to Montreal to bring the troops; that he had heard, by letter, that Oswego had fallen into the hands of the French, but it was not yet confirmed; that it was understood the English intended to invest Carillon, but did not know what course the French intended to take, should they neglect that step; that they kept a hundred and fifty *batteaux* on the lake, thirty-five of which plied between Montreal and Carillon; that Monsieur Montcalm commanded at Frontenac, with five thousand men, but he did not know whether they were regulars or militia; that a great many vessels had arrived at Quebec, with provisions and military stores; that he had heard the English had several ships in the St Lawrence; that Monsieur le Compte Levi commanded Carillon, and came last year from France; that, since the capture of the two last lighters (before mentioned), the number of men on board the large schooner had been increased from twelve to thirty men.

On his return Rogers was ordered by Lord Loudoun to wait upon Colonel Burton, at Saratoga, by whose direction he marched, with his company, from Fort William Henry to South bay; thence east to Wood Creek, crossing the creek southerly, opposite Saratoga, and made report to Colonel Burton. During this tour he apprehended four deserters from Otway's regiment, going over to the enemy, who were sent back to Fort Edward in charge of Lieutenant Stark.

At Saratoga the party met Captain Richard Rogers from the Mohawk, with the Stockbridge Indians in company, and all returned to Fort Edward, where an encampment was formed. Part of the Indians were sent out on the east side of Lake Champlain, to alarm the enemy at Ticonderoga; while Captain Robert Rogers, with a detachment of his own company, and that of Richard Rogers, proceeded down Lake George in whale-boats, leaving the remainder of the corps to serve as flankers to the parties conveying provisions to Fort William Henry.

September 7. Captain Robert Rogers embarked on Lake George, with fourteen men, in a whale-boat, which they concealed the evening following on the east side, four miles south of the French advanced guard. There he left seven, men in charge of Mr. Chalmer, a volunteer (sent by Sir John St. Clair), with directions, upon discovering the enemy's boats proceeding up the lake, to convey the news, with all possible speed, to Fort William Henry. With the other seven, he arrived, on the 9th, within half a mile of Ticonderoga. The enemy were engaged in raising the walls of the fort, and had erected a large block-house near the south-east corner of the fortress, with ports for cannon. East of the fort was a battery commanding the lake.

Five houses were discovered close to the water side, south of the works, one hundred and sixty tents on the south-west side, and twenty-seven *batteaux* hauled up on the beach. Next morning, with one private, he took a view of the falls between the two lakes, where several discharges of muskets had been heard the evening before. Mr. Henry had been sent to learn the cause, and soon joined Rogers, reporting that the French were building a small fort at the head of the falls, on the east shore; also, that he had discovered their advanced guard on the west side; and estimated both parties at five hundred men. The French were also found engaged in building a saw-mill, at the lower part of the falls. The party returned to their boats and provisions, which Mr. Chalmers had left. He, having executed his orders, had returned to camp, whither the party followed his track, and arrived on the 11th instant.

September 24. General Abercrombie ordered three commissioned officers of the rangers, with twenty privates each, to reconnoitre Wood Creek. South bay, and Ticonderoga, who alternately kept up a continual scout for some time.

October 22. The greater portion of the army now lay at Fort Edward, under General Abercrombie; and Lord Loudoun arriving at this time, it was supposed that, notwithstanding the season was so far advanced, an attempt would be made upon the French forts. But his lordship, supposing the lakes would freeze, as they generally do in December, and that no communication could be kept up with Fort William Henry, contented himself with keeping the field until Monsieur Montcalm retired to winter quarters.

October 22. Rogers embarked, with twenty men, being ordered to bring a prisoner from Ticonderoga. He had passed the narrows, twenty miles from the place of embarkation, when his boat was hailed by Captain Shephard, who had been taken prisoner in August last. He knew his voice, and took him on board, with three men, one of whom was taken with him. He left Canada fifteen days before. Continuing his course, Rogers landed, on the night of the 17th, on the west shore, concealed his boats, and travelled by land until within a mile of the fort. The next day two videttes of the French picket guard were discovered, one of whom was posted on the road leading to the woods. Rogers, with five men, marched directly down the road in the middle of the day, until challenged by the sentry. He answered in French, "Friends." The sentinel was thereby deceived, until the party came close to him, when, perceiving his mistake, in great surprise he cried out, "*Qui êtes-vous?*"

The captain answered, "Rogers," led him from his post in great haste, and, with his party, reached Fort William Henry on the 31st of October. The prisoner reported that he belonged to the regiment of Languedoc, and left Brest last April, twelve month; had since served at Lake Champlain, Crown Point, and Carillon; was with General Dieskau last year at Lake George; that the French lost in that engagement a great number of troops; that Ticonderoga at this time mounted thirty-six pieces of cannon, namely, twelve eighteens, fifteen twelves, and nine eight-pounders; that Crown Point was defended by eighteen pieces of cannon, the largest of which were eighteens; that Monsieur Montcalm's forces this year at Carillon were three thousand regulars, and two thousand Canadians and Indians; that General Montcalm was away with one battalion; that the force at Carillon consisted of five battalions and eight hundred Canadians; that the Indians had all gone home, but two hundred of them talked of returning to spend the winter at Carillon.

Also, that the advanced guard on the west side, above the falls, were all drawn in, and that on the east consisted of six hundred men, who were to decamp on the 1st of November; that five battalions of infantry of the line and sixty Canadian militia lay encamped half a league from Carillon; that the remainder of the army were in the fort; that the barracks were sufficient for five hundred men, whom he understood were to quarter there; that the French had one schooner and two hundred *batteaux* on Lake Champlain, and but five or six on Lake George; that the Chevalier Levi commanded in General Montcalm's absence, and that the Canadians were under the orders of Messieurs Corné and Columbié; that, when the general went away, he said "he had done enough this year, and would take Fort William Henry in the spring;" that the French had taken four of Rogers' whale-boats on Lake Champlain; that, when taken, he was within a gunshot and a half of the fort; and that their camp was healthy.

From this time the rangers were constantly employed in patrolling the woods about Fort Edward, until November 19, 1756, when they made an excursion down the lake. Captain Abercrombie, nephew of the general, had the curiosity to accompany the expedition; and, although nothing was effected, save obtaining a view of the French garrison, he was delighted with the novelties of a scout, and the noble scenery through which he was conducted. The party returned, on the 25th, at evening. About this time his lordship drew off the main body of his troops, to be quartered at Albany and New York. Both armies now retired to winter quarters. The rangers were stationed at Forts William Henry and Edward, and were augmented by two new companies from Halifax (N. S.), under Captains Hobbs and Spikeman. These two companies were posted at Fort William Henry, and the other two at Fort Edward. Captain Richard Rogers was sent to New-England for recruits. He waited upon the Boston Government to obtain pay for the rangers' services in the winter of 1755; but could obtain none, although Lord Loudoun generously supported the claim.

January 15, 1757. Capt. Robert Rogers marched with Lieutenant Stark, Ensign Page, of Richard Rogers' company, and fifty privates, to Fort William Henry, where they were employed in providing provisions, snow-shoes, &c., until the 17th, when being joined by Captain Spikeman, with Lieutenant Kennedy, Ensign Brewer, and fourteen men of his corps, together with Ensign James Rogers, with twenty men of Hobb's company, and Mr. Baker, a volunteer of the 44th regiment of the line, the whole party proceeded down Lake George on the ice, and at night encamped on the east side of the first narrows.

Next morning a portion of the party, who had become lame in consequence of yesterday's exertions, were sent back, which reduced the force remaining to seventy-four, officers included. On the 18th they encamped twelve miles down the lake, on the west side. On the 19th they marched three miles down the lake, and then took to the land with their snow-shoes; and having travelled eight miles northwest, encamped three miles from the lake. On the 20th they marched east all day, and encamped on the west side, three miles from Lake Champlain.

January 21. The party marched eastward until they came to the lake half way between Crown Point and Ticonderoga, where they discovered a sled passing from the latter to the former. Lieutenant Stark, with twenty men, was directed to head the sled, while Rogers, with five of the party, cut off its retreat, leaving Captain Spikeman with the centre. Ten other sleds were discovered following down the lake. Rogers endeavoured to give Mr. Stark notice before he shew himself on the lake, but could not. He sallied out, and they hastily turned back toward Ticonderoga. The rangers pursued and captured seven prisoners, three sleds and six horses; the remainder escaped.

The captives were separately examined, and reported that two hundred Canadians and forty-five Indians had just arrived at Ticonderoga, and were to be reinforced that evening by fifty Indians from Crown Point; that six hundred regular troops were in that fortress, and three hundred and fifty at Ticonderoga, where they expected a large army which, in the spring, was to besiege the English forts; that they had large magazines of provisions; that the troops were well equipped, and in condition to march at a moment's warning, and intended to waylay and distress the convoys between the English forts. In consequence of this information, and knowing that those who escaped would give immediate notice of the party, orders were given them to march with all expedition to the fires which had been kindled the night before, and prepare for battle, if offered, by drying their guns, as the day was rainy.

This was effected, and the party marched in single file—Captain Rogers and Lieutenant Kennedy in front, Lieutenant Stark in the rear, and Captain Spikeman in the centre; Ensign Page and Rogers between the front and centre, and Mr. Brewer between the centre and rear—Sergeant Walker having command of a rear guard.

In this manner the party advanced half a mile over broken ground, and passed a valley fifteen rods in breadth, when the front, having gained the summit of the opposite hill, on the west side, fell in with the enemy drawn up in the form of a crescent to surround the party, and were immediately saluted with a volley of two hundred shot, at a distance of five yards from the nearest, and thirty from the rear of the party. This fire took place about 2 o'clock p.m., and proved fatal to Lieutenant Kennedy and Mr. Gardner, a volunteer, beside wounding several, and Captain Rogers in the head. Rogers ordered his men to retire to the opposite hill, where Lieutenant Stark and Mr. Brewer had made a stand, with forty men, to cover the retreat. They were closely pursued, Captain Spikeman and others killed, and several made prisoners.

Lieutenant Stark repulsed them by a brisk fire from the hill, killing a number, and affording those retreating an opportunity to post themselves to advantage. Mr. Stark then took a position in the centre, with Ensign Rogers, Sergeants Walker and Phillips acting as reserves to protect the flanks and watch the enemy's motions. Soon after the party had thus formed for battle, the enemy attempted to outflank them, but were bravely attacked by the reserve, who gave the first fire, which stopped several from returning to the main body. The rangers were then pushed closely in front, but having the advantage of the ground, and being sheltered by large trees, they maintained a constant fire, which killed a number, and compelled the others to retire upon their main force. The enemy attempted to outflank them once more, but were again gallantly repulsed by the reserve. In this affair, Mr. Baker was killed.

A constant fire was kept up till sunset, when a shot through his wrist disabled Captain Rogers from loading his gun. The action continued until darkness prevented the parties from seeing each other. The rangers gallantly maintained their position till the fire of the enemy ceased, and he retired. During this action, the Indians practiced several stratagems to induce the rangers to submit: sometimes assuring them that reinforcements were at hand, who would cut them to pieces without mercy; that it was a pity so many brave men should be lost; that, in case of surrender, they should be treated with compassion. Calling Rogers by name, they assured him of their friendship and esteem; but he, and the brave men who fought by his side, were neither to be dismayed by their threats, nor flattered by their professions. They were resolved to conquer, or die with arms in their hands.

After the action, a considerable number were so severely wounded that they could not travel without assistance; but as the French garrison was so near, it was thought best to take advantage of the night and retreat. The spirits of the wounded were kept up as well as possible, and the party reached Lake George, six miles south of the French advanced guard, next morning. The wounded men were now exhausted, and could march no farther. Lieutenant Stark volunteered, with Thomas Burnside and another, to proceed to Fort William Henry and procure sleighs for the wounded. They reached the fort at 8 o'clock that night, and next morning sleighs arrived, though the distance was forty miles. Lieutenant Bulkley, of Hobbs' company, came out with fifteen men as far as the first narrows of Lake George; and the survivors of the expedition, consisting of forty-eight effective and six wounded men, arrived with their prisoners on the same evening (Jan. 23, 1757), at Fort William Henry.

Before the sleighs came to their relief, the men, looking back upon the lake, observed a dark object following at a distance on the ice. Supposing it might be one of their wounded stragglers, a sleigh was sent back for him. He proved to be Joshua Martin. His hip had been shattered by a ball which passed through his body, and he had been left for dead on the field of battle; but recovering himself, had followed his comrades' tracks to the lake, and there came in sight of them. He was so exhausted that he sank down the moment the sleigh reached him. He recovered of his wound, became a lieutenant, served through the war, and died at Goffstown at an advanced age.

The number of the enemy in this action was two hundred and fifty French and Indians. Accounts received afterward reported their loss on the spot, and those who died of their wounds, to be one hundred and sixteen—the whole force of the rangers being but seventy-four, officers included. The officers and men who survived the first onset, behaved with the most undaunted bravery, and vied with each other in their respective stations.

******

In regard to this fight, the late Mr. John Shute observed that Rogers did not on this occasion obey his own rules, written out for the guidance of the corps. After taking the sleds, a council of war advised to return by another route than that by which they came, which was their usual practice, and would have saved them the loss incurred by this conflict. The first notice the party had of the enemy was the noise made in cocking their guns, which Shute supposed was occasioned by some rangers preparing to fire at game. He was struck senseless by a ball which ploughed the top of his head. On coming to himself, he observed a man cutting off the ribbon of Rogers' queue, to bind up his wrist, through which a ball had passed.

On the night retreat the rangers made a circuit to avoid a large fire in the woods, supposing the enemy were there. This caused them to lose time, so that Joshua Martin, who had kindled the fire by a large dry pine tree to warm himself, was enabled to follow and come in sight of them on the lake; otherwise he must have perished. Stilson Eastman, and the late Colonel Webster, of Plymouth, corroborated the statement of Mr. Shute that the conduct and courage of John Stark saved the party, and that to his activity, enterprise, and example, the corps of rangers were indebted for much of their celebrity during the "seven years' war."

******

RETURN OF KILLED, WOUNDED AND MISSING, IN THE ACTION OF
JANUARY 21, NEAR TICONDEROGA.

CAPTAIN ROBERT ROGERS' COMPANY.

Killed.	Wounded.	Missing.
Mr. Gardner, volunteer,	Captain Rogers,	William Morris,
Mr. Baker, volunteer,	Joshua Martin,	Sergeant Henry,

Thomas Henson.   Thomas Burnside.   John Morrison.
Total—3 killed, 3 wounded, 3 missing.

CAPTAIN RICHARD ROGERS' COMPANY.

Killed.	Wounded.	Missing.
John Stevens,	David Page.	Benjamin Goodall,
Ensign Caleb Page.		David Kimball.

Total—Killed 2, wounded 1, missing 2.

CAPTAIN HOBBS' COMPANY.

Killed.
Sergeant Jonathan Howard,
Phinehas Kemp,
John Edmunds,
Thomas Farmer,
Edmund Lapartaquer.
Total—Killed 5.

CAPTAIN SPIKEMAN'S COMPANY.

Killed.	Wounded.	Missing.
Captain Spikeman,	Sergeant Moore,	Thomas Brown.
Lieutenant Kennedy,	John Kahall.	
Robert Avery,		
Samuel Fisk.		

Total—Killed 4, wounded 2, missing 1.

Total of the four companies—Killed 14, wounded 6, missing 6.
(the missing men were prisoners.)

Captain Rogers forwarded this report to Major Sparks, at Fort Edward, and wrote to Capt. Abercrombie, recommending such officers as were deserving to fill the vacancies occasioned by the late action, as follows:

Lieutenant Stark to be captain of Spikeman's corps, Sergeant Joshua Martin to be ensign of Richard Rogers' company, to which he received the following answer:

Albany, February 6, 1767.

Dear Sir—The general received your report by Major Sparks. He returns you and your men thanks for your good behaviour, and has recommended to my Lord Loudoun that they have pay for their prisoners.

On receiving an account of your skirmish, we sent an express to Boston recommending your brother James for lieutenant of

Spikeman's company.

Please send the names of the officers you recommend for your own company, and your recommendation shall be duly regarded. You cannot imagine how all ranks of people are pleased with your men's behaviour. I was so pleased with their appearance when I was out with them, that I took it for granted they would behave well whenever they met the enemy. I am happy to learn that my expectations are answered. I am sorry for Spikeman and Kennedy, as well as for the men you have lost, but it is impossible to play at bowls without meeting rubs. We must try to revenge them. Few persons will believe it, but upon honour I should have been glad to have been with you, that I might have learned the manner of fighting in this country. The chance of being shot is all stuff, and King William's principle is the best for the soldier, "that every bullet has its billet," and that it is allotted how every man shall die; so that I am certain everyone will agree that it is better to die with the reputation of a brave man, fighting for his country in a good cause, than by shamefully running away to preserve one's life, or by lingering out an old age to die in one's bed without having, done his country or king any service.

The histories of this country, particularly, are full of the unheard-of cruelties committed by the French, and the Indians, at their instigation; wherefore I think every brave man ought to do his utmost to humble that haughty nation, and reduce her bounds of conquest in this country to narrower limits.

When General Abercrombie receives his lordship's instructions respecting the rangers, I shall send you notice of it. In the meantime, I hope you'll get the better of your wound. As long as you and your men continue to behave so well, you may command

Your most humble servant,

James Abercrombie, *Aide-de-Camp.*

To Captain Robert Rogers.

The wound of Captain Rogers becoming worse, he repaired to Albany for medical aid, and there received from General Abercrombie the following instructions:

Instructions for Captain Robert Rogers.

His Excellency, the Earl of Loudoun, having given authority to me to augment the companies of rangers under your command to one hundred men each: *viz.*, one captain, two lieutenants, one ensign, upon English pay; four sergeants at 4*s*. each, New York currency; and one hundred privates at 2*s*., 6d. each, do. per day. And whereas, certain privates are serving at present in your companies on higher pay than the above, you are at liberty to discharge them, in case they refuse to serve under the new establishment, as soon as you have men to replace them. If they remain and serve, you may assure them that they will be noticed, and be the first provided for. Each man is to be allowed ten dollars bounty money, to find his own clothing, arms, and blankets, and sign a paper subjecting himself to the articles of war, and to serve during the war. You are to enlist no vagrants, but such men as you and your officers are acquainted with, and who are every way qualified for the duty of rangers. Complete the companies as soon as possible, and proceed to Fort Edward.

James Abercrombie, Major General.

At this time Rogers wrote to Lord Loudoun, asking his aid in obtaining the amount due to himself and men for services in the winter of 1756. He replied that, as these services were antecedent to his command, it was not in his power to reward them. General Amherst afterward gave a similar answer. His men afterward sued and recovered judgments against him for £828, 3*s*., 3d., beside costs. For this, and for his own services during that severe season, he never received any consideration.

Captain Hobbs dying about this time. Lieutenant Bulkley succeeded him as captain. From March 5th to April 15th Rogers was confined with the smallpox at Fort Edward, during which time his officers were employed in recruiting, according to the foregoing instructions. Soon after his recovery, he received the following letter:

New York, April 23, 1767.
Sir—As another company of rangers has been sent to Albany, with orders to proceed to our forts, you will inform Colonel Gage that it is Lord Loudoun's order that the two companies at Fort William Henry, and your own at Fort Edward, proceed immediately to Albany, and embark for this place. Show this letter to Colonel Gage, that he may inform Colonel Munro of his lordship's orders, and that quarters may be provided for your companies at Albany. See that your companies are well equipped, and are good men; if they are found insufficient, the

blame will rest on you. If the officers of the new company are ignorant of the woods about Fort William Henry, your brother must send some officers and men to inform them of the different scouting grounds.

I am, sir, your humble servant,

James Abercrombie,
Aide-de-Camp.

To Captain Robert Rogers, Albany.

Richard Rogers, with his own and Bergen's new company of rangers from New-Jersey, being left at Fort William Henry, Stark's (at New York Captain Stark was taken with the smallpox, and did not accompany the expedition), and Bulkley's from the same fort, and Robert Rogers' company from Fort Edward, proceeded to Albany, and thence to New York, where Shephard's new company, from New-Hampshire, joined them. There they embarked on board a transport, and left Sandy Hook June 10th, with a fleet of one hundred sail, for Halifax; where they soon arrived, and encamped on the Dartmouth side of the harbour, while the main army lay on the Halifax side.

July 3. Rogers went to Lawrencetown, where a portion of his men were employed in making hay for the horses to be employed on the Louisburg expedition. Part of them covered the hay-makers, while others went on scouts, one of which brought in two deserters from the 45th regiment. Toward the end of July, forty rangers were sent across the isthmus of Nova Scotia to the settlements on the Bay of Fundy, and a party down the north-west arm, to scour the woods for deserters, who brought in several, both of the army and navy. At this time Admiral Holbourn arrived with a fleet from England, having on board several regiments of troops, which were landed and encamped at Halifax. All the scouts were now called in, but certain intelligence having been received that a French fleet of superior force had arrived at Louisburg, the intended expedition was abandoned, and the rangers remanded to the western frontiers. During the summer numbers of the rangers were carried off by the smallpox, and several officers were sent on the recruiting service.

The rangers embarked for New York, and proceeded in small vessels up the Hudson to Albany, where the recruits soon after arrived. They then proceeded to Fort Edward, which was now the only cover to the northern frontiers of New York, and the more eastern provinces, Fort William Henry having been taken in August previous by the French.

★★★★★★

Captain Richard Rogers died of smallpox a few days before the siege of this fort; but the enemy, after its surrender, dug him up and scalped him. In consequence of the articles of capitulation, the two companies of rangers were disbanded and dismissed. After the surrender, Samuel Blodget, the ranger sutler, was found concealed under a *batteau*. He was allowed to go free, after being plundered of everything but his scalp. He was afterward a sutler in the revolutionary army; became a considerable merchant, a judge, and was the projector of the first canal at Amoskeag falls, on Merrimack River. He lived to a great age, and died at Manchester, respected as an enterprising and public individual.

During Lord Loudoun's absence at Halifax, Fort William Henry was taken, after a siege of nine days, by the Marquis de Montcalm, while General Webb lay at Fort Edward, fifteen miles distant, with more than four thousand regular troops, and made no effort for its relief. The garrison capitulated on condition of quarter, which was shamefully broken by the enemy, and many of the prisoners massacred or carried away captive by the savages. Previous to the expedition against this fortress, ten *sachems* were sent by the French general as messengers to the northwestern tribes, to invite them to become the allies of France. In consequence of this summons, among others, a party of a tribe called "Cold Country Indians," appeared at the siege. They were cannibals, and many prisoners were by them roasted and eaten. The journal of a French officer, who was in Montcalm's army, and afterward taken in the West Indies, states "that the Indians roasted several of their English captives, and compelled the survivors to partake of the horrid banquet."—*Hutch, Hist.*

Two savages seized a lad named Copp, and were leading him away by his shirt sleeves, when a ranger, named Benjamin Richards, a bold, athletic man. hearing his cries, broke from the ranks and rushed after them. He snatched away the boy, leaving the shirt sleeves in their hands, and regained his place in the ranks.

★★★★★★

General Webb, now commanding Fort Edward, kept the rangers constantly employed patrolling the woods between that post and Ticonderoga. Lord Howe accompanied one of these scouts, being desirous of learning their method of marching, ambushing, and retreating; and, on their return, expressed his good opinion of them very generously.

Lord Loudoun now added to the corps a number of volunteers from the regulars, to be trained to wood service under Captain Rogers' inspection, to be hereafter employed as light infantry. Several of them belonged to the 42nd regiment of Highlanders. (This celebrated regiment in after times repulsed the French on the shores of Aboukir, and covered the landing of Sir Ralph Abercrombie's army in Egypt.)

These volunteers formed a separate company under Rogers' immediate orders. For their instruction, he reduced to writing several rules, and a course of discipline, of which experience had taught him the necessity.

December 1, 1767. Lord Loudoun visited Fort Edward, and after giving directions for quartering the army, and leaving a strong garrison under the command of Colonel Haviland, he returned to Albany. The rangers and their volunteers were quartered in huts on an island in the Hudson, near Fort Edward, and were employed in various scouts, which the health of Rogers did not permit him to accompany, until December 17th; when, by order of Colonel Haviland, he marched with one hundred and fifty men to reconnoitre Ticonderoga, and if possible take a prisoner. He advanced six miles in a snow storm, and encamped, the snow being then three inches deep, and before morning it fell to the depth of fifteen. He however pursued his route.

December 18. Eight of the party being fatigued and unwell, returned to camp. The remainder proceeded nine miles to the east side of Lake George, near the place where Mons. Montcalm landed his troops when he besieged Fort William Henry. There they discovered a large quantity of cannon balls and shells, which had on that occasion been concealed by the French, and made such marks at the place, as would enable them to find the articles again. This was their first visit to the ruins since their return from Halifax,

December 19. The march continued on the north-west side of the lake, nine miles, to the head of North-west bay.

December 21. So many of the men became tired, and returned, as to reduce the force to one hundred and twenty-three, officers included, who marched ten miles farther, and encamped for the night. Here each man was ordered to leave one day's provisions.

December 22. They marched ten miles, and encamped near the great brook running into Lake George, eight miles from the French advanced guard. December 23. They proceeded eight miles—the next day six more, and halted six hundred yards from Ticonderoga. Near the mills five Indians' tracks were discovered, supposed to have been made the day before by a hunting party. On the march this day, between the advanced guard and the fort, three places of rendezvous were appointed in case they should be broken in action. Rogers informed the officers and men that he should rally the party at the post nearest the fort; and if broken there, retreat to the second; and at the third make a stand, until night should afford an opportunity of retiring in safety. The road from the fort to the woods was then ambushed by an advanced guard of twenty men. and a rear guard of fifteen.

At 11 o'clock a sergeant of marines came from the fort up the road toward the advanced party, who suffered him to pass to the main body, which secured him. He reported the garrison at three hundred and fifty regulars, fifty artificers, and five Indians; that they had plenty of provisions, and that twelve masons were employed blowing rocks in the intrenchment, assisted by a number of soldiers; that Crown Point was garrisoned by one hundred and fifty regulars and fourteen Indians; that the Marquis de Montcalm was at Montreal; that five hundred Attawawa Indians wintered in Canada; that five hundred rangers had been raised in Canada, and were commanded by an experienced officer, well acquainted with the country; he did not know that the French intended an attack on the English fort this winter, but expected a large force of Indians, as soon as the ice would bear, to go down to that post; and all the bakers in Carillon were employed in making biscuit for these scouts.

About noon a Frenchman came near the rangers on his return from hunting. A party was ordered to pursue to the edge of the clearing, take him prisoner, fire a gun or two, and retreat to the main body, and thus by stratagem entice the enemy from their fort. The orders were promptly obeyed, but no one ventured out. The last prisoner gave the same information as the first, and also, that he had heard the English intended to attack Ticonderoga as soon as the lake was frozen hard enough to bear them. Finding that the enemy would not come out, the party killed seventeen head of cattle, and set fire to the wood collected for the garrison. Five large piles were consumed. The French discharged cannon at those who kindled the fires, but did them no injury. At 8 o'clock in the evening the party commenced their march, and on the 27th, with their prisoners, reached Fort Edward. On their return, they found at the north end of lake George the boats the French had taken at Fort William Henry, and a great number of cannon balls concealed. As the boats were under water, they could not destroy them.

On his return from this scout, Captain Rogers was ordered to New York to confer with Lord Loudoun in respect to the augmentation of the corps of rangers. His lordship gave him a friendly reception, and the following instructions:

By His Excellency, John, Earl of Loudoun, Lord Mackline, and Taireensen, &c, &c.; one of the sixteen peers of Scotland, Captain General of Virginia, and Vice Admiral of the same; Colonel of the 13th regiment of Foot, Colonel-in-Chief of the Royal American regiment. Major General and Commander-in-chief of all His Majesty's forces raised or to be raised in North America. (His lordship's list of titles remind one of the Spanish traveller, for whose catalogue of names the landlord could not find room in his house.)

Whereas, I have thought proper to augment the rangers with five additional companies: *viz.*, four from New-England, and one Indian company, to be forthwith raised and employed in his majesty's service; and having entire confidence in your knowledge of the men fit for that service, I therefore, by these presents, empower you to raise such a number of non-commissioned officers and privates as will complete the companies upon the following establishment: *viz.*, each company to consist of one captain, two lieutenants, one ensign, four sergeants and one hundred privates.

The officers are to receive British pay, that is, the same as officers of the same rank in the line; the sergeants 4*s.*, New York currency, and the privates 2*s.*, 6*d.* per day. One month's pay for each of said companies shall be advanced, on condition that it is to be deducted from the first warrants which shall be issued hereafter for the subsistence of said companies. The men are to provide themselves with good blankets and warm clothing; the same to be uniform in each company. They will supply their own arms, which must bear inspection.

The Indians are to be dressed in their own costume, and all are to be subject to the articles of war.

You will dispatch the officers, appointed to these companies, immediately upon the recruiting service, with directions to enlist none for a less term than one year, nor any other than able bodied men, accustomed to the woods, good hunters, and every way qualified for rangers. They are all required to be at

Fort Edward on or before the 15th of March next, and are to be mustered by the officer commanding that garrison.

Given under my hand, at New York, the 11th day of January, 1758.

Loudoun.

By His Excellency's command—

J. Appy, Sec'y.

To Captain Robert Rogers.

In pursuance of these instructions, officers were dispatched to the New England colonies, and the levies were completed on the 4th of March. Four of them were sent to join General Amherst, at Louisburg, and the others remained under the order of Captain Rogers. He was at the whole expense of raising these companies, for which he received no allowance; and by the death of one captain, to whom he had delivered one thousand dollars as advanced pay, as by his instructions he had a right to do, he was obliged to account to government for the same, for which he never received a farthing.

February 28. Colonel Haviland ordered a scout from Fort Edward, under Captain Putnam, who commanded a company of Connecticut provincials, together with a party of the rangers, giving out publicly that upon Putnam's return Rogers would be sent to the French forts with four hundred rangers. This was known to officers and soldiers at the time of Putnam's departure. While this party was out, a servant of Mr. Best, the sutler, was taken by a flying party from Ticonderoga, and one of Putnam's men deserted to the enemy. Captain Putnam returned, reporting that six hundred Indians lay not far from the enemy's quarters.

March 10. Colonel Haviland ordered Rogers to the vicinity of Ticonderoga, not with four hundred men as had been given out, but with one hundred and eighty, officers included. He had with him one captain, one lieutenant, and one ensign of the line, as volunteers: *viz.*, Messrs. Creed, Kent and Wrightson; also, one sergeant and a private, all of the 27th regiment; a detachment from the four companies of rangers, quartered on the island near Fort Edward: *viz.*, Captain Bulkley, Lieutenants Phillips, Moore, Campbell, Crafton and Pottinger; Ensigns Ross, Waite, McDonald and White, with one hundred and sixty-two privates.

Captain Rogers engaged in this enterprise, with so small a detachment of brave men, with much uneasiness. He had every reason to believe that the prisoner and deserter had informed the enemy of the movement intended, and the force to be employed. Yet Colonel Haviland, knowing all this, sent him out with *but* one hundred and eighty men. He probably had his reasons, and could perhaps justify his conduct; but that affords no consolation to the friends of the brave men who were thus rashly thrown in the way of an enemy of three times their force, and of whom one hundred and eight never returned.

The detachment first marched to Half-way Brook, in the road leading to Lake George, and there encamped for the night. On the 11th they proceeded as far as the first narrows on Lake George, and encamped that evening on the east shore. After dark a scout was sent three miles down, to ascertain if the enemy were coming toward our fort, who returned without discovering them. The troops were, however, on their guard, and parties were kept out walking upon the lake all night, while sentries were posted at all necessary places on shore.

March 12. The rangers left their camp at sunrise, and, having advanced about three miles, perceived a dog running across the lake. A party was therefore sent to reconnoitre an island where it was supposed the Indians were in ambush; but, as none were found there, it was thought expedient to take to the shore, and thus prevent being discovered from the surrounding hills. They halted at a place called Sabbath-day Point, on the west shore, and sent out scouts to look down the lake with perspective glasses. At dark the party proceeded down the lake. Lieutenant Phillips, with fifteen men, several of whom preceded him on skates, acted as an advanced guard, while Ensign Ross flanked them on the left under the west shore, near which the main body was kept marching as closely as possible to prevent separation, the night being extremely dark.

In this manner they came within eight miles of the French advanced guard. When Mr. Phillips sent back a man on skates to desire the detachment to halt. Upon this the men were ordered to sit down upon the ice. Mr. Phillips soon after appeared, reporting that he had discovered what he supposed to be a fire on the east shore, but was uncertain. (It was afterward learned that a scout of French had a fire there at the time, but on discovering the advanced party, put it out, and carried the news to the fort). He and Mr. White were sent to ascertain the fact. They returned in an hour, fully persuaded that a party of the enemy were encamped at the place. The advanced guard was called in, and the whole force marched to the west shore, where in a thicket they concealed their sleighs and packs. (These Indian sleighs were pieces of split wood shaved thin, about sixteen inches wide and six feet long, turned up in front, so as to slide easily over the snow, with two arms and a cross-piece, by which they were drawn. Thus, an old ranger described them.)

Leaving a small guard with the baggage, the party marched to attack the enemy's encampment, if it could be found. On reaching the place where the supposed fire had been seen, and finding no enemy, they concluded Mr. Phillips had mistaken patches of snow or rotten wood for fire, (which in the night and at a distance resemble it.) They then returned to their packs, and passed the night without fire. On the morning of the 13th a council of officers determined that the best course was to proceed by land upon snow-shoes, lest the enemy should discover the party on the lake. Accordingly, the march was continued on the west shore, along the back of the mountains, which overlooked the French advanced guard, and the party halted two miles west of them, where they refreshed themselves until three o'clock. This halt and rest was to afford the day scout from the fort time to return home, before they advanced to ambush some of the roads leading to the fortress that night, in order to trepan the enemy in the morning.

The detachment now advanced in two divisions, one headed by Captain Bulkley, and the other by Captain Rogers. Ensigns White and Waite led the rear guard, while the other officers were properly posted with their respective divisions. On their left they were flanked by a rivulet, and by a steep mountain on their right. The main body kept close under the mountain, that the advanced guard might better observe the brook, on the ice of which they might travel, as the snow was now four feet deep, which made travelling difficult even with snowshoes. In this manner they proceeded a mile and a half, when the advance reported the enemy in sight, and soon afterward, that his force was about ninety-six, chiefly Indians. The party immediately threw down their knapsacks, and prepared for action, supposing the enemy's whole force were approaching our left upon the ice of the rivulet.

Ensign McDonald was ordered to take command of the advanced guard, which, as the rangers faced to the left, became a flanking party to their right. They marched within a few yards of the bank, which was higher than the ground they occupied, and, as the ground gradually descended from the rivulet to the foot of the mountain, the line was extended along the bank so far as to cover the enemy's whole front at once. When their front was nearly opposite his left wing, Captain Rogers fired his gun as the signal for a general discharge. The first fire was given by the rangers, which killed more than forty, and put the remainder to flight, in which one-half of the rangers pursued and cut down several more with their hatchets.

Imagining the enemy totally defeated, Ensign McDonald was ordered to head their flying remains, so that none should escape. He soon ascertained that the party already routed was only the advanced guard of six hundred Canadians and Indians, who were now coming up to attack the rangers. The latter now retreated to their own ground, which was gained at the expense of fifty men killed. There they were drawn up in good order, and fought with such intrepidity, keeping up such a constant and well-directed fire, as caused the enemy, though seven to one in number, to retreat a second time. The rangers being in no condition to pursue, the enemy rallied, and made a desperate attack upon their front and wings. They were so warmly received that their flanking parties soon retreated to their main body with great loss. This threw the whole into confusion, and caused a third retreat. The rangers' numbers were now too far reduced to take advantage of their disorder, and, having rallied, the enemy attacked them a fourth time.

Two hundred Indians were now discovered ascending the mountain on the right, in order to fall upon our rear. Captain Rogers ordered Lieutenant Phillips, with eighteen men, to gain the heights before them, and drive the Indians back. He succeeded in gaining the summit, and repulsed them by a well-directed fire. Captain Rogers now became alarmed lest the enemy should go round on the left, and take post on the other part of the hill, and directed Lieutenant Grafton, with fifteen men, to anticipate them. Soon afterward he sent two gentlemen, who were volunteers, with a few men to support him, which they did with great bravery.

★★★★★★

These gentlemen were both officers of the line, and went out as volunteers, desirous of witnessing the novelty of an Indian fight. Rogers previously requested them to retire, and offered a sergeant to conduct them. They at first accepted the offer; but, boing unused to snow-shoes, unacquainted with the woods, and seeing the rangers hardly pressed by the Indians, painted most hideously, and causing the mountains to echo with their horrid yells, like gallant men, came back to their aid. After the light they escaped, and wandered in the forest and mountains for seven days, enduring great hardships, until the morning of the 20th, when they reached Ticonderoga, and surrendered to a party of French officers, who, observing them, ran out and prevented their capture by a party of Indians. The French treated them in a kind and hospitable manner, and in due time they were exchanged.

★★★★★★

The enemy now pressed so closely upon the English front, that the parties were often intermixed, and in general not more than twenty yards asunder. A constant fire continued from the commencement of the attack, one hour and a half, during which time the rangers lost eight officers and one hundred privates killed on the spot. After doing all that brave men could do, they were compelled to break, and each man to look out for himself. Rogers ran up the hill, followed by twenty men, toward Phillips and Grafton, where they stopped, and gave the Indians who were pursuing in great numbers another fire, which killed several and wounded others. Lieutenant Phillips was at this time about capitulating for himself and party, being surrounded by three hundred Indians. Rogers came so near that Phillips spoke to him, and said if the enemy would give good quarter, he thought it best to surrender; otherwise, he would fight while a man was left to fire a gun.

Captain Rogers now retreated, with the remainder of his party, in the best manner possible. Several men, who were wounded and fatigued, were taken by the savages who pursued his retreat. He reached Lake George in the evening, where he was joined by several wounded men, who were assisted to the place where the sleighs had been left. From this place an express was dispatched to Colonel Haviland, for assistance to bring in the wounded. The party passed the night without fire or blankets, which were lost with their knapsacks. The night was extremely cold, and the wounded suffered much pain, but behaved in a manner consistent with their conduct in the action.

In the morning the party proceeded up the lake, and at Hoop island met Captain John Stark bringing to their relief provisions, blankets and sleighs. They encamped on the island, and passed the night with good fires. On the evening of March 15, they arrived at Fort Edward.

Regarding this unfortunate enterprise, Rogers says:

The number of the enemy who attacked us was seven hundred, of which six hundred were Indians. From the best accounts, we afterward learned that we killed one hundred and fifty of them, and wounded as many more, most of whom died. I will not pretend to say what would have been the result of this unfortunate expedition, had our number been four hundred strong, as was contemplated; but it is due to those brave officers who accompanied me, most of whom are now no more, to declare that

151

every man in his respective station behaved with uncommon resolution and coolness. Nor do I recollect an instance, during the action, in which the prudence or good conduct of one of them could be questioned.

The only person whose conduct appears censurable was Colonel Haviland, for sending out so small a force, when he had every reason to believe that the enemy wag apprised of his intentions, and would without doubt have a superior force in readiness, to compel the rangers to an engagement under every disadvantage.

RETURN OF KILLED AND WOUNDED, IN THE ACTION OF MARCH 18, 1758.

The captain and lieutenant of the regular troops, acting as volunteers, were made prisoners. The ensign, a sergeant and one private, all volunteers from the same regiment, were killed.

Captain Robert Rogers' Company—
Lieutenant Moore, Sergeant Parnell, and thirty-six privates, killed.
Captain Shephard's Company—
Two sergeants and sixteen privates killed.
Captain James Rogers' Company—
Ensign McDonald killed.
Captain John Stark's Company—
Two sergeants and fourteen privates killed.
Captain Bulkley's Company—
Captain Bulkley, Lieutenant Pottenger, and Ensign Waite killed: 17 privates killed and missing.
Captain William Stark's Company—
Ensign Ross killed.
Captain Brewer's Company—
Lieutenant Campbell killed.

After the return of Captain Rogers from this scout, he was ordered to Albany to recruit his company, where he met with a friendly reception from Lord Howe, who advanced money to recruit men, and gave him leave to wait upon General Abercrombie, at New York. That general had now succeeded to the command-in-chief, in place of Lord Loudoun, who was about to embark for England. At this time, he received the following commission:

By His Excellency, James Abercrombie, Esquire, Colonel of His Majesty's 44th regiment of Foot, Colonel-in-Chief of the 60th

Royal Americans, Major General and Commander-in-Chief of all His Majesty's forces raised or to be raised in North America.

Whereas, it may be of great use to his majesty's service in America to have a number of men employed in obtaining intelligence of the strength, situation and motions of the enemy, and other services, for which rangers are qualified: Having, therefore, the greatest confidence in your loyalty, courage and skill, I do hereby constitute you major of the rangers in His Majesty's service, and captain of a company of the same. You are therefore to take the said rangers as major, and the said company as captain, into your care, and duly exercise and instruct as well the officers as the soldiers; who are hereby commanded to obey you as their major and captain, respectively. And you are to observe such orders as from time to time you shall receive from His Majesty, myself, or any other superior officer, according to the rules and discipline of war.

Given at New York, this 6th day of April, 1758, in the 31st year of our sovereign lord, the King of Great Britain, France and Ireland, defender of the faith, &c.

James Abercrombie.

By His Excellency's command—

J. Appy, Sec'y.

To Major Robert Rogers.

On the 12th of April Major Rogers reported himself to Lord Howe, at Albany, with whom he conversed respecting the different modes of distressing the enemy, and prosecuting the war with vigour the ensuing campaign. He then proceeded to Fort Edward to take orders from Colonel Grant, then commanding that post. Captain Stark was dispatched to Ticonderoga, on the west side of Lake George; Captain Jacobs (Indian), on the east side; Captain Shephard between the lakes, with orders to take prisoners from Ticonderoga. At the same time. Major Rogers marched, with eighteen men, to Crown Point Captain Burbank was also detached in quest of prisoners. These scouts were kept constantly out to reconnoitre the enemy from time to time.

April 29. Major. Rogers marched, with eighteen men, towards Fort William Henry, four miles, and encamped at Schoon Creek, the weather being rainy.

April 30. He proceeded north-east, and encamped by South bay.

May 1. He encamped near the narrows north of South bay.

May 2. He made a raft, crossed the lake, and encamped four miles from it, on the east side.

May 3. He steered north, and encamped three miles from Ticonderoga.

May 4. He marched north-east all day, and encamped three miles from Crown Point.

May 5. He killed a Frenchman, and took three prisoners. With them he reached camp on the 9th instant.

One of the prisoners reported that:

He was a native of Lorraine; that he had been eight years in Canada—of which time he had passed two years at Quebec, one at Montreal, and live at Crown Point; that at the latter place were two hundred soldiers, under Mons. Jonang; that Ticonderoga contained four hundred of the queen's regiment, one hundred and fifty marines, two hundred Canadians and seven hundred Indians, three hundred more being expected; that the French did not intend to attack the English fort, but were preparing to receive them at Ticonderoga; they had heard that Rogers was killed in the conflict of last March, but from prisoners taken by the Indians, at Dutch Hoosac, they learned that he was alive, and had sworn to revenge the barbarities with which his men had been treated, particularly Lieutenant Phillips and his party, who had been butchered in cold blood, after they had been promised quarter. This was talked of among the Indians, who blamed the French for encouraging them to do so.

★★★★★★

A note in the *History of Manchester*, refers to this circumstance as follows:

It is stated in a note, in Rogers' *Journal*, that Lieut. Phillips was killed in this battle; he and his party being tied to trees, and hewn to pieces in the most barbarous manner. This is a mistake. Lieut. Phillips escaped, lived to a good old age, and died in Northfield, N. H., somewhere about the year 1810. The writer of this has often heard Lieut. Phillips relate this and other of his escapes in the 'seven years' war.'"

In regard to Phillips, Judge Potter states that his Christian name was William. He was known as 'Bill Phillips.' He was a noted hunter, and lived in the vicinity of Concord, supporting himself principally by hunting. His father was a Frenchman, and his mother an Indian. He partly learned the trade of a blacksmith, but preferred to swing a hatchet or knife to making either; and had rather by far *steal* a hatchet, axe, or knife, than labour in their manufacture, or to purchase them, provided he had money. In a word, he was an excellent hunter and warrior; but, with these characteristics, he had some of the bad habits of both the French and the Indian. He was appointed a lieutenant by Lord Loudoun. He was not killed, as reported by Rogers, in the action of March 13th, 1758, but lived in the Merrimack valley until his death, in 1819. He married Eleanor Eastman, of Rumford (now Concord), daughter of Ebenezer Eastman. He supported himself by hunting and occasional blacksmith work. He became a drunkard, neglected his business, and *would steal*. His wife in consequence, left him, and joined the Shakers at Canterbury. He lived to a great age, and was supported for a time by the town of Concord. At length, he joined the settlement at Northfield. That town supported him till his death.

★★★★★★

Captains Stark and Jacobs returned on the 8th instant. The former brought in six prisoners, four of whom he recaptured near Ticonderoga; they, having escaped from New York and Albany, wert on their flight to the French forts. The latter, who had with him but one white man and eighteen Indians, took ten prisoners and seven scalps from a party of French. About the middle of May a flag of truce was sent to Ticonderoga on Colonel Schuyler's account, which put a stop to all offensive scouts till its return.

May 28. Orders were issued by Rogers to all officers and men of the rangers, and the two Indian companies on furlough, to join their respective corps before the 10th of June. These orders were obeyed, and parties kept on scouts until June 8th, when Lord Howe arrived at Fort Edward with one half of the army.

His lordship ordered Rogers, with fifty men, and his whale-boats, which were conveyed in wagons to Lake George, to proceed to Ticonderoga, to obtain at all events an accurate plan of the north end; also, of the ground from the landing-place to the fort; also, of Lake Champlain for three miles beyond it, and discover the enemy's force in that quarter.

With these orders, he marched on the morning of the 12th, and at night encamped on the site of Fort William Henry.

June 30. He proceeded down the lake in five whaleboats to the first narrows, and to the west end of the lake, where he took the plans required. Part of his men proceeding to reconnoitre the fort, discovered an extensive Indian encampment and a large number of Indians. While Rogers was at a distance from his men, engaged with two or three others taking plans of the fort and camp, the rangers were attacked by a superior number of the enemy who had come between them. Captain Jacobs, with his Mohegans, ran off at the first onset, calling to the rangers to do the same; but they stood their ground, discharged their pieces several times, and at last broke through the enemy, who surrounded them on all sides except their rear, which was covered by a river. They killed three of the enemy, but lost eight rangers in the skirmish. The party rallied at the boats, where Rogers joined them, and, having collected all but the slain, returned homeward.

On the 20th, at Half-way Brook, they met Lord Howe with three thousand men, to whom Rogers gave an account of his scout, and the plans he had requested. From him he obtained leave to wait upon General Abercrombie at Fort Edward. He ordered him to join Lord Howe next day with all the rangers, amounting to six hundred, and proceed with him to the lake.

On the 22d his lordship encamped near the site of Fort William Henry. The rangers advanced four hundred yards farther, and encamped on the west side. From this position three small parties were detached, one to the narrows of South bay, one along the west shore of Lake George, and a third to Ticonderoga, all proceeding by land. Another party of two lieutenants and seventeen men were sent down the lake in five whale-boats, on the lookout, and were all taken prisoners by two hundred French and Indians.

On the 28th of June General Abercrombie arrived at the lake with the remainder of his troops; and on the morning of July 5th the whole army, of nearly sixteen thousand men, embarked in *batteaux* for Ticonderoga.

The order of march afforded a brilliant spectacle. The regular troops occupied the centre, and the provincials formed the wings. For the advanced guard, the light infantry flanked the right, and the rangers the left of Colonel Bradstreet's *batteau* men.

In this order the army advanced, until dark, down the lake to Sabbath-day Point, when it halted to refresh. At ten o'clock at night the force moved onward. Lord Howe proceeding in front with his whale-boat, attended by Colonel Bradstreet, Major Rogers, and Lieutenant Holmes in other boats. Holmes was detached in advance to view the landing-place, and ascertain if the enemy were posted there. He returned at daybreak, and met the army four miles from the landing-place, near the Blue Mountains. He reported that he had discovered, by their fires, that a party of the enemy were posted at the landing-place.

At daylight his lordship. Colonel Bradstreet, and Major Rogers proceeded within a quarter of a mile of the landing-place, and perceived a small party in possession of it. His lordship thereupon returned to assist in landing the army, intending to march by land to Ticonderoga. At twelve o'clock the landing was effected, and the rangers posted on the left wing. Major Rogers was ordered to gain the summit of a mountain, which bore north one mile from the landing-place; thence to proceed to the river which enters the falls between the landing-place and the sawmills, and take possession of a rising ground on the side of the enemy; there to await farther orders. After a toilsome march of one hour, he gained the position, and posted his men, to the best advantage, within a quarter of a mile of the post occupied by the Marquis de Montcalm, with fifteen hundred men, as the scouts ascertained.

At twelve o'clock Colonels Lyman and Fitch, of the provincials, took post in their rear. While Rogers was informing them of the enemy's position, a sharp fire commenced in the rear of Lyman's regiment, who immediately formed his front, and desired Rogers to fall upon the left flank, which lie did. Rogers ordered Captain Burbank, with one hundred and fifty men, to retain their present position, and watch the motions of the French at the saw-mills. With his remaining force he fell upon the enemy's left, the river covering their right, and killed many of them. By this time Lord Howe, with a detachment from his front, had broken the enemy, and hemmed them in on each side; but, while advancing himself with too great intrepidity and zeal, he was unfortunately struck by a shot, and died instantly. (This intrepid and accomplished nobleman was beloved by both officers and soldiers, and his fall produced a general consternation.)

At six o'clock, July 7th, Rogers was ordered to the river, where he had been stationed the day before, there to halt on the west side, with four hundred and fifty men, while Captain Stark, with the remainder of the rangers, advanced with Captain Abercrombie, and Mr. Clerk, the engineer, to reconnoitre the place. They returned the same evening, and the whole army passed the night under arms. At sunrise, July 8th, Sir William Johnson arrived with four hundred and forty Indians. At seven o'clock the rangers were ordered to march. A lieutenant of Captain Stark led the advanced guard, which, when within three hundred yards of the entrenchments, was ambushed and fired upon by two hundred French. Rogers formed a front to support them, and they maintained their ground until the enemy retreated. Soon after this the *batteau* men formed on Roger's left, and the light infantry on his right. The enemy's fire did not kill a man of the rangers. Two provincial regiments now formed in Rogers' rear, at two hundred yards' distance.

While the army was thus forming, a scattering fire was kept up between the English flying parties and those of the enemy, without the breastwork. At half past ten, the army being drawn up, a sharp fire commenced on the left wing, where Colonel De Lancy's New York men and the *batteau* men were posted. Upon this Rogers, with the rangers, was ordered to drive the enemy within their works, and then to fall down, that the pickets and grenadiers might march through. The enemy soon retired within their works, and Major Proby, with his pickets, marched within a few yards of the works, where he unfortunately fell. The enemy keeping up a steady fire, the soldiers were drawing back, when Colonel Haldiman came up with the grenadiers to support them, followed by the battalions of the line. The colonel advanced very near the breastwork, which was eight feet high.

Some provincials and Mohawks also came up. The troops toiled, with repeated attacks, for four hours, being much embarrassed by trees felled by the enemy without their breastwork, when the general ordered a retreat, directing the rangers to bring up the rear, which they did in the dusk of the evening. On the 9th, at dark, the army reached the south end of Lake George, where the general bestowed upon them his thanks for their good behaviour, and ordered them to intrench. The wounded were sent to Fort Edward and Albany. The loss of the English was sixteen hundred and eight regulars, and three hundred and thirty-four provincials killed and wounded, while that of the French was five hundred killed and wounded, and many prisoners.

Soon after this Rogers went on a scout to South bay, and returned July 16th, having discovered one thousand of the enemy on the east side. This party fell upon Colonel Nichols' regiment, at Half-way Brook, and killed three captains and twenty men. (From these and other slaughters this brook is sometimes called "Bloody Brook.")

July 27. Another party of the enemy attacked a convoy of wagons between Fort Edward and Half-way Brook, and killed one hundred and sixteen men, sixteen of whom were rangers. Major Rogers attempted to intercept this party with seven hundred men, but they escaped. On his return an express met him with orders to march to South and East bays, and return. On this march nothing material occurred until August 8th. Early in the morning the march commenced from the site of Fort Ann; Major Putnam, with a party of provincials, marching in front, the rangers in the rear, and Captain Dalyell, with the regulars in the centre, the whole force amounting to five hundred and thirty, exclusive of officers. After marching one-third of a mile, five hundred of the enemy attacked the front. The men were immediately brought into line, Captain Dalyell commanding the centre, with the rangers and light infantry on the right, and Captain Giddings, with his Boston troops, on the left.

★★★★★★

Captain James Dalyell was appointed a lieutenant in the 60th, or Royal Americans, January 15, 1756, and obtained a company in the 2nd battalion of Royals, or 1st regiment of Foot, on the 13th of September, 1760. On the 31st of July, 1763, he led a detachment against Pontiac, then encamped beyond the bridge on the creek called "Bloody Run," near Detroit. The British party was obliged to retreat; but Dalyell, seeing a wounded sergeant of the 55th lying on the ground, gazing in despair after his retiring comrades, ran back to rescue the wounded man, when he was struck by a shot, and fell dead.

★★★★★★

Major Putnam being in front of his men when the fire began, the enemy rushed in and took him, one lieutenant, and two privates, prisoners, and threw his whole party into confusion. They afterward rallied, and performed good service, particularly Lieutenant Durkee, who, notwithstanding a wound in the thigh and one in his wrist, bravely maintained his ground, and encouraged his men throughout the action.

★★★★★★

Lieutenant Robert Durkee. This brave and skilful partisan served with distinction in the French war, and afterward removed to the settlement in the valley of Wyoming, Penn., and rendered valuable services in the revolutionary contest. He was slain at the Battle of Wyoming, July 3, 1778.—*Wilson's Orderly Book.*

★★★★★★

Captain Dalyell, with Gage's light infantry, and Lieutenant Eyers of the 44th regiment, behaved with great gallantry. They occupied the centre, where at first the fire was most severe. It afterward fell upon the right, where the enemy made four different attacks upon the rangers.

The officers and men behaved with so much courage, that in an hour the enemy broke and retreated; but with so much caution, and in such small squads, as to afford no opportunities to harass them by pursuit. The English kept the field, and buried the dead. They missed fifty-four men, twenty-one of whom came in afterwards, they having been separated from the rangers during the action. The enemy lost one hundred and ninety-nine killed, several of whom were Indians. The party was met, at some distance from Fort Edward, by three hundred men with refreshments, sent by Colonel Provost, and with them they arrived, on the 9th of August, at Fort Edward.

July 11. Colonel Provost, who now ranked as brigadier, ordered Rogers to pursue the track of a large body of Indians, which he heard had passed down the Hudson. The report proving groundless, he returned on the 14th, and proceeded to the camp at Lake George. August 29th, he reconnoitred Ticonderoga, and from that time until the army retired to winter quarters, was employed in various excursions to the French forts, and in pursuit of their flying parties.

Although little was effected by the expedition to Ticonderoga, the British arms were not everywhere unsuccessful. Colonel Bradstreet, with two thousand men, reduced Fort Frontenac at Cataraqua; and General Amherst, who had captured Louisburg, now assumed the chief command of His Majesty's forces, and established his headquarters at New York.

******

Fort Frontenac was square-faced, with four stone bastions, and nearly three quarters of a mile in circumference. Its situation was pleasant, the banks of the river presenting an agreeable landscape, with a fair view of Lake Ontario, distant one league, interspersed with many beautiful woody islands. It was erected to prevent the Indians from trading with the English, and became a place of great trade.

******

Major Rogers proceeded to Albany to settle his accounts with the paymaster, and while there addressed the following letter to Colonel Townshend, deputy adjutant general to his excellency, General Amherst:

Albany, January 28, 1769.

Sir—I herewith send you a return of the present condition of his majesty's rangers at Fort Edward, with a list of officers now recruiting in different parts of New England, who report nearly four hundred men enlisted, who are now wanted to protect our convoys between Albany and Fort Edward.

In order to urge the recruiting service, I would propose a visit to New-England, and wait upon the general at New York on my way, to represent the necessity of augmenting the rangers, and the desire of the Stockbridge Indians to re-enter the service. The rangers' arms are in the hands of Mr. Cunningham at New York, and are very much needed at Fort Edward. Will you be good enough to have them forwarded?

Respectfully, your obedient servant,

R. Rogers.

To Colonel Townshend.

P. S. General Stanwix informs me that a subaltern and twenty rangers are to be stationed at Number Four. I would recommend Lieutenant Stevens, who is well acquainted with the country in that quarter.

(Answer.)

February 5, 1759.

Sir—I received your letter with the enclosed return. The general commands me to inform you that he can by no means approve of your leaving Fort Edward. Your recruiting officers are ordered to send their recruits to Fort Edward, by an advertisement in the newspapers containing the general's orders, as you did not furnish their names and places of duty. The proposals for the Indians must be sent immediately to the general. The arms shall be sent forthwith. Lieutenant Stevens has been notified of the general's intention of leaving him at Number Four. It is a season of the year when you may expect the enemy's scouting parties, and you must see the necessity of remaining at Fort Edward. Your officers will join you as soon as possible. At another time the general would grant your request.

Your humble servant,

R. Townshend, D. A. G.

To Major Rogers.

Rogers proposed to the colonel an addition of two new corps of rangers, on the same footing as those already in service, and that three Indian companies should be raised for the next campaign. To secure them before they went out on hunting parties, he wrote to three of their chiefs: one, to King Uncas of the Mohegans, was as follows:

Brother Uncas—As it is for the advantage of King George to have a large body of rangers raised for the next campaign, and being well convinced of your attachment, I wish, in pursuance of General Amherst's orders, to engage your assistance early in the spring. Should you choose to come out as captain, you shall have a commission; if not, I shall expect Doquipe and Nunipad. You shall choose the ensign and sergeants. The company shall consist of fifty men or more. If the deserters from Brewer's corps will join you, the general will pardon them. You may employ a clerk, who shall be allowed the usual pay. I wish you success in raising the men, and shall be glad to be joined by you as soon as possible.

Your humble servant,

R. Rogers.

With letters to Indians, a belt of *wampum* is sent. The bearer reads the letter, and delivers that and the belt to the *sachem*, to whom they are directed.

Toward the last of February Sir William Johnson sent Captain Lotridge, with fifty Mohawks, to join Rogers in a scout to Ticonderoga.

On the 3rd of March Colonel Haldiman ordered Rogers to reconnoitre the enemy's forts. He marched, with three hundred and fifty-eight men, to Half-way Brook, and there encamped. One Indian, being hurt, returned. On the 4th he marched within a mile and a half of Lake George, and halted till evening, that he might pass the enemy undiscovered, should any of them be on the hill. He then marched on until two o'clock in the morning, and halted at the first narrows, whence several frost-bitten men wore sent back in charge of a careful sergeant. At eleven, on the night of the 5th, the party reached Sabbath-day Point, almost overcome with cold.

At two o'clock the march was resumed, and the landing-place reached at eight o'clock in the forenoon. Here a scout was sent out, who reported two working parties on the east side, but none on the west. This being a suitable opportunity for the engineer to make his observations, Rogers left Captain Williams in command of the regulars and thirty rangers, and proceeded with the engineer and forty-nine rangers, Captain Lotridge and forty-five Indians, to the isthmus which overlooks the fort, where the engineer made his observations. They then returned, leaving five Indians and one ranger to observe what numbers crossed the lake from the east side in the evening, that the party might know how to attack them in the morning.

At dark the engineer went again to the entrenchments with Lieutenant Tute and a guard of ten men. He returned without molestation at midnight, having completed his survey. Upon his return Captain Williams and the regulars were ordered back to Sabbath-day Point; they, being distressed with cold, and having no snow-shoes, it appeared imprudent to march them farther. Lieutenant Tute and thirty rangers were sent with them to kindle fires at the point.

At three o'clock Rogers marched with forty rangers, one regular, and Lotridge's Indians to attack the working parties when they crossed the lake early in the morning. He crossed South bay eight miles south of the fort, and at six o'clock bore down opposite to it, within half a mile of the French parties who were cutting wood. A scout of two Indians and two rangers reported that they were forty in number, and at work close upon the lake shore, nearly opposite the fort. Throwing off their blankets, the rangers ran down upon the choppers, took several prisoners, and destroyed most of the party in their retreat. Being discovered by the garrison, the party was pursued by eighty Canadians and Indians, supported by one hundred and fifty regulars, who, in a mile's march, commenced a fire upon their rear. The rangers, halting upon a rising ground, repulsed the enemy before their whole party came up, and resumed their line of march abreast.

After proceeding half a mile, their rear was again assailed; but, having gained an advantageous position upon a long ridge, they made a stand on the side opposite to the enemy. The Canadians and Indians came very near, but, receiving a warm fire from the rangers and Mohawks, they broke immediately, were pursued, and entirely routed before their regulars could come up. The party now marched without interruption. In these skirmishes one regular and two rangers were killed, and one Indian wounded. Thirty of the enemy were left dead. At twelve o'clock at night the party reached Sabbath-day Point, fifty miles from the place they left in the morning. (Considering that three skirmishes took place in the course of it, this must be considered an extraordinary march on snow-shoes.)

Captain Williams was up, and received them with good fires, than which nothing could have been more acceptable, as many of the men had their feet frozen, the weather being intensely cold, and the snow four feet deep. Next morning the whole party marched to Long island, on Lake George, and encamped for the night. During the march several rangers and Indians had leave to hunt on the lake shore, and brought in plenty of venison. Fearing that a party of Indians, who had gone up South bay, might do some mischief before his return. Major Rogers dispatched Lieutenant Tute, with the following letter to Colonel Haldiman:

Camp at Sabbath-day Point, 8 o'clock a. m.
Sir—I would inform you that sixty Indians, in two parties, have gone toward Fort Edward and Saratoga, and I fear they will strike a blow before this reaches you. Mr. Brheme, the engineer, has completed his business agreeably to his orders; since which I have taken and destroyed several of the enemy near Ticonderoga, as the bearer will inform. The Mohawks behaved well, and ventured within pistol shot of the fort. The weather is extremely severe, and we are compelled to carry some of our men whose feet are frozen.

Yours, &c.,

R. Rogers.

N. B. Two-thirds of my detachment have frozen their feet.

(Answer.)

Fort Edward, March 20, 1759.
Dear Sir—I congratulate you on your success, and send twenty-two sleighs to transport your sick. You will also bring as many boards (left at south end of Lake George, and wanted at Fort Edward), as you can conveniently. My compliments to Captain Williams and the gentlemen.

Your most obed't serv't,

Fred. Haldiman.

P. S. The signal guns have been fired to give notice to the different posts to be on their guard. Nothing has yet appeared. (A party of Indians near Fort Miller, eight miles below, heard these guns, and, supposing they were discovered, retreated.)

At Lake George the party met the sleighs and a detachment of one hundred men, and all returned in safety to Fort Edward, where Rogers received the following letter:

New York, February 26, 1759.
Sir—Your letter by Mr. Stark was yesterday received. The general approves of raising the Indians, but does not agree to raise any more companies of rangers until the present ones are completed. Your arms have been proved by the artillery, and answer well. They will be sent you as fast as possible. We have chosen one hundred men from each regiment, and selected officers,

to act this year as light infantry. They are equipped as lightly as possible, and are much wanted in our service. Brigadier Gage recommends you highly to the general. With him merit will not pass unrewarded, nor will he favour recommendations unless the person deserves promotion. Please return your companies when complete.

Your humble servant,

R. Townshend.

New York, February 13, 1759.

Sir—This will be delivered by Captain Jacob Nannawapateonks, who during the last campaign commanded the Stockbridge Indians, who, upon hearing that you had written concerning him, came to offer his services for the ensuing campaign. As you have not mentioned any terms, I refer him to you to receive his proposals. Report them to me, and inform me whether his service is adequate to them. After which I will give an answer.

Your most obed't serv't,

Jeff. Amherst.

To Major Rogers.

Before receiving this letter, Rogers had waited on the general at Albany, by whom he was well received, and assured of the rank of major in the line of the army from the date of his commission under General Abercrombie. Returning to Fort Edward, May 15th, he received the melancholy news of the death of Captain Burbank, who, during his absence, had been cut off with thirty men while on a scout. He was a good officer, and the scout upon which he was sent was needless and ill-advised.

★★★★★★

An Indian scalped Captain Burbank, and held up the trophy with great exultation, thinking it to be that of Major Rogers. The prisoners informed him of the mistake, and the Indians appeared to be sorry, saying he was a good man. He had some time previously shown some of them kindness, which Indians never forget.

★★★★★★

Preparations for the campaign were now hastened in every quarter. Levies from the provinces arrived, the ranger companies were completed, and in June a portion of the army under General Gage advanced to the lake. Rogers was ordered to send Captain Stark, with three companies, to join him. With the other three, Rogers remained under the orders of the general-in-chief, who directed several scouts to be made to the enemy's forts.

June 20. The second division of the army proceeded to the lake, the rangers forming the advanced guard. Here the general fulfilled his promise to Rogers, by declaring publicly, in general orders, his rank as major in the army from the date of his commission as major of rangers. The army lay here collecting its strength, and procuring information of the enemy, until July 21st, when it was again embarked for Ticonderoga, in little more than a year from the time of the memorable repulse before the lines of that fortress.

June 22. The rangers were in front, on the right wing, and were the first troops landed at the north end of Lake George. They were followed by the grenadiers and light infantry, under Colonel Haviland. The rangers marched across the mountains in the isthmus, thence, through a by-path in the woods, to the bridge at the saw-mills; where, finding the bridge uninjured, they crossed to the other side, and took possession of a rising ground. From this they drove a party of the enemy, killed several, took a number of prisoners, and routed the whole party before Colonel Haviland's corps had crossed the bridge. The army took possession of the heights near the saw-mills, where it remained during the night. The enemy kept out a scout of Canadians and Indians, who killed several men, and galled the army severely.

July 28. At an early hour the general put the troops in motion. The rangers were ordered to the front, with directions to proceed across Chestnut plain, the nearest route to Lake Champlain, and endeavour to strike the lake near the edge of the cleared ground, between that and the breastwork; there to await farther orders. The general had by this time prepared a detachment to attack the main breastwork on the hill, which they carried; while two hundred rangers carried a small intrenchment near Lake Champlain, without much loss. From the time when the army came in sight, the enemy kept up a constant fire of cannon from their walls and batteries. The general employed several provincial regiments in transporting cannon and stores across the carrying-place, which service they performed with great expedition.

July 24. This day engineers were employed in raising batteries, with the assistance of a large portion of the troops, the remainder being employed in preparing fascines, until the 26th, at night.

******

The brave Colonel Townshend was killed this day by a cannon ball. He was deeply lamented by the general, to whom he acted as deputy adjutant general. Roger Townshend, fourth son of Charles, Viscount Townshend, was commissioned lieutenant colonel February 1, 1758, and served as adjutant general in the expedition against Louisburg, and deputy adjutant general in the campaign of 1759, with the rank of colonel. He was killed in the trenches at Ticonderoga, by a cannon ball, July 26, 1759. His remains were conveyed to Albany for interment. His spirit and military knowledge entitled him to the esteem of every soldier, and his loss was universally lamented.—*Wilson's Orderly Book.,*

★★★★★★

Scouts of rangers were during this interval kept out in the vicinity of Crown Point, by whose means the general received hourly information from that post. Orders were now given to cut away a boom, which the French had thrown across the lake opposite the fort, which prevented the English from passing in boats to cut off the French retreat. To effect this object, two whale-boats and one English flat-boat were conveyed across the land from Lake George to Lake Champlain. In these, after dark, Rogers embarked with sixty rangers, and passed over to the other shore, opposite the enemy's camp; from thence intending to steer along the east shore, and silently saw off the boom, which was composed of large timber logs, fastened together with strong chains.

At nine o'clock the party had nearly reached their destination, when the French, who had previously undermined the fortress, sprung their mines, which blew up the fort with a tremendous explosion, and the garrison commenced a retreat in their boats. Rogers and his party availed themselves of this favourable opportunity of attacking them, and drove several boats on shore; so that in the morning ten boats were taken on the east shore, containing a large quantity of baggage, fifty casks of powder, and a quantity of shot and shells; which Rogers reported to the general at ten o'clock next morning.

On the 27th Rogers was ordered with a party to the saw-mills, to waylay flying parties of the enemy who were expected to return that way. There he remained until August 11th, when he received the following order:

> You are this night to send a captain, with a suitable proportion of subalterns, and two hundred men, to Crown Point, where they will post themselves in such a manner as not to be surprised; and, if attacked, they are not to retreat, but to maintain their ground until reinforced. Jeff. Amherst.

Captain Brewer was detached with this party, and the general, following next morning with the whole army, took possession of Crown Point the same day. Captain Brewer had executed his orders in a most satisfactory manner.

August 12. This evening the encampment was arranged, the rangers' station being in front of the army. The next day the general directed the ground to be cleared, and employed a large portion of the troops in erecting a new fort. Captain Stark, with two hundred rangers, was employed in cutting a road from Crown Point through the wilderness to Number Four. (Charlestown, N. H.) While the army lay at Crown Point, several scouts were sent out, who brought prisoners from St. John's, and penetrated far into the enemy's back country.

On the 12th of September, the general, being exasperated at the treatment of Captain Kennedy by the St. Francis Indians, to whom he had been sent with a flag of truce and proposals of peace, but who, with his party, had been made prisoners by the Indians, resolved to inflict upon them a signal chastisement, and gave orders as follows:

> You are this night to join the detachment of two hundred men which was yesterday ordered out, and proceed to Missisqui bay. From thence you will proceed to attack the enemy's settlements on the south side of the St. Lawrence, in such a manner as shall most effectually disgrace and injure the enemy, and redound to the honour and success of His Majesty's arms. Remember the barbarities committed by the enemy's Indian scoundrels on every occasion where they have had opportunities of showing their infamous cruelties toward his majesty's subjects. Take your revenge, but remember that, although the villains have promiscuously murdered women and children of all ages, it is my order that no women or children should be killed or hurt. When you have performed this service, you will again join the army wherever it may be.
>
> Yours, &c.,
>
> Jeff. Amherst.

Camp at Crown Point, September 13, 1759.
To Major Rogers.

★★★★★★

The plan for this expedition was formed on the day previous; but that all due caution might be observed, it was announced, in public orders, that Rogers would proceed another way, while he had secret orders to proceed to St. Francis.

★★★★★★

The account of this expedition is contained in Rogers' official dispatch, and is in substance as follows:

On the evening of the twenty-second day after our departure from Crown Point, we came in sight of the Indian town of St. Francis, which we discovered by climbing a tree at three miles' distance. Here my party, consisting of one hundred and forty-two, officers included, were ordered to refresh themselves. (Captain Williams of the royal troops, on the fifth day out, accidentally burnt himself with powder, and was obliged to return, taking with him forty men sick or hurt.) At eight o'clock Lieutenant Turner, Ensign Avery, and myself reconnoitred the town. We found the Indians engaged in a high frolic, and saw them execute several dances with great spirit and activity. (The prisoners afterward informed me that the Indians celebrated a wedding the night before the destruction of their town.) We returned to our camp at two o'clock a.m., and at three advanced with the whole party within three hundred yards of the village, where the men were lightened of their packs, and formed for action.

Half an hour before sunrise we surprised the village, approaching it in three divisions, on the right, left, and centre; which was effected with so much caution and promptitude on the part of the officers and men that the enemy had no time to recover themselves, or to take arms in their own defence, until they were mostly destroyed. Some few fled to the water; but my people pursued, sunk their canoes, and shot those who attempted to escape by swimming. We then set fire to all the houses except three, reserved for the use of our party.

The fire consumed many Indians who had concealed themselves in their cellars and house-lofts, and would not come out. At seven o'clock in the morning the affair was completely over. We had by that time killed two hundred Indians, and taken twenty women and children prisoners. Fifteen of the latter I suffered to go their own way, and brought home with me two Indian boys and three girls.

★★★★★★

These prisoners, when brought to Number Four, claimed Mrs. Johnson as an old acquaintance, she having been with their tribe as a prisoner some time before. One of them was called Sebattis. The bell of the Catholic chapel was also brought away, and a quantity of silver brooches taken from the savages who were slain.

******

Five English captives were also found, and taken into our care. When the detachment paraded, Captain Ogden was found to be badly wounded, being shot through the body, but still able to perform his duty. Six privates were wounded, and one Stockbridge Indian killed. I ordered the party to take corn out of the reserved houses, for their subsistence home, which was the only provision to be found. (One ranger, instead of more important plunder, placed in his knapsack a large lump of tallow, which supported him on his way home, while many, who had secured more valuable plunder, perished with hunger.) While they were loading themselves, I examined the captives, who reported that a party of three hundred French and Indians were down the river, four miles below us, and that our boats were waylaid. I believed this to be true, as they told the exact number of the boats, and the place where they had been left. They also stated that two hundred French had three days before gone up the river to Wigwam Martinique, supposing that I intended to attack that place.

A council of war now concluded that no other course remained for us than to return by Connecticut River to Number Four. The detachment accordingly marched in a body eight days upon that course, and, when provisions became scarce, near Memphremagog lake, it was divided into companies, with proper guides to each, and directed to assemble at the mouth of Ammonoosuc River, as I expected to find provisions there for our relief. Two days after our separation. Ensign Avery, of Fitch's regiment, with his party, fell upon my track, and followed in my rear. The enemy fell upon them, and took seven prisoners, two of whom escaped, and joined me the next morning. Avery and his men soon afterward came up with us, and we proceeded to the Coös *intervales*, where I left them under the orders of Lieutenant Grant.

I then proceeded with Captain Ogden, and one private, upon a raft, and arrived at this place yesterday. Provisions were in half an hour after dispatched up the river to Mr. Grant, which will reach him this night Two other canoes, with provisions, have been sent to the mouth of Ammonoosuc River. I shall go up the river tomorrow, to look after my men, and return as soon as possible to Crown Point. Captain Ogden can inform you of other particulars respecting this scout, as he was with me through the whole of the expedition, and behaved nobly.

Your most obedient servant,

R. Rogers.

Number Four, November 5, 1759.

To General Amherst.

The following additional particulars, stated by Major Rogers, exhibit the daring and hazardous character of this enterprise, and the hardships endured, dangers encountered, and difficulties surmounted, by the brave men by whom it was accomplished. He says:

I cannot forbear making some remarks upon the difficulties and distresses which attended the expedition, under my command, against St. Francis, situated within three miles of the river, St. Lawrence, in the heart of Canada, half way between Montreal and Quebec. While we kept the water, it was found extremely difficult to pass undiscovered by the enemy, who were cruising, in great numbers upon the lake, and had prepared certain vessels to decoy English parties on board, to destroy them; but we escaped their designs, and landed at Missisqui bay in ten days. Here I left my boats, and provisions sufficient to carry us back to Crown Point, under the charge of two trusty Indians, who were to remain there until we returned, unless the enemy should discover the boats; in which case they were to follow my track, and bring the intelligence.

On the second day after this, they joined me at night, informing me that four hundred French had found my boats, and two hundred were following my track. This report caused us much uneasiness. Should the enemy overtake us, and we obtain an advantage in the encounter, they would be immediately reinforced, while we could expect no assistance, being so far advanced beyond our military posts. Our boats and provisions also being taken, cut off all hope of retreat by the route we came; but, after due deliberation, it was resolved to accomplish our object, and return by Connecticut River.

Lieutenant McMullen was dispatched by land to Crown Point, to desire General Amherst to relieve us with provisions at Ammonoosuc River, at the extremity of the Coös *intervales*, that being the route by which we should return, if ever. We now determined to outmarch our pursuers, and destroy St. Francis before we were overtaken. We marched nine days through a spruce bog, where the ground was wet and low, a great portion of it being covered with water a foot deep. When we encamped at night, boughs were cut from the trees, and with them a rude kind of hammock constructed to secure us from the water.

We uniformly began our march at a little before daybreak, and continued it until after dark at night. The tenth day after leaving the bay, brought us to a river, fifteen miles north of St. Francis, which we were compelled to ford against a swift current. The tallest men were put up stream, and holding by each other, the party passed over, with a loss of several guns, which were recovered by diving to the bottom.

We had now good marching ground, and proceeded to destroy the town, as before related, which would probably have been effected, with no other loss than that of the Indian killed in the action, had not our boats been discovered and our retreat that way cut off. This tribe of Indians was notoriously attached to the French, and had for a century past harassed the frontiers of New-England, murdering people of all ages and sexes, and in times of peace, when they had no reason to suspect hostile intentions. They had, within my own knowledge, during six years past, killed and carried away more than six hundred persons. We found six hundred scalps hanging upon poles over the doors of their *wigwams*.

It is impossible to describe the dejected and miserable condition of the party on arriving at the Coös *intervales*. After so long a march, over rocky, barren mountains, and through deep swamps, worn down with hunger and fatigue, we expected to be relieved at the *intervales*, and assisted in our return. (In one of these swamps a party was led about for three days by a squaw, and finally brought back to their tracks. This she did to afford the Indians an opportunity to overtake them.)

The officer dispatched to the general reached Crown Point in nine days, and faithfully discharged his commission; upon which the general ordered an officer to Number Four, to proceed from thence, with provisions, up the river to the place I had designated, and there to wait as long as there were any hopes of my return. The officer remained but two days, and returned, carrying with him all the provisions, about two hours before our arrival. (This gentleman was censured for his conduct; but that reproach afforded no consolation to the brave men to whom his negligence caused such distress and anguish; and of whom many actually died of hunger.) We found a fresh fire burning in his camp, and fired guns to bring him back, which he heard, but would not return, supposing we were an enemy.

In this emergency, I resolved to make the best of my way to Number Four, leaving the remainder of the party, now unable to proceed farther, to obtain such wretched subsistence as the wilderness afforded (ground-nuts and lily-roots, boiled, will support life), until I could relieve them, which I promised to do in ten days.

Captain Ogden, myself, and a captive Indian boy, embarked on a raft of dry pine trees. The current carried us down the stream, in the middle of which we kept our miserable vessel with such paddles as could be split and hewn with small hatchets. On the second day we reached White River falls, and narrowly escaped running over them. The raft went over and was lost; but our remaining strength enabled us to land, and pass by the falls, at the foot of which Captain Ogden and the ranger killed several red squirrels and a partridge, while I attempted to construct a new raft. Not being able to cut the trees, I burned them down, and burned them off at proper lengths. This was our third day's work after leaving our companions.

The next day we floated to Wattoquichie falls, which are about fifty yards in length. Here we landed, and Captain Ogden held the raft by a withe of hazel-bushes, while I went below to swim in, board the raft, and paddle it ashore. This was our only hope of life; for we had not strength to make another raft, should this be lost. I succeeded in securing it, and next morning we floated down to within a short distance of Number Four. Here we found several men cutting timber, who relieved and assisted us to the fort A canoe was immediately sent up the river with provisions, which reached the men at Coös in four days, being the tenth day after my departure.

Two days afterward I went up the river with two canoes, to relieve others of my party who might be coming that way. I met several parties: *viz.*, Lieutenants Cargill, Campbell and Farrington; also, Sergeant Evans, with their respective parties; and proceeding farther, fell in with several who had escaped of

Turner's and Dunbar's parties, which, twenty in number, had been overtaken and mostly taken or killed by the enemy. Expresses were sent to Suncook (Pembroke, N. H.) and Pennacook, (Concord, N. H.) upon Merrimack River, directing that any who should stray that way should be assisted. At Number Four, the following letter was received from the general.

Crown Point Nov. 8, 1759.

Sir—Captain Ogden has delivered your letter of the 5th, which I have read with great satisfaction. Every step you have taken was well judged, and deserves my approbation. I am sorry Lieutenant —— conducted so ill in coming away with the provisions, from the place where I ordered him to wait for you.

An Indian came in last night, who left some of your men at Otter river. I sent for them, and they have come in. This afternoon came in four Indians, two rangers, a German woman, and three other prisoners. They left four of your party some days since, and supposed they had arrived. I hope the residue may get in safe. The only risk will be in meeting the enemy's hunting parties.

I am, sir, your obed't serv't,

Jeff. Amherst.

After the party had recruited their strength, such as were able to march started for Crown Point, where they arrived December 1, 1769. Since leaving the ruins of St. Francis the party had lost three officers: Lieutenant Dunbar of Gage's light infantry, Lieutenant Turner of the rangers, and Lieutenant Jenkins of the provincials, with forty-six sergeants and privates.

The rangers at Crown Point were all dismissed before Roger's return, excepting two companies, commanded by Captains Johnson and Tute. The general had left him orders to continue in that garrison during the winter, with leave to proceed down the country, and wait upon him at New York. After reporting to the general at that city what intelligence he had obtained respecting the enemy, he was desired, at his leisure, to draw a plan of the march to St. Francis. He returned by way of Albany, which place he left February 6, 1760, with thirteen recruits. On the 13th, while on the way between Ticonderoga and Crown Point, he was attacked by sixty Indians, who killed five of his men, and took four prisoners. With the remaining four he escaped to Crown point, and would have pursued the party; but Colonel Haviland thought the step would be imprudent, as the garrison was very sickly.

★★★★★★

This officer was the same who sent him out in March, 1768, with a small, force, when he knew a superior one lay in wait for him. He was one of those sort of men who manage to escape public censure, let them do what they will. He ought to have been cashiered for his conduct on that occasion. He was one of the many British officers who were meanly jealous of the daring achievements of their brave American comrades, but for whose intrepidity and arduous services, all the British armies, sent to America during the seven years' war, would have effected little toward the conquest of Canada.

★★★★★★

His sleigh was taken, containing £1,196, York currency, beside stores and necessaries. Of the money, £800 belonged to the crown, which was allowed him. The remainder, £396, being his own, was lost.

March 31. Captain Tute, with two regular officers and six men, went on a scout, and were all taken prisoners. The sickness of the garrison prevented pursuit. The following letter was received from the general.

New York, March 1, 1760.

Sir—The command of his majesty, to pursue the war in this country, has determined me to complete the companies of rangers which were on foot last campaign. Captain Waite yesterday informed me that his company could easily be filled up in Massachusetts and Connecticut, and I have given him a warrant for $800, and beating orders.

I have also written to Captain John Stark, in New Hampshire, and Captain David Brewer, in Massachusetts, inclosing to each beating orders for their respective provinces. I send you a copy of their instructions, which are to send their men to Albany as fast as recruited.

Your humble servant,

Jeff. Amherst.

To Major Rogers.

(Answer.)

Crown Point, March 15, 1760.

Sir—Since the receipt of yours, I have dispatched Lieutenant McCormick, of Captain William Stark's corps, and Lieutenants Fletcher and Holmes to recruit for my own and Captain Johnson's companies. I have no doubt they will bring in good

175

men to replace those who have been frost bitten, who may be discharged or sent to the hospital. The smallness of our force has prevented any incursions to the French settlements in quest of a prisoner, which may be obtained at any time.

Yours respectfully,

R. Rogers.

March 9. The general wrote to Major Rogers that he had given a company of rangers to Captain Ogden, and to desire someone to be sent to Stockbridge to engage Lieutenant Solomon (Indian) to raise a company of Indians for the ensuing campaign. Mr. Stuart, adjutant of the rangers, was accordingly sent to explain to Solomon the conditions of the service. The Indians agreed to enter the service, but, as many of them were out hunting, they could not be collected at Albany until the 10th of May. In the meantime, the ranger companies at Crown Point were completed.

May 4. Sergeant Beverly, having escaped from Montreal, arrived at Crown Point after seven days' journey. He had lived in the house of Governor Vaudreuil, and reported that, on the tenth of April, the enemy withdrew their troops from Isle aux Noix, excepting a garrison of three hundred, under Monsieur Bonville; that they had already brought away half the cannon and ammunition; that two French frigates, of thirty-six and twenty guns, and several smaller vessels, lay all winter in the St. Lawrence; that all the French troops in Canada had concentrated at Jecortè on the 20th of April, excepting slender garrisons in their forts; all the militia who could be spared from the country, leaving one male to every two females to sow the grain, were also collected at the same place, under General Levi, who intended to retake Quebec, (taken by General Wolfe, in 1769); that ninety-nine men were drowned in their passage to Jecortè; that he saw a private, belonging to our troops, at Quebec, who was taken prisoner April 15th.

He stated that the garrison was healthy; that Brigadier General Murray had four thousand troops fit for duty in the city, and an advanced guard of three hundred men at Point Levi, which place the enemy attempted to occupy in February last with a considerable force, and began to fortify a stone church near the point; but that General Murray sent over a detachment of one thousand men, which drove the enemy from their position, with the loss of a captain and thirty French soldiers; that General Murray had another military post, of three hundred men, on the north side of the river, at Laurette, a short distance from the town; that all along the land-ward side of the town was a line of block-houses, under cover of the cannon; that a breast-work of fraziers extended from one to the other of the block-houses; that General Murray had heard that the enemy intended to beat up his quarters, but was not alarmed.

Also, that a party from Quebec surprised two of the enemy's guards at Point Trimble, who were all killed or taken, one guard being composed entirely of French grenadiers; that two more English frigates had passed up the river, and two other men-of-war lay near the Isle of Orleans; that the French told him that a fleet of ten sail of men-of-war had been seen at Gaspee bay, and had again put to sea on account of the ice, but did not know whether they were French or English; that the French intended, on the 1st of May, to draw off two thousand men to Isle aux Noix, and as many more to Oswegatchie, and did not intend to attack Quebec unless the French fleet entered the river before the English; that, on the 6th of May, one hundred Indians departed for our forts—the remainder had gone to Jecortè.

And that the Attawawa and Cold Country Indians would join General Levi in June, ten *sachems* having been dispatched last fall to solicit aid of those natives from the far north-west; that many deserters from the corps of Royal Americans are at Quebec, in the French service; that they were to be sent, under the charge of Monsieur Boarbier, up the Attawawa River to the colony between the lakes and the Mississippi; that most of the enemy's Indians intend going there; that many of the French who have money intend to secure it by going to New-Orleans; that he saw at Montreal Reynolds and Hill, who were last fall reported to Colonel Haviland as deserters—they were taken near River-head block-house while in quest of cattle; two more rangers will be here in two days with fresh tidings from Montreal, if they can escape; that Lougee, the famous partisan, was drowned in the St. Lawrence a few days after his return with the party which surprised Captain Tute.

And that the Indians keep a sharp look-out upon the Number Four roads, where they intercept plenty of sheep and cattle on their way to Crown Point. General Murray had hanged several Canadians, who were detected conveying ammunition from Quebec to the enemy; that the two Indian captains, Jacob, are still in Canada; one is with Captain Kennedy on board a vessel, in irons; the other ran away last fall, but returned, having frozen his feet; he is at Montreal.

Soon after this Major Rogers went down Lake Champlain to reconnoitre the Isle aux Noix, the landing-places, &c. He then proceeded to Albany, and gave the general all the information he possessed in regard to the passage into Canada by the Isle aux Noix; as, also, by Oswego and la Gallette.

The general, having learned by express that Quebec was besieged by the French, formed the design of sending Major Rogers, with a force, into Canada, with directions, if the siege continued, to lay waste the country, and, by marching from place to place, to endeavour to draw off the enemy's troops, and protract the siege, until the English vessels should ascend the river. He was to be governed entirely by the motions of the French Army. If the siege was raised, he was to retreat; if not, to harass the country, even at the expense of his party. The orders were as follows:

> You are to proceed with a detachment of three hundred men: *viz.*, two hundred and seventy-five rangers, with their officers, a subaltern, two sergeants, and twenty-five men from the light infantry regiments, down the lake, under convoy of the brig, and lay up your boats in a safe place upon one of the islands while executing the following orders:
>
> You will send two hundred and fifty men on the west side, in such a manner as to reach St John's without being discovered by the enemy at Isle aux Noix. You will endeavour to surprise the fort at St. John's, and destroy the vessels, boats, provisions, or whatever else may be there for the use of the troops at Isle aux Noix. You will then proceed to Chamblée, and destroy every magazine you can find in that quarter.
>
> These proceedings will soon be known at Isle aux Noix, and the enemy will endeavour to cut off your retreat; therefore, your safest course will be to cross the river, and return on the east side of the Isle aux Noix. Upon landing on the west side, you will send an officer, with fifty rangers, to Wigwam Martinique, to destroy what he may there find on both sides of the river, and then retreat. You will take such provisions as are necessary, and direct Captain Grant, with his vessels, to wait for your return at such places as you may direct.
>
> Your men should be as lightly equipped as possible. They should be strictly cautioned respecting their conduct, and obedience to their officers. There should be no firing, no unnecessary alarms, and no retreating without order. The men are to stand by each other, and nothing can injure them. Let every man who has a proper musket be furnished with a bayonet. You are not to suf-

fer the Indians to destroy women or children, nor your men to load themselves with plunder. (The Stockbridge Indians had not arrived, but orders were left for them to follow the track of Rogers.) They shall be rewarded on their return as they deserve.

Jeff. Amherst.

With these instructions the general delivered him a letter, directed to General Murray at Quebec, with orders to have it conveyed to him as soon as possible. He then returned to Crown Point, and about the 1st of June embarked from thence in four vessels, taking on board their boats and provisions, that the enemy might have no opportunity of discovering their design.

June 3. Lieutenant Holmes, with fifty men, landed at Missisqui bay, with orders to proceed to Wigwam Martinique. A sloop was directed to cruise for him, and on his return to take him and his party on board, upon his making certain signals. From this place Rogers dispatched Sergeant Beverly, with the general's letter to General Murray, with these instructions:

> You will take under your command John Shute, Luxford Goodwin, and Joseph Eastman, and proceed, under the convoy of Lieutenant Holmes, to Missisqui bay, and land in the night; otherwise, you may be discovered by a party from Isle aux Noix. You will then steer a north-easterly course, and proceed with all possible dispatch to Quebec, or to the English Army at or near that city, and deliver the letter intrusted to your care to Brigadier Murray, or the officer commanding His Majesty's forces in and upon the River St. Lawrence.
>
> You have herewith a plan of the country, that you may know the considerable rivers between Missisqui bay and Quebec. The distances are marked in the plan, as is the road I travelled last fall to St. Francis, which road you will cross several times. The rivers you will know by their descriptions, when you come to them. The River St Francis, about midway of your journey, is very still water, and may be easily rafted where you will cross it; lower down it is so rapid that its passage must not be attempted. The Chaudière River is rapid for some miles above its mouth, and should be well examined before you cross it After passing this river, lay your course east, leaving Point Levi on the left:, and strike the St. Lawrence near the lower end of the Isle of Orleans, as General Murray may possibly be encamped on that

or the Isle of Quadoa.

You are directed to look out for the English fleet, and may venture on board the first line-of-battle ship you see, whose commander will convey you to the general, who will pay you fifty pounds, and give farther orders as soon as you have rested from your march.

Major Rogers, with his party, now crossed Lake Champlain to the west shore, and, embarking in boats, on the 4th landed two hundred men twelve miles south of Isle aux Noix. Captain Grant, with his sloops, was directed to cruise down the lake near the fort, to attract the notice of the enemy until Rogers could get into the country. In consequence of the rain, and the risk of spoiling their provisions, he lay with his party, during the whole day of the 5th, concealed in bushes.

In the afternoon of that day several French boats appeared on the lake, continuing as near to our vessels as they could with safety, until after dark. Concluding these boats would watch the vessels all night, Rogers went on board after dark, in a small boat, and ordered them to retire to the Isle of Motte. The enemy, who were out all night, discovered his landing, and sent a force from the island to cut off the party. The scouts counted their number as they crossed from the fort in boats, making it three hundred and fifty men. At eleven o'clock the left of the rangers was briskly attacked. Their right was protected by a bog, which the enemy did not venture over; through which, however, by the edge of the lake, seventy rangers, under Lieutenant Farrington, passed, and fell upon their rear.

At the same time, they were attacked in front, and immediately broke. They were pursued a mile, where they separated into small parties, and took refuge in a thick cedar swamp. The rain now came on again, and the party was recalled to the boats, where they found that Ensign Wood, of the 17th regiment, had been killed, and Captain Johnson shot through the body, the left arm, and wounded in the head. Of the rangers sixteen were killed and eight wounded; two light infantry men were wounded. Forty of the French fell; their commander. Monsieur la Force was wounded (mortally), with several of his men. Fifty muskets were taken.

After the action the party embarked with their killed and wounded, and returned to the Isle of Motte, near which the brig lay. One of the vessels, having on board the corpse of Mr. Wood, and that of Captain Johnson (who died on the passage thither), was dispatched to Crown Point, with orders to return with provisions. The dead were buried upon a small island, and the party prepared for a second landing.

Being now joined by the Stockbridge Indians, Rogers determined to execute his orders, and, to conceal his motions, left the following orders for Captain Grant:

You will immediately fall down the lake, with your vessels, to Wind-mill Point, and there cruise two or three days, to attract the attention of the enemy from my motions. When I suppose you are near the point, my party will land on the west side, opposite the north end of the Isle of Motte, near the river which enters the bay at that place.

If we are not attacked, we shall return on the east side, and endeavour to join you near Windmill Point, or somewhere between that and the Isle of Motte. Our signal will be a smoke, and three guns discharged in succession, at a minute's interval, the signal to be repeated in half an hour.

But, should we be attacked before reaching our destination, in case we have the worst of it, you may expect us to make the above signals on the west side, between the Isle of Motte and the place of our action, on the 6th instant. As the time of our return is uncertain, I advise your not coming south of the Isle of Motte, as a contrary wind may prevent your getting in to my relief. Sergeant Hacket and ten rangers will remain with you during my absence. I advise you not to send parties to the island to take prisoners until the fifth day after my landing, as the loss of a man may be a serious misfortune at this time, and discover our intentions to the enemy. Mr. Holmes will probably return between the 11th and 16th days from his departure from the Missisqui bay; one of the sloops may cruise for him off the bay.

On the 9th of June, at midnight, Rogers landed, with two hundred men, on the west shore, opposite la Motte, and marched with all dispatch for St. John's. On the evening of the 15th they came to the road leading from that place to Montreal. At eleven at night they advanced within four hundred yards of the fort. The enemy was stronger than was expected, with seventeen sentinels so well posted as to render a surprise impossible.

The scout was discovered, and alarm guns fired; upon which the party retired at two o'clock, and proceeded down river to St. d'Estrées. This place was reconnoitred at daybreak. The fort was a stockade, proof against small arms, and containing two large store-houses. The enemy were carting hay into the fort, and the rangers, watching their opportunity, when a cart was entering the gateway, rushed forward from their concealment, and captured the place before the gate could be closed. In the meantime, other parties proceeded to the houses near the garrison (fifteen), which were all surprised without firing a gun. In the fort were twenty-four soldiers, and in the houses seventy-eight prisoners—men, women, and children. Several young men escaped to Chamblée.

Ascertaining, from an examination of the prisoners, that Chamblée could not be attacked with success, they burned the fort and village, with a large magazine of hay and provision. They killed all the cattle and horses; and every *batteau*, canoe, wagon, and everything which could be of service to the enemy, was destroyed. To the women and children Rogers gave a pass to Montreal, directed to all officers of the several detachments under his command. After this the party continued their march to the east side of Lake Champlain. While passing Missisqui bay, opposite the Isle aux Noix, their advanced guard engaged with that of a detachment of eight hundred French, who were in quest of them; but, as the enemy's main body was a mile behind, their advanced party retreated.

The party continued their march to the lake, where a party had been sent forward to repeat the signals, and found the boats waiting, in which they all embarked, thus escaping the enemy, who appeared in full force a few minutes after. Mr. Grant had performed his duty like an able and faithful officer, patiently waiting with his vessels, and securing the retreat of the party.

Several of the prisoners had been at the siege of Quebec, and reported that the French lost five hundred men, and, after bombarding the place twelve days, had retired to "Jack's quarters," where General Levi had left five hundred regulars and four hundred Canadians; that the remainder of his troops were quartered by threes and twos upon the inhabitants from that place to St. John's; that in Montreal one hundred troops were stationed, the inhabitants themselves performing duty; that Chamblee fort contained one hundred and fifty men, workmen included; that the remnant of the Queen's regiment were in the village; that St. John's fort had twelve cannon and three hundred men, including workmen, who were obliged to take up arms at a moment's notice; that three hundred men and one hundred pieces of cannon were stationed at the Isle aux Noix.

On the 21st the twenty-six prisoners, under a guard of fifty men, were dispatched in a vessel to Crown Point, the others of the party remaining to cover Mr. Holmes' retreat He joined them the same evening, having failed in his enterprise by mistaking a river which falls into the Sorelle for that called Wigwam Martinique, which falls into the St. Lawrence near St. Francis. On the 23rd the party reached Crown Point, and encamped on Chimney Point, directly opposite.

The general wrote to Rogers, from Canajoharie, soon after his return, expressing his satisfaction of his conduct in this enterprise. Preparations were made for the army to advance into Canada, and, on the 16th of August, the embarkation was effected in the order following: Six hundred rangers and seventy Indians, in whale-boats, formed the advanced guard, at the distance of half a mile from the main body. Next followed the light infantry and grenadiers in two columns, under Colonel Darby. The right wing was composed of provincials, commanded by Brigadier Ruggles (of Boston), who was second in command. The left was made up of New-Hampshire and Boston troops, under Colonel Thomas. The 17th and 27th regiments formed the centre column under Major Campbell. Colonel Haviland was posted in front of these, between the light infantry and grenadiers. The Royal Artillery, under Colonel Orde, followed in four *rideaux*.

In this order the troops moved down the lake forty miles the first day, and encamped on the west side. On the 18th, embarking with a fresh south wind, they proceeded within ten miles of the Isle of Motte. The roughness of the water split one of the rangers' boats, by which accident ten were downed.

On the 9th the army encamped on the Isle of Motte. On the 20th they proceeded twenty-two miles farther, and came in sight of the French fort. At ten o'clock a.m. Colonel Darby landed his infantry and grenadiers, the rangers following without opposition, and occupied the ground over against the fort. Batteries were raised the next day, and shells thrown into the place.

On the 25th Colonel Darby proposed to capture the enemy's *rideaux* and vessels lying at anchor. Two companies of regulars, four of rangers, and the Indians, were selected for the service, under Colonel Darby. Two light howitzers and a six-pounder were silently conveyed through the trees, and brought to bear upon the vessels before the enemy were aware of the design. The first shot from the six-pounder cut the cable of the great *rideau*, and the wind blew her to the east shore, where the English party were stationed. The other vessels weighed anchor, and steered for St. John's, but grounded in turning a point two miles from the fort. Rogers then led a party down the east shore, and, crossing a river thirty yards wide, arrived opposite the vessels.

From thence a portion of his men kept up a fire, while others, armed with tomahawks, swam off and boarded one of them. In the meantime, Colonel Darby captured the *rideau*, had her manned, and secured the other two. Colonel Haviland sent down men to work the vessels, and ordered the party to join the army that night.

At midnight the French evacuated the island, and reached the main land, leaving their sick behind. Next morning Colonel Haviland took possession of the fort.

On the second day after Monsieur Bonville's retreat, Colonel Haviland ordered the rangers to pursue him as far as St. John's, about twenty miles down the lake, and await the arrival of the army, but by no means to approach nearer to Montreal.

At daylight they reached St. John's in boats. The place was on fire, and the enemy had retreated. Two prisoners informed that Monsieur Bonville was that night to encamp half way on the road to Montreal; that he left St John's at nine o'clock the night before; that many of his troops were sick, and they thought some of them would not reach the place of encampment until late in the afternoon. It was now seven o'clock in the morning, and a portion of the men were directed to fortify the houses standing near the lake shore, while the remainder should pursue Monsieur Bonville. At eight o'clock Rogers left the boats, under the protection of two hundred rangers, while, with four hundred others and the two Indian companies, he pursued the track of the French Army, now consisting of fifteen hundred French and one hundred Indians.

Rogers followed with such diligence as to overtake their rear guard of two hundred men two miles before they reached their ground of encampment. They were immediately attacked, broken, and pursued to the main body. (In this attack the rangers fired the last hostile guns for the conquest of Canada. This was the finishing skirmish.) The rangers pursued in good order, expecting General Bonville would make a stand. But, instead of this, he pushed forward to the river, where he intended to encamp; which he crossed, and broke down the bridge, thus putting a stop to the pursuit. The enemy encamped within a good breast-work, which had been prepared for their reception. In the pursuit the rangers lessened their numbers, and returned in safety. In the evening Colonel Haviland's detachment arrived at St. John's, and next day proceeded down the Sorelle as far as St. d'Estrées, and fortified their camp.

From this place Rogers proceeded, with his rangers, down the Sorelle, to bring the inhabitants under subjection to his Britannic majesty. They entered the settled parts of the country by night, collected all the priests and militia officers, and directed them to assemble all the inhabitants who were willing to surrender their arms, take the oath of allegiance, and keep their possessions. After this he joined. Colonel Darby, at Chamblée, where he had brought several pieces of light artillery to reduce the fort; but, as the garrison consisted of but fifty men, they soon after surrendered at discretion.

September 2. The army having nothing farther to perform, and favourable intelligence having been received from Generals Amherst and Murray, Major Rogers, with the rangers, was detached to join the latter, and on the 6th reached Longueville, four miles below Montreal, and next morning reported himself to General Murray, whose camp was directly opposite. General Amherst had at this time arrived, and landed his army within about two miles of the city. Early in the morning General Vaudreuil, the commander-in-chief of all the Canadas, proposed to General Amherst a capitulation.

The articles of surrender were signed on the 8th, and on the same evening the English troops took possession of the gates of Montreal. Next morning the light infantry and grenadiers of the whole army, under Colonel Haldiman, with two pieces of cannon and several howitzers, entered the city. Among the trophies here recovered were the colours of Pepperell's and Shirley's regiments, which had been captured at Oswego. Thus, at the end of five campaigns, the whole Canadian territory became subject to the King of Great Britain.

On the 12th of September General Amherst issued the following orders:

By His Excellency, Jeffrey Amherst, Esquire, Major General and Commander-in-Chief of His Majesty's Forces in North-America, &c.

To Major Rogers, of His Majesty's Independent Companies of Rangers:

You will, upon receipt of this, proceed with Waite's and Hazen's companies of rangers to Fort William Augustus, taking with you one Joseph Poupao, *alias* la Fleur, an inhabitant of Detroit, and Lieutenant Brheme, assistant engineer.

From that fort you will continue your voyage by the north shore to Niagara, thence transporting your boats over the carrying-place to Lake Erie. Major Walters, commanding at Niagara, will render you any assistance you may require, and deliver up Monsieur Gamelin, who was made prisoner at the taking of that fortress, to be conducted, with said la Fleur, to their habitations at Detroit; where, upon taking the oath of allegiance to His Majesty, whose subjects they have become by the capitulation of the 8th, they are to be protected in the peaceable enjoyment of their property.

You will next proceed to Presque Isle, (Erie, Pennsylvania), and make known your orders to the commander of that post. You will there leave your whale-boats and most of your detachment, proceeding with the remainder to join General Monckton, wherever he may be. Deliver him your dispatches, and obey such orders as he may give you for relieving the garrisons of Detroit, Michilimackinac, and their dependencies; for collecting the arms of the inhabitants, and administering the oath of allegiance. This you will see administered to the said Poupao. You are to bring away the French troops and arms to such place as General Monckton shall direct. After completing this service, you will march your detachment back to Presque Isle or Niagara, according to the orders you receive from General Monckton, and, leaving your boats in charge of the officer at one of those posts, march your detachment by land to Albany, or wherever I may be, to receive farther orders.

Given under my hand, at headquarters, in the camp at Montreal, 12th September, 1760.

Jeff. Amherst.

By His Excellency's command—

J. Appy, Sec'y.

An additional order was given him, to be shown only to commanders of the different posts he might touch at. The objects of the expedition were to be kept secret, lest the Indians, through whose country he must pass, should impede his march. The order was as follows:

Major Walters, or the commander at Niagara, will judge whether there is sufficient provision at Presque Isle, and Major Rogers will accordingly take provisions from Niagara or not, as the case may be. The route from Montreal to Fort William Augustus will require eight days' provisions; from that post he will take a sufficient quantity to proceed to Niagara. Major Rogers knows whither he is going, and what provisions he will want. A quantity should also be in store at Presque Isle, for the party General Monckton will send.

Jeff. Amherst.

Montreal, 12th September, 1760.

September 13, 1760. In pursuance of these orders. Major Rogers and his party embarked at Montreal, in fifteen whale-boats. The detachments consisted of Captains Brewer and Waite, Lieutenant Brheme, of the engineers, Lieutenant Davis, of the royal artillery, and two hundred rangers. At night they encamped at La Chien. Next morning, they reached Isle de Prairies, and surveyed the Indian settlements at Cayawaga and Canasedaga.

September 16th. They reached an island in lake St. Francis, and the next night encamped on the western shore, at the foot of the upper rifts. Next day they ascended the rifts, and passed the night on the north shore, opposite a number of islands.

September 19th. At evening they reached the Isle de Galettes, and spent the next day in repairing the boats which had been damaged in passing the rapids. Ten sick rangers were sent to Colonel Fitch, at Oswego, to proceed thence to Albany.

September 21st. At twelve o'clock they left the island, but the wind being unfavourable, they passed Oswegatchie, and encamped three miles above, on the north shore.

September 22nd. The course was continued up the river, and the party halted in the evening, at the narrow passes near the islands. The wind abating, at midnight they embarked, rowed the remainder of the night and the next day, until they reached the ruins of old Fort Frontenac, where a party of Indian hunters from Oswegatchie were encamped. The next day proving stormy, with snow and rain squalls, the engineer took a plan of the old fort, situated at the bottom of a fine safe harbour. Five hundred acres had been cleared around the fort; a few pine trees were still standing, and the situation was pleasant. The soil, though covered with clover, appeared rocky and barren. The Indians were highly pleased with the news of the surrender of Canada, and supplied plenty of venison and wild fowl.

September 25th. They steered S. two miles, then W. six miles, to the mouth of a river thirty feet wide; thence S. four miles, where the party halted to refresh. In the afternoon they steered for a mountain, bearing S. W., which was reached in the night, and proved to be a steep rock, one hundred feet high. They rowed all night, and breakfasted on shore at eight next morning. They then proceeded, and at eight in the evening were one hundred miles from Frontenac.

September 27th. This day being windy, the party hunted and killed many deer. The land was poor and rocky, as is generally the case on the north shore of Lake Ontario. The timber is chiefly hemlock and pine.

September 28th. They steered S. W., leaving on the right a large bay, twenty miles wide, the western side of which terminates in a point, and a small island. Proceeding fifteen miles W. by 8., they entered the mouth of a river, called by the Indians the "Grace of Man;" there they encamped, and found fifty Mississaqua Indians fishing for salmon. Upon the first appearance of the boats, the whole party ran down to the shore to testify their joy at the sight of English colours, and fired their muskets until the party landed. They presented the major with a deer, just killed, and split in halves, with the skin on, which is a significant token of their great respect. They pretended to be well pleased with the success of the English.

In the evening they invited the men to fish with them. They went out, and in half an hour filled a bark canoe with salmon. They returned, much pleased with the sport, and the attentions of their tawny companions. Their mode of taking the fish was a curious one: one person held a pine torch, while another struck the fish with a spear. The soil near the river was good, and the country level. The timber was chiefly oak and maple, or the sugar tree.

September 29th. The party proceeded fifteen miles farther on a W. S. W. course, and came to a river called "the Life of Man." Here twenty Mississaquas were hunting, and paid them compliments similar to those of their brethren. They presented Major Rogers with a young bear, split in halves. The rangers here caught plenty of salmon. The land was level, the soil rich, and of a dark colour. The shore of the lake was quite low.

September 30th. The wind was fair, and, by the aid of sails, they reached Toronto in the evening, having run seventy miles. Many long points, extending into the lake, caused frequent alterations of their course. They passed a bank twenty miles long, behind which was a heavy growth of oak, hickory, maple, poplar, and white wood. The soil was principally clay. A tract of three hundred acres, cleared, surrounded the remains of the old fort of Toronto. Deer were plenty.

A party of Indians, at the mouth of the river, fled to the woods, but returned next morning, expressing great joy at the news of the success over the French. They said that the party could reach Detroit in eight days; that, when the French resided here, the Indians brought furs from Michilimackinac down the river Toronto; that the portage was only twenty miles from that to a river falling into Lake Huron, which was broken by several falls, but none of any consequence; and that there was a carrying-place of fifteen miles, from some westerly part of Lake Erie to a river running through several Indian towns, without any falls, into Lake St. Clair. Toronto appeared an eligible place for a factory, from which the British government might easily settle the north side of Lake Erie.

October 1. They steered south, across the west end of Lake Ontario, and reached the shore four miles from Fort Niagara, where they passed the night, and repaired the boats.

October 2. The party embarked with orders for the boats to be in line; and, if the wind should rise, a red flag was to be hoisted, upon which signal the boats were to close, so as to be enabled to assist each other in case of leaks. By this measure Lieutenant McCormick's boat's crew was saved, with no other loss than the men's knapsacks. They halted next day at Niagara, and were supplied with blankets, coats, shoes, shirts, *moccasins*, &c. They also received eighty barrels of beef, and exchanged two whale-boats for as many *batteaux*, which proved leaky.

October 3. In the evening a party proceeded up the Niagara river seven miles, to the falls, with provisions. Next morning, they were followed by the whole detachment, who immediately commenced the portage of the baggage and provisions. While they were thus occupied, Messrs. Brheme and Davis took a survey of the great cataract of Niagara, the roaring of which had been heard at several miles distance.

Modern travellers who yearly visit this, one of the grandest creations of nature, can imagine the arduous labours of these hardy rangers in transporting their boats and baggage up the bank of this river, from the foot of the cataract, which is one hundred and fifty feet in height, to ascend which, even at the present time, without a load, by aid of steps and stairs, is a laborious undertaking.

The rangers were more than one day engaged in conveying their boats and baggage round the falls. On the fifth of October Rogers, with Lieutenants Brheme, Holmes and eight rangers embarked, in a birch-bark canoe, for Presque Isle, leaving Captain Brewer in command, with orders to follow to the same post. Rogers encamped that night eight miles up the Niagara River, and at noon next day entered the waters of Lake Erie. Leaving a small bay, (now Buffalo harbour), or creek upon his left, he reached the south shore at sunset, and, thence proceeding west until eight o'clock, drew up his canoe on a sandy beach, forty miles from the last night's encampment.

October 7. The wind being fresh, he made but twenty-eight miles in a south-west course.

October 8. Pursuing a southerly course, he reached Presque Isle in the afternoon. Here the party remained until three o'clock, when the eight rangers were sent back to meet and assist Captain Brewer; while, with three men, in a bark canoe furnished by Colonel Bouquet, commander of the post, Rogers, with Messrs. Bhreme and Holmes, proceeded to French Creek, and that night encamped half way on the road to Fort du Boeuf, which they reached at ten o'clock next day. After three hours' rest they passed on to the lower crossings. The land on both sides appeared rich, and covered with large and valuable timber. They passed the night of the 11th at the Mingo Cabins, and on the 12th lodged at Venango.

Thence they proceeded down the Alleghany River, and, on the 17th delivered their dispatches to General Monckton, at Pittsburg. The general promised to forward his instructions by Mr. Croghan, and to dispatch Captain Campbell, with a company of Royal Americans, to his support. On the 20th Rogers started on his return to Presque Isle, which he reached October 30th. Mr. Brewer had arrived there three days before, having lost several boats and part of the provisions. Captain Campbell arrived next day.

The boats were now repaired, and Rogers, having learned that a vessel expected from Niagara, with provisions, had been lost in a gale on the lake, dispatched Captain Brewer, with a drove of forty cattle supplied by Colonel Bouquet, to proceed by land to Detroit. Mr. Waite was sent back to Niagara for more provisions, and directed to cruise along the north shore of Lake Erie, and wait for farther orders about twenty miles east of the strait, between Lake St. Clair and Lake Erie.

Captain Brewer was furnished with a *bateau* to ferry his party over the creeks, two horses, and Captain Monter, with twenty Indians of the Six Nations, Delawares, and Shawanese, to protect him from the hostile tribes of the west. The following order of march was adopted on the re-embarkment of the party from Presque Isle:

The boats are to row two deep—Major Rogers' and Captain Croghan's boats in front; next Captain Campbell's corps, followed by the rangers—Lieutenant Holmes commanding the rear guard with his own boat; and that of Mr. Waite will hold himself in readiness to assist any boat in distress. Should the wind blow so hard that the boats cannot preserve their order, a red flag will be hoisted in the major's boat. The other boats will then steer for the flag, and make their landing as well as may be. Officers and men were advised to pay no attention to the waves of the lake, but, when the surf was high, to ply their oars, and the men at the helms to keep the boats quartering, in which case no injury can happen. Ten of the best steersmen of the rangers will attend Captain Campbell's party. The officers of the boats will hearken to the steersmen in all cases in a storm. If thought best to proceed in the night, a blue flag will be hoisted in the major's boat, which is the signal for the boats to dress. Mr. Brheme is to pay no regard to this order of march, but to steer as is most convenient for making his observations.

On landing, the regulars are to encamp in the centre; Lieutenant Holmes and Mr. Croghan, with their men, on the left wing; and Mr, Joquipe with his Mohegans, will constitute a picket, and encamp in front. The *generale* shall be beat, when ordered by the major, as the signal for embarking. No guns are to be fired unless by permission, or in case of distress. No man must leave the lines unless by order. Captain Campbell will parade and review his men as often as he thinks proper. Mr. Croghan will regularly report to the major the intelligence received from the Indians during the day.

November 4. The detachment left Presque Isle, and, proceeding slowly, with bad weather, reached Chogagee River on the 7th, where they met a party of Attawawas returning from Detroit. They were informed of the reduction of the Canadas, and that this party were on their way to Detroit to bring away the French garrison. Rogers offered them a belt, and proposed to them to go with him and witness the result. They retired to hold a council, promising an answer next day. In the evening the calumet or pipe of peace was smoked, all the officers and Indians smoking in turn from the same pipe. The peace being thus concluded, the party went to rest; but, as the sincerity of the Indians was doubted, a strict guard was kept. In the morning the Indians said their young warriors would go, while the old ones would stay and hunt for their families.

Rogers gave them a string of *wampum*, and charged them to send some of their chiefs with the party who drove the cattle on shore, to spread the news of his arrival, and prevent any annoyance from their hunters. Bad weather detained the English party here until the 12th, during which time the Indians held a plentiful market of venison and wild turkeys in their camp. After passing the mouths of several small streams, the party reached a small river a few miles beyond Sandusky, and encamped. From this place a letter was dispatched to the commandant of Detroit, as follows:

> Sir—That you may not be alarmed at the approach of English troops, I send this in advance, by Lieutenant Bhreme, to inform you that I have General Amherst's orders to take possession of Detroit and its dependencies, which, according to a capitulation, signed on the 8th of September last by the Marquis de Vaudreuil and General Amherst, now belong to his Britannic Majesty. I have with me letters from the Marquis de Vaudreuil to you directed, which I will deliver on arriving at or near your fort. I have also a copy of the capitulation.
>
> I am, sir, your obed't serv't,
>
> R. Rogers.

To Captain Beleter.

The land on the south shore of Lake Erie has a fine appearance. The country is mostly level, and heavily timbered with oak, hickory, maple, beach, and locust; and for plenty and variety of game was at this time not surpassed by any country in the world.

On the 20th of November Rogers followed Mr. Bhreme, proceeding nine miles to a river three hundred feet wide. Here several Huron *sachems* gave information that four hundred Indian warriors were assembled at the mouth of the strait to oppose his passage, and that Monsieur Beleter had incited them to defend their country; and that themselves were messengers to demand his business, and whether the person sent forward told the truth that all Canada was surrendered to the English. Rogers confirmed the account. He told them that Detroit was to be given up to him, gave them a large belt, and spoke as follows:

> Brothers, with this belt I take you by the hand. Go to your people at the strait, and tell them to go home to their towns until I arrive at the fort. There I will send for you, after Monsieur Beleter is sent away, which will be in two days after my arrival. You shall live happily in your own country. Tell your warriors to mind their French fathers no more, for they are all prison-

ers to the English, who have left them their houses and goods upon their swearing by the Great One, who made the world, to become as Englishmen. They are your brothers, and you must not abuse them. When we meet at Detroit, I will convince you that what I say is true.

November 22. The party encamped upon a river twenty yards wide, where fuel was procured with difficulty, the western shore of Lake Erie abounding in swamps. Next day they rowed ten miles to Cedar point. Here several Indians they had seen the day before came to them. They said their warriors had gone up to Monsieur Beleter, who was a strong man, and intended to fight. On the 24th the party proceeded twenty-four miles, and encamped upon a long point. That night sixty Indians came with congratulations, and offered to escort them to Detroit. They reported that Mr. Bhreme and his party were confined, and that Monsieur Beleter had set up a high flag-staff, with a wooden effigy of a man's head at the top of it, and upon that a crow; that the crow meant himself, and the head meant Rogers, whose brains he should pick out. This, they said, had no effect on them, for they told him the reverse would be the true sign. At the mouth of the strait the *sachems* desired Rogers to call together his officers. He did so, and the 26th was spent in conciliating their savage dispositions to peace and friendship. On the 27th Monsieur Babec brought the following letter:

Sir—I have read your letter, but, having no interpreter, cannot fully understand it. Your officer informs me that he was sent to give notice of your arrival to take possession of this post, according to the capitulation of Canada. I beg you will halt at the mouth of the river, and send me Monsieur Vaudreuil's letter, that I may conform to his instructions. I am surprised that no French officer accompanies you, as is usual in such cases.

I have the honour, &c.,

De Beleter.

To Major Rogers.

Soon after this Captain Barrenger, with a French party, beat a *parley* on the western shore. Mr. McCormick went over to him, and returned with an officer, bearing the following letter:

Sir—I have already, by Mr. Barrenger, informed you the reasons why I could not answer particularly your letter delivered by your officer on the 22nd. I am unacquainted with his reasons for not returning to you. I have sent my Huron interpreter to that nation to stop them, should they be on the road, not knowing whether they are disposed in your favour or my own; and to direct them to behave peaceably; to inform them that I knew my duty to my general, and should conform to his orders. Be not surprised, sir, if you find the inhabitants of this coast upon their guard. They were told you had several Indian nations with you, and had promised them the plunder of the place. I have, therefore, directed the inhabitants to take up arms, which may be for your safety as well as ours; for, should these Indians become insolent, you may not be able to subdue them alone.

I flatter myself, sir, that when this comes to hand, you will send some of your gentlemen with Monsieur Vaudreuil's letter and the capitulation.

I have the honour to be, &c.,

Pign. Beleter.

To Major Rogers.

November 28. The detachment encamped five miles up the river, having rowed against the wind. On the 29th Captain Campbell, with Messieurs Barrenger and Babec, were dispatched with this letter:

Sir—I acknowledge the receipt of your two letters yesterday. Mr. Bhreme has not yet returned. The enclosed letter from Monsieur Vaudreuil will inform you of the surrender of Canada; of the indulgence granted the inhabitants, and the terms allowed to the troops of His most Christian Majesty. Captain Campbell will show you the capitulation. I beg you will not detain him, as I have General Amherst's orders immediately to relieve the place. My troops will halt without the town till four o'clock, when I shall expect your answer. Your inhabitants being under arms will not surprise me, as I have as yet seen no others in that condition, excepting savages awaiting my orders. The inhabitants of Detroit shall not be molested, they and you complying with the capitulation. They shall be protected in their estates, and shall not be pillaged by my Indians, nor yours who have joined me.

Yours, &c.,

R. Rogers.

To Captain De Beleter, Commander of Detroit.

The detachment landed half a mile below the fort, and drew up in front of it in a field of grass. Here Captain Campbell joined them, with a French officer, who, with Captain Beleter's compliments, informed Major Rogers that the garrison was at his command. Lieutenants Mc-Cormick and Leslie, with thirty-six Royal Americans, immediately took possession of the fort. The troops of the garrison piled their arms; the French flag was hauled down, and that of the English run up in its place. Upon this about seven hundred Indians, who were looking on at a little distance, gave a shout, exulting in the verification of their prophecy that the crow represented the English instead of the French. They appeared astonished at the submissive salutations of the inhabitants, and expressed great satisfaction at the generosity of the English in not putting them all to death.

They declared that in future they would fight for a nation thus favoured by the Great Spirit. The commander delivered Major Rogers a plan of the fort, with an inventory of the stores and armament, and before noon of December 1st the militia had been collected, disarmed, and taken the oath of allegiance. Monsieur Beleter and his troops were ordered to Philadelphia, under the charge of Lieutenant Holmes and thirty rangers. Captain Campbell, with the Royal Americans, was ordered to garrison the fort. Captain Waite and Lieutenant Butler were detached, with twenty men, to bring the French garrisons from Forts Miami and Gatanois. A party was directed to remain there, if possible, through the winter, to watch the enemy's motions in Illinois. Mr. McKee, with a French officer, was sent to Shawanese Town, on the Ohio, to bring off the French troops.

As provisions grew scarce at Detroit, Captain Brewer, with most of the rangers, was ordered to Niagara, leaving Lieutenant McCormick, with thirty-seven privates, to accompany Major Rogers to Michilimackinac. Rogers concluded a treaty with the several tribes living in the vicinity of Detroit, and departed for Lake Huron.

December 10. He encamped at the north end of Lake St. Clair, and the next evening at the entrance of a considerable river, where a large body of Indians were hunting.

December 12. He came to the entrance of Lake Huron, and met many Indians hunting on both sides of the outlet He coasted along the west shore for three days, making one hundred miles, when the ice cakes obstructed his farther passage. He consulted the Indians as to the practicability of a journey to Michilimackinac by land. They declared it an impossibility at this season without snow-shoes. Rogers was therefore obliged to return. He was so impeded by the ice, that he did not reach Detroit until the 21st of December.

December 23. Rogers left the command of Detroit to Captain Campbell, and departed for Pittsburg. He marched along the lake shore, and reached Sandusky January 2, 1761. The soil from Detroit is excellent, being well timbered with black and white oak, hickory, locust, maple, sassafras, and white wood. Several immense black walnuts are also found on the south shore of Lake Erie. (One of these trees stood, in 1824, near Cataraugus Creek, N.Y., which was thirty feet in circumference. The trunk was hollow, and used for a refreshment shop for travellers passing along the road. A section of it was afterward carried down the New York canal to place in a bar-room at New York.)

Along the west end of Lake Erie Rogers reports that plenty of wild apples were found. He passed through many rich savannahs (or prairies), of many miles' extent, without a tree, and clothed with long jointed grass, nearly six feet high, which, decaying every year, adds fertility to the soil. Sandusky bay is fifteen miles long, and about six miles wide. Here Rogers halted to refresh at a village of Wyandots. The next day he passed through a meadow, saw several *wigwams*, and halted at a small village of ten *wigwams*. Here he saw a spring issuing from the side of a small hill, with such force as to rise three feet. He judged that it discharged ten hogsheads in a minute. He continued his march through the prairies, killing plenty of deer and wild turkeys, and encamped in the woods.

January 4. He crossed a river twenty-five yards wide, where were two *wigwams*. A few yards onward, in a south-east course, he came to another *wigwam* of Wyandots who were hunting there. From this he proceeded south, and crossed the same river he passed in the morning. Several deer were killed during the day's march.

January 5. He encamped on Muskingum Creek, there eight yards wide.

January 6. He travelled fourteen miles farther, and encamped by a fine spring.

January 7. After travelling six miles he came to Muskingum creek, there twenty yards wide; and an Indian town, called the Mingo Cabins, lies about twenty yards from the creek on the east side. Only three Indians were at home, the remainder being out on a hunting party. They had plenty of cows, horses, hogs, &c.

January 8. This day was passed with the Indians, repairing moccasins and preparing provisions.

January 9. The party travelled twelve miles south-east, and encamped on a long meadow, where the Indians were hunting.

January 10. They made eleven miles, and on their march killed three bears and two elks.

January 11. They fell in with a party of Wyandot and Six Nations Indians hunting together.

January 12. They travelled six miles, and in the evening killed several beavers.

January 13. The party travelled six miles north-east, and came to Beaver Town, a village of the Delawares. The town covers a good tract of land, on the west side of the Muskingum, which is joined by a river opposite the town. The latter is thirty yards wide, and the former forty. Their junction forms a fine stream, which flows with a swift current toward the south-west. The Indians have here three thousand acres of land cleared. The warriors number one hundred and eighty. The country from Sandusky to this place is low and rich. No pine timber was noticed, but plenty of white, black, and yellow oak, black and white walnut, cypress, chestnut, and locust. The party rested here until the 16th, and obtained a supply of corn from the Indians.

January 16. They marched nine miles to a small river.

January 19. After passing several creeks, they came to a small river where the Delawares were hunting.

January 20. They reached Beaver creek in sight of the Ohio. Three Indian *wigwams* were seen on the west side.

January 21. They travelled south-east twenty miles, and encamped with the Indians.

January 25. They reached the Ohio, opposite Fort Pitt. From this post Lieutenant McCormick was ordered to cross the country to Albany, with the rangers, while Major Rogers proceeded by the common road over the mountains to Philadelphia, and thence to New York, where he reported his proceedings to General Amherst February 14, 1761.

Extracts from General Orders in the Campaign of 1759.

June 12, 1759. "It is the general's orders that no scouting parties or others in the army under his command shall, whatsoever opportunity they have, scalp any women or children belonging to the enemy. They may bring them away if they can; but, if not, they are to leave them unhurted; and he is determined that, if they should murther or scalp any women or children who are subjects of the King of England, he will revenge it by the death of two men of the enemy, whenever he has occasion, for every man, woman, or child murthered by the enemy."

June 22, 1759. "Commanding officers may send their men for greens; but they must go only a short distance from the fort, and never without a covering party. No soldier, except with a party, is to go beyond the outposts of the camp."

June 24. "Effects of late Lieutenant Watts, of late Forbes' regiment, to be sold at auction at the head of the colours of said regiment."

The following extract from general orders regards a field of green peas, in the vicinity of Crown Point, August 5, 1759:

As there is a field of pease found, they shall be divided amongst the army; and the corps are to send tomorrow two men per company with arms, a sergeant per regiment, and an officer per brigade; each corps and the artillery taking two *batteaux*, and assembling in the front of the fort at five in the morning. Gage's light infantry sends a captain, two subalterns, and a partie of men in the English boat, with the three-pounder, to cover the *batteaux*; Lieutenant Willamoze to shew where the pease are; and major of brigade, Skeene, will proportion out the quantity each regiment is to take, taking care that they pluck them properly, and to take none but what is fit to be gathered, and that they do not spoil them in gathering them. They are then to return altogether to camp; and the pease muste be equallie divided amongst the messes.

Similar parties were frequently sent out to obtain spruce for brewing beer for the army.

EXTRACT FROM GENERAL ORDERS, AUGUST 6, 1759:

An officer and fifty rangers to assemble at Gage's light infantry at five o'clock tomorrow morning. They will take six *batteaux*, and proceed two miles down the lake, where they will cut spruce. The officer will take the French prisoner who is on the general's guard, who will shew him where the spruce is; and a man who can talk German to the interpreter. A party of Gage's light infantry will go in the English boat to guard the *batteaux*. The officer will deliver the spruce under the care of the sergeant's guard at the fort.

★★★★★★

Opposition writers for the British press, commenting upon the slow progress of General Amherst, insinuated that if, instead of wasting so much time in gathering peas and brewing spruce beer, at Crown Point, he had advanced into Canada to cooperate with the expedition of the daring and heroic Wolfe, the campaign of 1759 would have terminated with the capitulation of Canada the same season which witnessed the surrender of Quebec.

★★★★★★

Extracts from General Orders to Major Rogers.

June 9. "Major Rogers will furnish forty men for a covering party."

June 17. "Major Rogers will take care the ground in front is clear;" meaning the ground where the provincials who were not marksmen were to fire five rounds each for practice, officers of their several regiments attending to see that the men levelled well.

June 20. "Major Rogers, with the rangers, and Major Gladwin, with Gage's light infantry, will form the advanced guard, and are to take great precautions in keeping out flanking parties to the left, as well as to the right."

June 22. "Major Rogers is on all detachments to take rank as major, according to the date of his commission as such, next after majors who have the king's commission, or one from his majesty's commander-in-chief."

June 25. "The three eldest companies of light infantry under Major Holmes, two hundred rangers and Indians under Major Rogers, the whole under the command of Colonel Haviland, to be ready to march when dark."

July 16. 1759. "Eight of the provincial regiments are to give thirteen men each, and two of the provincial regiments fourteen men, for the ranging service; the men to be told they will be paid for it the difference between the provincial pay and that of the rangers. Commanding officers of those battalions to turn out all volunteers willing to serve in the rangers tomorrow morning at ten o'clock. Major Rogers will attend, and choose the number each regiment is to turn out of such volunteers."

July 18. "The men that have chose to serve with the rangers to join them this afternoon at five o'clock, and follow such orders as they shall receive from Major Rogers."

Ticonderoga, 25 July, 1759. "Sixty of Major Rogers' rangers will march with the commanding officer to the trenches this night, and will be employed at a proper time to alarm the enemy, by firing into their covered way, and keeping their attention from the workmen."

July 27. "Major Rogers will send a company of rangers tomorrow morning, with all the boats, to the fort. The companies posted on the lake side from Colonel Haviland's corps will join their corps at reveille beating; after which Major Rogers will put trees across the foot path that has been made by the lake side. Major Rogers will receive his orders from the general. . . . . Major Ord will send this night for the two twelve-pounders that are at Major Rogers' camp."

July 28. "The rangers will be posted beyond the sawmills, on the right, as ordered by Major Rogers."

August 4. "Major Rogers is to send a sufficient party of men, with an officer, to take three *batteaux* tomorrow morning, very early, to Ticonderoga to apply to Serjeant Airy, who will load them with spruce beer, which they are immediately to bring to camp here."

August 5. "The camp not be alarmed by Major Rogers firing on the other side of the lake."

August 6. "Major Rogers to send a party of men, with an officer, to take two *batteaux* immediately to Ticonderoga, to apply to Serjeant Airy for spruce beer, which they are to load and bring to camp here without the loss of time.

"Major Rogers will send one captain, two subalterns, and sixty men as a covering party, with some Indians, and an officer with them, to shew the commanding officer of the working party the best wood on the other side of the lake. The covering party must not fire any dropping shots at game.

"A captain and sixty rangers to set out tomorrow morning, at 5 o'clock, with six *batteaux*; Gage's light infantry will send at the same time the English boat to cover the *batteaux*, and the English boat to stay out till towards evening. The captain of the rangers will take out the French deserter from the general's guard, and must go to the place that the deserter will shew him; at which place the French have supplied themselves with spruce, and they must bring as much spruce to camp as they can."

August 10. "A detachment of two hundred rangers, and one hundred of Gage's light infantry, and one company of light infantry, and one of grenadiers, to assemble tomorrow, in their whale-boats, as soon as reveille is beat in the front of the fort. Gage's light infantry will be commanded by a captain and three subalterns, and are to take the two boats, with the three-pounders, and one boat, with a two-pounder. The whole must take one day's provision with them. Major Rogers will command the rangers; and the whole detachment is to be commanded by Lieut. Col. Darby, who will receive his orders from the general."

PUNISHMENTS INFLICTED DURING THE CAMPAIGN OF 1759.

	Shot or hanged.	Whipped.
May 29	3	0
June 14	1	5
" 28	0	1
July 13	1	0
" 19	0	7
August 2	2	3
" 8	0	1
" 14	0	2
October 4	1	1
	8	20

Commissary Wilson' Orderly Book.

Thomas Burnside

Thomas Burnside was one of the celebrated corps of rangers whose exploits contributed a very important portion of materials for the history of the "seven years' war" in America. If His Majesty, Frederic of Prussia, acted during that war, in Europe, the part of general, as he may be considered, for his cousin and ally, George of England, humbler individuals in America were striving to attain the same object—that of humbling the power of France.

Among those individuals was Mr. Burnside. Although reported as wounded in the bloody skirmish near Ticonderoga, January 21, 1767, he volunteered, as an attendant of Lieutenant Stark, to convey the account of it to Fort William Henry, a distance of forty miles, and request sleighs to bring in the wounded.

After the peace of 1763, he settled at Stratford, in Coös County, N. H., and soon afterward that township contained two inhabitants—Mr. Burnside and his neighbour ———. The former, desirous of becoming one of his majesty's justices of the peace, inquired of the facetious Colonel Barr, of Londonderry, how he should proceed to obtain his commission. He advised him to procure a firkin of butter, and a piece of Londonderry linen, both of Scotch Irish manufacture, as presents to Governor Wentworth, and proceed to Portsmouth and make his application in person.

Accordingly, with his presents, he called upon Governor Wentworth, at his seat (Little Harbor), and preferred his request. The latter inquired how many inhabitants the township contained. Burnside replied, "Oh, only me and my neighbour, and we cannot live any longer without a justice of the peace."

Amused by this most singular application, the governor inquired who was the most suitable person to be appointed. "Myself," was the reply; "for my neighbour is no more lit for it than the devil is." The commission was granted, and the new justice immediately qualified.

Observing, upon the sideboard, several well filled decanters and glasses, Burnside said: "Suppose, when I get home, my neighbour should ask me what your excellency offered me to drink, what shall I tell him?"

"Help yourself, Mr. Justice," replied the latter.

After refreshing himself with a glass of brandy and water, Burnside returned to his "White mountain" region, much gratified with his easily acquired official dignity, and with his first visit to the provincial capitol.

The foregoing is one instance of the system of bribery countenanced by and made a source of profit to the royal governors in their appointments and charters. In the grants of townships, the grantees invariably set off a liberal allowance of farm lots, for the governor, his secretary and treasurer, "to them and their heirs forever." The American Revolution, however, a convulsion unanticipated and unprecedented in the history of the world, "indefinitely postponed" all these admirable schemes for future family wealth and power. Confiscation settled the account of most of these so easily obtained grants of land.